W9-DAN-265

Taking Measure

X. J. Kennedy. Photo by Dorothy M. Kennedy, June, 1995

Taking Measure

The Poetry and Prose of X. J. Kennedy

Bernard E. Morris

Selinsgrove: Susquehanna University Press
London: Associated University Presses

Associated University Presses
2010 Eastpark Boulevard
Cranbury, NJ 08512

Associated University Presses
16 Barter Street
London WC1A 2AH, England

Associated University Presses
P.O. Box 338, Port Credit
Mississauga, Ontario
Canada L5G 4L8

The paper used in this publication meets the requirements of the American National Standard for Permanence of Paper for Printed Library Materials Z39.48-1984.

Library of Congress Cataloging-in-Publication Data

Morris, Bernard E., 1935–
Taking measure : the poetry and prose of X. J. Kennedy / Bernard E. Morris.
p. cm.
Includes bibliographical references and index.
ISBN 1-57591-063-2 (alk paper)
1. Kennedy, X. J.—Criticism and interpretation. I. Title
PS3521.E563 Z78 2003
811′.54—dc21 2002070572

PRINTED IN THE UNITED STATES OF AMERICA

To my wife, Silvana, the spirit of song

Contents

Acknowledgements

CHAPTERS FOUR AND SIX AND MATERIAL RELATING TO THE CRITICAL response to X. J. Kennedy's poetry appeared in *Paintbrush* 25 (autumn 1998). The author wishes to thank the editor, Ben Bennani, for his part in making this book a reality.

Introduction

X. J. KENNEDY HAS HAD A LONG, ACTIVE, AND DISTINGUISHED CAREER AS A poet, an author of popular textbooks and children's literature, and a public speaker. He is a favorite among both adults and children as a reader of poetry. His understanding of what poetry is and should do and his experience in making poetry an oral and public experience place him among the most widely appreciated poets of our time. He is exceedingly generous both of his time and his energy in supporting the community of poets and poetry readers. Privately modest and self-effacing, he is outspoken and unwavering in promoting excellence in writing, reading, and teaching poetry. He is a staunch defender of traditional forms without dismissing formless poetry altogether, and though he opposes the view that good modern poetry exists only in open forms, he accepts all forms of poetic expression and is sagacious in his commentary on it. His critical statements are always instructive, and his criticism is never tainted by acrimony or personal attack. His eye is always on the poetry, the best that one can achieve.

While this book has been making slow progress, Kennedy has continued writing and publishing poetry and prose and traveling all over the nation to participate in literary conferences, to give readings, and to promote education and poetry any way he can. All the while, his own poetry has been consistently praised for its wit, formal excellence, and piercing commentary on the modern American experience. One of Kennedy's more remarkable achievements is to have written so much formal verse for so long that he has come to be labeled a traditionalist by many critics, yet his poetry has never been old-fashioned, nor has he allowed traditional forms to define his poetic limits. His most rewarding poems mingle form and perception to a degree that continues to surprise and edify. Well aware of the darker side of the human condition, Kennedy has maintained a strong faith in the generative nature of poetry. For him, poetry is a means of carrying the past forward, so he believes that we are obligated not only to preserve it but to assimilate it, to read it, and, if we can, to create it. For him, the poetic past is a window through which we can see ahead, and poetry is an instrument for making our vision intelligible to others.

Those who read Kennedy's poetry carefully and with an open mind recognize that it is not simply the work of another "widely respected poet" or "one of America's finest poets who writes in traditional forms," as the book blurbs would have it. His work is important because it preserves something necessary to our sensibility and understanding of ourselves and our world. It helps us see that the present can create from the past the promise of a better future. Without his sardonic wit, sharp visions, and formal excellence, the world would not mean as much.

Taking Measure

Chapter 1
The Poetry of Design

X. J. KENNEDY REMAINS ONE OF OUR MOST OUTSPOKEN DEFENDERS OF rhyme and meter and an acknowledged master of the couplet, quatrain, and other traditional structures. He believes with Ezra Pound and others that the important part of poetry is its form;[1] its meaning is secondary. A poem whose interest is only in its prose meaning has little merit in his view.[2] "The meaning of a poem is not only the connotations of the words," he once told an interviewer, "but all the emotional effects . . . the sound of it, the rhythms of it."[3] In his reviews, he is ever interested in how something is said, and often his chief interest is how the poet achieves formal effects. Those poets he most admires are the best crafters, Marianne Moore, L. E. Sissman, James Hayford, W. D. Snodgrass, to name only a few contemporaries. He has long argued that traditional forms offer poets many benefits, and his own poetry demonstrates as much. Traditional forms enable a poet to seek order and unity in a world better understood by the kind of shaping such forms offer, and they engage the poet's total self. As he told John Ciardi in 1971, traditional form helps poets know when they are going wrong and leads them to what they really want to say.[4] Writing in meter and rhyme takes pains, but such labor "is likely to produce valuable poems," Kennedy believes, and the demands these formal elements put on the writer tend to discourage the unskilled and those who seek primarily to be published or simply to gush forth. More important, perhaps, traditional forms provide a standard, a kind of backdrop against which poets may place modern situations, points of view, situations, and sensibilities. Reworking a familiar form can make the poem surprising, more illuminating, or enlarging. An accomplished poet such as Miller Williams, for example, "knows that forms convey unexpected power when a poet chooses to shatter their rules."[5] Kennedy himself is above all a weaver of the old and the new. One of his fundamental convictions is that the future of poetry rests on a synthesis of what has been written and what is being written. The medium of this exchange is not only language but traditional forms.

In his criticism and his poetry, Kennedy has suggested that those who write free verse and those who use traditional forms are involved essentially in the same enterprise and quest: to make sense of inner and outer realities and to share the sense—and nonsense—they make of their experience. Czeslaw Milosz spoke recently of the value provided by poetry in general: "When the world is deprived of clear-cut outlines, of up and down, of good and evil, it succumbs to a peculiar nihilization. . . . Poetry, if it is good, matters greatly in the face of this deprivation because it looks at the singular, not the general. It cannot look at things of this Earth other than honestly, with reverence, as colorful and variegated; it cannot reduce life with all its pain and ecstasy into a unified tonality. By necessity, it is on the side of being. Naming is a defense of hope."[6] To the extent that a poet, irrespective of formal commitments, seeks to put a name on experience, some value is shared and hope is sustained, though Kennedy believes that, because the "made" poem implies permanence, formal poets "are the only ones to affirm some hope of the future."[7] He has "no quarrel with any poet who seriously practices the difficult craft of honest open verse,"[8] but the chief problem with those who write free verse is that they skimp on craft. Those who reject traditional forms probably have not mastered them well enough to feel free within them.[9] Kennedy expressed this same sentiment in one of his epigrams: "A worn tradition is a joy to quit / For anyone no good at wearing it."[10] They do not "distinguish between the spontaneous masterpiece and the spontaneous horse-piddle." They never or seldom revise, so in love are they with their "effortless outpour."[11] In American poetry today, a "desperate sincerity" is "valued more highly than brilliance of craftsmanship." Though many new poets care about rhythm and seek new cadences, they show little interest in meter and rhyme. Their poems "demand that we concentrate not on their patterns or textures, but on what they say."[12] Yet Kennedy has held to the conviction that "'it don't mean a thing if it ain't got that swing.'"[13] Meter for him is "an absolute need." The demands of writing a well-crafted poem are almost essential to the creative endeavor. Writing sonnets, for example, can lead a poet to "discover a deeper individuality." Kennedy refers to W. H. Auden's idea that "metrical verse . . . requires its practitioners not merely to adopt its conventions, but to adapt those conventions to their own needs. In so doing, each practitioner tends to discover an individual voice."[14]

He tried open forms, Kennedy once confessed, but after only a few lines he wanted his "good old rhymed pacifier."[15] He needs "the challenge of old-fangled technical difficulties."[16] Yet throughout his career he has shown a poet's interest in open form, borrowing some of its features and flirting with its lax structures in varying degrees of seriousness. In "Satori," a light-hearted frolic that he never reprinted, he mimics some of the features of "beatnik poetry," triple spacing between "stanzas," three of which are only one line long, omitting rhyme in all but two of the lines, lowercasing the personal pronoun *i*, and including references to the cosmos, Buddha, Bird Parker, and other Beatnik favorites.[17] He teases his target in such lines as this: "I'm the mote in the eye in the dot in the i / in the poster for Pepsi-Cola." In an early uncollected poem "Alternatives," Kennedy tried his hand at an even more radical approach, joining words and altering spelling to capture the sound—and sense—of a certain kind of speech:

> Whatflavor shit
> joo like to eat bub
> sez Life, we got
>   1. chucklet
>   (teaching
>   history of the he-
>   roiccouplet)
>   2. wanilla
>   (editing Stockingloom
>   Weekly)
>   3. strawbree
>   (owning wife 1.3 lens &
>   taking pornographs),
> huh ?[18]

In a number of other poems, however, Kennedy takes a more serious approach to open form. One of them, "Two Views of Rhyme and Meter," makes a statement about free verse itself. The structure is decidedly open. Line lengths are irregular; only one of the lines is longer than the title, most of them containing only one or two words. Word alignment, spacing, line breaks, and indentations are all used to create visual and rhetorical effects associated with open-form poetry. Even punctuation is omitted in a way typical of open form: "Meter / Is the thrust rest thrust of loins and peter." In this artfully haphazard arrangement, the rhymes that do appear seem like a forlorn afterthought or a sporadic attempt to control the lines that threaten to fall into complete disarray.

Yet Kennedy's use of open form is not always adversarial or satirical. In "Evening Tide" the absence of rhyme and the dispassionate tone suggest a sterile world in which people suffer a lingering paralysis, even dismemberment: "On its recliner by dusk set afloat / Father's head lolls, its dome of beer half-emptied." A child's cry "Comes blundering in again and again, a stick of driftwood." The imagery joins with the relatively sterile form to depict a disembodied scene. "In a Secret Field" also shows Kennedy's skill in crafting a powerful image with little more than rhythm and sound in a poem of only six lines:

> Stealthily
> The snow's soft tons
>
> By the air
> Unbearable
>
> Accumulate.

This poem resembles a haiku in its brevity and imagery. The five words in the first two lines are linked by alliteration and modulation of the "o" sound: "Stealthily / The snow's soft tons. . . ." Assonance unites the two lines of the second stanza—"By the air / Unbearable . . . ,"and the final line leaves the reader with a vivid image of how the snow has fallen, an image created by the sound and rhythm of this one word. Structurally, too, Kennedy suggests the nature of the snow as the lines "fall" together and accumulate like the falling snow. Without using rhyme, he has the rhythm bear most of the weight of making the image come alive.

Whether he is experimenting with open form or confronting the difficulties of traditional forms, Kennedy makes craft the overriding element in his own poetry. He once said that he writes his poems without much concern for sense and likes to write "formally tight, constipated, closed poems," including the ballad, ode, elegy, sonnet, limerick, and epigram.[19] These latter two forms have occupied him recently more than any other, and they well suit his gift for satire, wit, rhyme, and pithy expression. In all his poems, most of the lines are rhymed, most contain three to five stresses each, and most of the meters are iambic. Exercising great freedom, imagination, and skill in the use of these elements, he relies heavily on stanzaic patterning, favoring the quatrain—a quarter of his collected poems use the quatrain—and the couplet, which allows him to build a poem with paired lines as a base unit, extending the poem for as long as his inspiration lasts, then closing quickly with force and wit.

One can see the effectiveness of Kennedy's crafting couplets in "Terse Elegy for J. V. Cunningham," in which the couplet is used to produce startling results:

> Though with a slash a Pomp's gut he could slit,
> On his own flesh he worked his weaponed wit
> And penned his patient skill and lore immense,
> Prodigious mind, keen ear, rare common sense,
> Only those words he could crush down no more
> Like matter pressured to a dwarf star's core.
>
> (ll. 5–10)

Kennedy's modern sensibility is especially evident in the simile in the last line, which joins modern science to metaphysical wit. Kennedy wants his poem to reflect the kind of poetry Cunningham wrote: concise, skillfully structured, epigrammatic, and elevated, its "heroic" quality reminiscent of neoclassical verse. But the couplet is of general interest to Kennedy, and he is especially adept at crafting it. Its brevity and potential for either balance or opposition enable him to deliver sharp, summary comments on human nature, including his own.

The uses to which the couplet can be put so as to create peculiar but apt effects may be seen in a later poem from *Dark Horses.* The poem's title, "The Withdrawn Gift," hints at the way Kennedy uses the couplet structure to create balance and opposition to mirror the poem's content. In the poem's four couplets, a gesture is opposed; an offer is withdrawn; a connection is attempted but ultimately denied; a scene is concluded but wholeness is not achieved; and charity is defeated by pride. Balance in opposites: this is the couplet's special character, and Kennedy has chosen the couplet to write a poem about a man who offers a homeless person a coin but is stopped by his wife:

> And so the quarter in my hand
> I'd meant to toss him did not land.
>
> Denying him, I felt denied
> A swig from that brown-bagged bottle, pride.
>
> (ll. 5–8)

Like a couplet in which the meaning or impression of the first line is reversed by the second, this poem suggests at the start that the speaker is moved by pity toward the homeless man, but the poem's final line withdraws this impression, showing that the speaker's motive is pride. The final couplet also, ironically, brings the homeless man and the speaker together, balancing them in perpetual opposition. Both are denied something, and both are in some way destitute: the homeless man lacks means, and the speaker lacks charity. As the two lines of a couplet are mirror images of each other, sharing the same structure and rhyming, so these two figures, the derelict and the speaker, are also mirror images of each other. But the couplet's lines are very different in meaning, as these two men are different in character; though their respective conditions differ in fact, their essential nature is the same: the homeless man sits back "in his self-made pond / Of piss (ll. 3–4)," just as the speaker has made his own foul pond, pride.

The couplet also can accommodate any wordplay Kennedy wishes to explore, and his penchant for such play is evident everywhere in his poetry. The couplet also makes the most of metric manipulation, so if the canvas is not vast, it gains in force by being well focused, concentrated, and swift. Brevity also allows him to increase the number of sound effects, puns, and other witty features without the risk of their overwhelming the poem and the reader. The two-line epigram "Voice from a Borne Pall," for example, uses the letter *b* to begin eight of the poem's nineteen words to simulate the sound of a drum beat and pace the meaning: "Bare-boned, born bare, I bared me when I married / And now past bearing can't bear to be carried." The poem also plays on the meanings and sounds of the words *bare, bear, born / borne, married,* and *carried.* The number of puns, together with the many alliterated words, makes the poem a rich container of witty sound effects, too rich to be sustained for very long, but very effective in couplet form. Kennedy uses this feature elaborately in his nonsense verse.

In an epigram from *Emily Dickinson in Southern California,* on marriage, Kennedy condenses an entire history of misery and ultimate revenge into one couplet: "On his wife's stone, though small in cost and small, / Meek got a word in edgewise after all." The irony of "though small in cost and small" combines with "got a word in edgewise" to express Meek's determination to enjoy a last bit of revenge. The headstone and its price are small because Meek is, well, meek, not given to large, bold gestures, but this individual is effective nonetheless. His choice serves a double purpose, revenge and economy, just as the poem, small and full of meaning, serves Kennedy's. The meanings of "edgewise" echo Meek's disadvantage in conversations with his wife; they also refer to the shape of the headstone and suggest the blade of this final thrust. The phrase "after all" contributes much to the poem's wit. Literally ending the poem, it nevertheless invites something more to complete the tale, such as "after all the woman did to this poor, long-suffering man. . . ." That small word, *all*, condenses years of suffering, volumes of complaints. Kennedy may even have intended a sly jab at the reader: by getting his own word in "edgewise after all," he gets the better of the reader, using a seemingly simple poem to engage the reader in a witty game of parry and thrust. Such a reading is always possible with Kennedy, who designs his poems so that each one includes the reader in addition to what it does with its subject.[20]

Kennedy often uses the couplet to shape an effective epigram, a form which he has produced with such skill and frequency that it has gained him much praise.[21] His affection for the epigram, ranging in length from two lines to ten, is reflected in the fact that he includes several of them in his major collections and supplied the contents of one whole issue of the little magazine *The Epigrammatist.* He has used the epigram to mock human folly and pretension throughout his poetic career. Sometimes he arranges epigrams into a loose series and gives them titles such as *Japanese Beetles,*[22] and "Last Lines," or he arranges them by subject, as he does in *The Epigrammatist,* with or without a title. Although specific targets vary, Kennedy focuses on human pretension, folly, and futile aspirations. Ever present, too, is Kennedy's witty use of language, especially the pun, and humor, which is sometimes light, sometimes dark, as it is in "City Churchyard," a later collection reprinted, appropriately, in *Dark Horses.*

In "City Churchyard" Kennedy uses the couplet to etch brief portraits in a series of nine imaginary epitaphs, and the accumulated effect is to inscribe a cheerless message: human aspirations are ultimately futile and death brings an ironic justice. The justice, in this case, is to be encapsulated in a Kennedy couplet, which uses language and structure to deliver a final, ironic sentence. The Lecher's epitaph mocks the man by turning his tombstone into a phallic symbol with which he salutes the passerby: "I who could once erect a throbbing bone / Salute you now with rigid, skinned-back stone." The irony of the two lines is that the "throbbing bone" the Lecher "could once erect" has been replaced by a lifeless stone that he did not erect, a permanent symbol of the ultimate futility of priding oneself on sexual prowess. The Watchmaker introduces the idea of time. Even in his epitaph he is conscious of the sweep of the second hand: "And here you stand and stare while minutes fly." The result is a lessening while one is alive, but in death, the Watchmaker laments, "even less am I." This theme takes a personal turn in Kennedy's contribution to *The Epigrammatist,* which concludes with a couplet that expresses Kennedy's own epitaph: "Earth was I made from, back to earth I went. / Envy me now: I'm in my element." The concluding word, *element,* carries several meanings: the literal one, earth; the abstract one, heaven or the afterlife; and the realm of poetry or poetry making. Appropriately, he has come to the end of his journey through this volume, and now his labors are done.

Bulsh, a work from 1970, represents Kennedy's most ambitious commitment to the couplet. The poem consists of twenty-nine closed pairs replete with coarse language, ribald humor, and satirical commentary, the whole carried forward by a thin plot: "Saint Bulsh" is a vain, vulgar, lazy prelate who fancies plump girls; nuns are advised to "keep bulldogs in their pew / Lest Bulsh's fingers play the Wandering Jew," and, while "on the crapper," he dreams of ascending to "the throne of Peter." Satan offers him "pink wriggling altar boys" while Bulsh continues to sate his appetite for drink and lechery. In the end, however, justice reigns: "On Resurrection morn it sore surprised / Bulsh to stand up and go unrecognized." Each couplet, set off from the others by spacing and numbers, is a discrete, satiric attack on licentiousness and bloated self-indulgence. Besides demonstrating that a classic form can serve low humor as well as high, the string of couplets sets up an ironic contrast between Bulsh's undisciplined, riotous life and the couplet's precise balance, controlled rhythms, orderly rhymes, and well-crafted wit. Kennedy mounts an attack against spiritual despoliation with an instrument of classical precision and orderly craft, wringing humor from Bulsh's disreputable behavior but implying a serious indictment of religious indulgence. Kennedy depicts what humans—especially religious authorities—can become if they allow their base nature unrestrained expression, and his couplet delivers the message with an implicit corrective: cultivate the higher faculties with integrity and self-restraint.

In Kennedy's hands, traditional forms always offer opportunities to turn out something new, fresh, and surprising, something crafted to fit a new vision. Revision and vision interact to create new poetry, even when he goes beyond the couplet and epigram in using a well-established form, as he does in "Ode."[23] The traditional ode has a solemn theme and complex structure and contains elevated public or private expression. By contrast, Kennedy's poem is typical of the traditional ode in neither stanzaic form, rhyme pattern, subject, nor language. The four quatrains are rhymed *abba*, some lines containing four stresses, others five. This structure represents an ironic contrast to the poem's subject: Kennedy's hindquarters, described as an "Old tumbril," a "Divided face," "Vesuvius upside down," the "Cave of the Winds," and so on. Although the language is decorous, the imagery is not: the poet and his posterior "Never see eye to eye"; the rump lets out a horselaugh, whistles, and shares with the poet a "dirty deed." Underlying the coarseness and humor is a serious and high-minded purpose: like Everyman, Kennedy feels the weight of this part of himself morally and physically. Surely, he thinks, it subverts the human spirit, housed in and dependent on a body burdened by this unattractive and "dirty" appendage. If the classical ode expresses the human spirit at its most elevated, what should a poet do in considering the other, necessary, lower part of human existence? Invert the traditional ode's form. In this way, Kennedy brings not only the "stuck-up spirit" but the tradition itself "back down to earth."

The complexity of Kennedy's use of traditional forms—it is never a mere question of loyalty with him—is evident in such poems as "Long Distance," which captures in thirteen tightly constructed lines the gaping distance between a poet desperate to be published and the speaker who can offer little solace and no useful advice. As the caller reads a villanelle to the editor, the phone oozes "warm blood." We do not know whether the caller cannot get published because he writes in outmoded forms (like Kennedy himself) or because he writes poorly—the editor asks, "how about / Not just redoing what the Georgians did?" The poet has called "To ask what's wrong, why editors resist / The moistened lips they thrust up to be kissed." The image in this second line closes the stanza and unites sound and rhythm in a way that open form cannot achieve. The reader hears the rhyme and is struck all-the-more forcibly by the image because of it. Rhyme seals the image of the caller as a sycophant while pairing his lips with resisting editors, and the stresses of the lines reinforce the weight of this message by falling on each of the rhyming words, *resist/kissed*. In the next stanza, stresses again drive home the consonance of sound and sense as "phone" rhymes with "moan," making this pairing seem inevitable: "One reads a villanelle you'll love. The phone / Oozing warm blood, you listen. Pillow talk. / The more he reads the more, outside, winds moan" (ll. 4–6). The word *moan* opens this world to the larger context of nature, which includes the rain that "Strums on the roof with amputated finger." Something universal is involved in the inability of caller and editor to connect. Ironically, the only warmth felt is the "warm blood." The monotonous beat of the finger is echoed by the poem's rhythms, "Dead air," in one line, and "Rain" in another, and the precise, complete rhymes of the first stanzas dissolve into half rhymes in the final one, "anger" and "finger," suggesting a world becoming somewhat unhinged and left in that state.

Critic Forrest Read explains how Kennedy merges description with the poem's structural features in "B Negative," particularly in the following stanza:

> And now I lay bifocals down. My feet
> Forget the twist that brought me to your street.
>   I can't make out your face for steamed-up glass
> Nor quite call back your outline on the sheet.
>
> (ll. 21–24)

Noting the use of a *Rubaiyat* stanza, Read comments: "Here [Kennedy's] bifocal vision has fused with the experience itself. The literal event, the device of recollection, and the stanzaic form enforce each other to embody that replete tone which speaks from beyond the line on which the poet is working. The rhythm springs us into a truly surprising insight as the voice comes to us from a distinct place, at a distinct time, from a suddenly palpable figure. Here the dance of Kennedy's mind, and of the mind's selected images and symbols, does not merely work with its own furnishings, which are, like furniture, detachable and movable, but has entered a world where it is part of an expanded landscape."[24] The use of the *Rubaiyat* stanza is particularly apt, for it adds to the poem, as Read points out, "a genuine expression of one who without hope lives in desire."[25] The stanza enables Kennedy to develop his poem within a structural context that continues throughout the poem to comment ironically on its other meanings. The reader hears two voices simultaneously, Kennedy's and Omar Khayyám's. Thus a traditional stanza becomes the means by which Kennedy renews and revises the past while developing a complex perspective on a contemporary subject.

In his review of *Cross Ties,* Moore Moran focuses on Kennedy's "keen awareness of the function of meter and rhythm, and the differences between the two (meter, of course, dealing with poetic feet and their positions and variations within the line; rhythm being the natural pronunciation of words within or without poetic feet)."[26] Moran illustrates his point with a close look at the first line of "Lilith," "Adam's first wife had soft lips but no soul," saying:

> Except for "Adam," the words here are all monosyllabic. Which means both unaccented and accented positions within each foot must accommodate a complete word.
>
> This is packing things a bit tight, yet the poet's ear is true and the line reads comfortably. More important, a wizardly touch is added to the line's rhythm by the word "soft" taking the accented position in the third foot—opposing the word "lips" in the unaccented position in the foot following. So that "soft" receives more weight metrically, but rhythmically "lips" retains dominance. The effect is that "soft lips" reads almost like a spondee, bringing an otherwise shopworn phrase to life through the impact of unexpected balanced sound. Add to this the distant alliteration of "soft" and "soul," and the line becomes even more impressive.[27]

One of Kennedy's first poems, also one of his most structurally complex, is "Nude Descending a Staircase."[28] It is a surprisingly short poem, three quatrains, considering all that it accomplishes. Its descriptions emphasize the woman's movement as she steps down stairs: she is "snowing flesh . . . She sifts in sunlight down the stairs . . . We spy . . . / A constant thresh of thigh on thigh / Her lips imprint the swinging air / That parts to let her parts go by." The metaphors in the poem encompass both the woman in the poem and the structural workings of the poem itself. The woman is a "One-woman waterfall," and her descent down the stairs parallels the descent of the poem from line to line down the page. If her flesh snows, so does, by implication, the flesh of the poem, the words. If descending, she "sifts in sunlight down the stairs," so the poem sifts in meaning down and through the stanzas. The poem, like the photographs on which the poem is based, creates the illusion of motion and meaning; the poem both moves and means. The final line completes the poem's design, which contains the power to continue as long as the poem is read. This closure synthesizes illusion and reality. The paradox that is central to this concept—finite and static elements can create motion, unending life—is deftly expressed in the last line: "Collects her motions into shape." Though it concludes the poem, this line does not stop the poem from continuing to work in the reader's mind. The idea, the vision, has become independent of it as long as it lives in the mind of the reader.

In a brief but trenchant analysis of "Nude Descending a Staircase," Ronald Sharp also notes Kennedy's ability to fuse structural elements into a poetic analog that celebrates the relationship between shape and motion, but he shows how Kennedy's language helps to fuse structure and meaning. Kennedy, Sharp says, "literally embodies the notion that for poem and nude alike their most beautiful shape is their motion":

> The waterfall is only part of a carefully constructed pattern of images ("snowing"-l.1, "sifts"-l.3, "thresh"-l.5) that have two things in common: the suggestion of downward motion and of parts or segments. The nude's descent is like the falling of snow or water, sifting of flour, and the threshing of grain (the latter two by implication, of course): the parts separate out and collect at the bottom . . . There is, however, another sense in which the medium she moves through is the poem itself, which is also in motion and which, like the air, "parts to let her parts go by" (l.8) . . . To use the same word as noun and verb to describe a thing as well as an action is, in the context of this poem, to blur the distinction. By directing our attention to that blur, Kennedy literally embodies the notion that for poem and nude alike their most beautiful shape is their motion.[29]

Nancy Sullivan gives this notion a more philosophical expression, seeing the form of "Nude" as a tour de force that embodies multiple realities in depicting the nude's descent, breaking free of the "time-space-place reality. Everything is seen at once." Quoting José Ortega y Gassett, Sullivan believes the poem offers a " 'harmonious multiplicity of all possible points of view.' "[30]

Kennedy tried his hand in transcribing visual art into poetic design in "Nude Descending a Staircase," and he succeeded in memorable fashion. In "A Beardsley Moment" he turns again to this challenge, using as his subject an illustration done by Aubrey Beardsley, the famous nineteenth-century English illustrator. While performing this task, the poem offers a display of features associated with Beardsley, and in that way, imitates the work of art it describes. The poem creates with its impressions a Beardsley drawing by playing on sound and imagery in a tone that both teases and attacks and that is both elaborate and risqué:

Adoze upon her vast aplomb
  The tittering-stock of palace mice,
Lulled by the ticking of her bombe
  Of deliquescent orange ice

Victoria forgets to reign. . . .

(ll. 1–5)

The vocabulary is as self-conscious and rare as the scene itself, which highlights the artificial nature of Beardsley's art. The second quatrain underscores the sense of weariness prevalent in the illustration—the queens "slackening hand" lets fall a crochet hook while the erotic element is evident in the form of "Priapic doodads down the walls." Dryads are present, and "Mignonette," whose pubic hair can be seen "Beneath drawers of lace fishing-net," tosses aside "swansdown shoes" while "A satyr carves." Kennedy's choice of details through the rest of the poem is as careful as his choice of rhythms and sounds: "Sly hoptoads with the heads of dwarves . . . a whimpering unicorn . . . centaurs, pearl-rope-draped, in drag . . ." (11. 15–18), all as colorful and figurative as the drawing itself, and all creating a verbal tapestry in which meaning shapes the design that contains it.

The way Kennedy employs rhyme demonstrates his belief that supposedly exhausted forms still retain power and flexibility, but rhyme succeeds best if it is so apt to the thought it encloses that the reader is surprised by the conjunction of sound and sense, like *resist/kissed* in "Long Distance." The rhyme cannot distract too much from the sense or appear so forced that the poet's skill is doubted and the effect undermined. Occasionally, the conjunction of sound and sense strikes with visceral force and seems inevitable. Any number of Kennedy's poems achieve this degree of effectiveness in the use of rhyme. In "First Confession," for example, off rhymes contribute emphatically to the poem's meaning by suggesting a disjunction exists between religious faith and personal feeling, as in the poem's opening stanza, *scuffed* and *coughed,* and elsewhere in the poem, *done* and *burned, doled* and *sol, light* and *priest.* As we hear the rhymes strike, we sense that the speaker's devotion to church doctrine is similarly "off," too, like an out-of-tune church bell. The poem also makes the point that the confessional booth joins sinner and confessor into a spiritual but disjointed whole, as the poem's rhyme does formally. In this way, the formal elements construct an emblem of the poem's subject.

"Rotten Reveille" uses rhyme to suggest the disordered mind of the poem's central character: a woman suffering the morning-after effects of too much drink. Such off rhymes as "thought/knots" and "Month/Menthe," for example, reflect the poem's theme of mental disarray. Sound generally plays an important part in the poem's thematic development. Alliteration reinforces as it imitates the dull thud of the woman's headache: "dreams / Drizzle to day dreams and dissolve to thought." The repetition of "dreams" suggests the sound of screaming, and three repetitions of "thought," followed by "ought," "not," and "knots," further the effect. This harsh chorus of sounds continues through the poem:

> From the bricked alley came the shriek of drums,
> Brakedrums, bringing to an abrupt stop
> The express truck delivering new Book-of-the-Month
> Too early. Crème de Menthe
> In the glass used to marinate by night
> Her dentures helped.
>
> (ll. 5–10)

The piercing sounds of "shriek," "green," and "mean" in these lines are counterpointed by the heavy sound of "bricked," the repetition in "drums/Brakedrums," and the frequent use of *d* and *p* sounds. These sounds reinforce the woman's mental condition, and together with the poem's other effects make the woman's hangover powerfully felt.

Using sound, including rhyme, to reinforce the poem's theme is among Kennedy's most effective strategies. He more than once quotes Robert Frost's comment that sound and sense in a poem are inseparable, or should be.[31] Although free verse and blank verse also use sound as a unifying element, rhyme simply magnifies the importance of sound in a poem. It is an instrument of such potency and potential that poets besides Kennedy wonder how a poet can reject its use. Kennedy suspects that many poets write unrhymed poetry because they lack the skill to rhyme well.[32] Be that as it may, Kennedy uses rhyme, together with other traditional elements, to make his poems resound with meaning. He even addresses the subject in "Two Views of Rime and Meter," a light and satirical poem that offers a serious definition of rhyme while illustrating its effectiveness. The first part of the poem dismisses rhyme as mere sound, the "thud / thud / thud of a bent wire / carpetbeater"; it is the "dust" that results from the carpetbeater's repetitive action. The second part of the poem counters this negative view of rhyme. Instead of dull repetition, the recurrence of sound and the concomitant action of "returning" to the same "place" is associated with the act of sexual intercourse and, more significantly, procreation. One "feels" a rightness as the poem's rhythms and stresses work together in unison, the way motion and emotion combine in the sex act. The poem ironically uses the devices associated with free verse as well as children's verse to make its argument in favor of rhyme, placing the words in the first stanza to reflect their meaning:

What's meter
but the thud
    thud
    thud of a bent wire
carpetbeater

(ll. 1–5)

In the last stanza the first three lines graphically suggest the male genitalia, a middle line flanked by two short lines:

Meter
Is the thrust rest thrust of loins and peter,
And rhyme,
to come at the same time.

(ll. 11–14)

Line length also reflects the sexual subject, short-long-short-long, as do the rhythms and stresses. Once this picture has been created, the poem reveals even more subtle meanings. As rhyme matches sound and word, it brings together two people, two minds, in a fruitful, even procreative act. From the union of two comes one poem. *E pluribus unum.*

Design in general has been an essential element of Kennedy's poetry from the beginning of his poetic career. The arrangement of his first collection, *Nude Descending a Staircase,* suggests a stage production, its three parts interspersed by a section titled "Intermission with Peanuts." *Cross Ties,* too, is arranged in this way, including no fewer than four intermissions with the book's other five sections. Kennedy thus shows a penchant for making structure, be it a whole volume or individual poem, an integral part of his meaning. In his poems, design is of course a central feature, everywhere evident and multifarious. In "First Confession," for example, the formal features, such as the quatrains, the rhymes, the metric rhythms—all trappings of a secular tradition—announce a commitment to that tradition and to a way of life that leads away from the church. By placing the poem first in this first collection and titling it "First Confession," Kennedy invites the reader to see this poem as his own first confession and the "I" as himself. In this light, the conflict between the poet and his own Catholicism is confessed to a reader who is in the position of the confessor, and the poem becomes a metaphor of the confession booth. Implicit in the poet's formal choices is a parallel confession as well: Kennedy has chosen a secular path, not a religious one, and he uses secular forms to declare his independence of religious forms. The poem's final lines express a defiance of church authority and the price of defiance: "I knelt . . . And stuck my tongue out at the priest: / A fresh roost for the Holy Ghost" (ll. 22–24). Traditional forms are, in this poem at least, a framework for working through the conflict between the religious and secular impulses. Ironically, without church ritual, we would have no secular poem.

If "First Confession" represents a personal declaration of independence and a commitment to a secular authority, Kennedy had no intention of becoming a mere imitator of traditional forms, however skilled he was at breathing life into them. In such poems as "Long Distance," he derides the mere imitator. When the editor asks the caller, "how about / Not just redoing what the Georgians did?" we may assume that Kennedy asks the same of himself whenever he thinks of any new poem. His artistic credo has always emphasized creative originality wed to ideal form. What Sam Hamill says of the Japanese poet Matsuo Basho applies equally to Kennedy: Basho's "fundamental teaching remained his conviction that in composing a poem, 'There are two ways: one is entirely natural, in which the poem is born from within itself; the other way is to make it through the mastery of technique.'"[33] To make a poem through the mastery of technique—this phrase recalls what Kennedy himself says of the "made" poem, one that comes from a skillful use of formal elements in discovering and expressing the spontaneous idea and emotion. Writing a sonnet, he once said, offers "the challenge of trying to do something a little bit new in such an old form."[34] Kennedy has always shown an awareness of the rich historical inheritances, seeing in them an opportunity to weave new patterns.

He seems to challenge himself on this point in an early poem and in one his most recent poems. "Emily Dickinson in Southern

California," published in 1974, is an expansive imitation of Dickinson's poetic style. The ninety-two lines are divided into eight numbered sections of varying lengths.[35] The first and fourth lines of the quatrains have four stresses each; the second and fourth lines, three stresses each. The rhyme scheme is *abcb,* and some of the rhymes are slant. Within this structural framework, Kennedy follows the speaker, Dickinson, as she journeys west, through California, where she finds sunbathers, expensive houses, and smog. At the end a spirit named Hopelessness appears and admonishes her, suggesting that her search is unrealistic, for she seeks something "other—than this Earth / And all its Goods. . . ." (47–48). The poem, considerably longer than Dickinson's typical poem, captures Dickinson's rhythms and style, showing Kennedy's ability to create a lengthy original work using a very idiosyncratic, highly personal form not his own. This skill has played an important role in his creation of new lyrics for old tunes—as "Song to the Tune of 'Somebody Stole My Gal'" demonstrates—and in his translations of French and German poetry.

This ability is also evident in one of his most recent poems, "For Allen Ginsberg."[36] In these four quatrains, Kennedy uses William Blake's "The Tyger"[37] as a kind of receptacle into which he pours a tribute to the guru of free, spontaneous verse.[38] Kennedy is poking good-natured fun not only at "Ginsberg, Ginsberg, burning bright" but also at himself, for he has long protested the notion that traditional forms are "boxes" into which a poet pours his thoughts.[39] To a great extent, he does just that when he imitates the forms of Emily Dickinson or William Blake, or even the thoughts of a French or German poet in his translations, but in doing so Kennedy demonstrates another of his critical precepts,[40] that a skilled poet can create something original even in the most similar of forms.

Perhaps the fullest expression of Kennedy's poetic skills may be found in the way he coalesces structure and meaning so that they reinforce each other. The poem's structure becomes an expression of the poem's subject as much as the language itself. Rhythm, line length, spacing, rhyme scheme, and stanzaic structure all combine with sound and sense to express what the poem is about. Kennedy is especially adept at creating images that combine all of these elements and strike with both surprise and insight. "Nude Descending a Staircase" is not an unusual instance of this skill. Early on, some critics were perceptive enough to see how Kennedy's skill in making form and meaning coalesce. A reviewer for the *Times Literary Supplement* sees in some of the poems the mastery of form that has become a Kennedy trademark. He singles out the final stanza of "Mining Town" as an instance:[41]

> Born in this town, you learn to sleep on edge,
> Always on edge, to grow up like a tree
> Locked to the wind's sharp angle. When fear tells
> It tells out of the corner of an eye,
> A rickety house balancing in uncertainty.
>
> (ll. 12–16)

The reviewer says that "The stumble of that final line beautifully enacts what it says," identifying one of the key elements in Kennedy's poetry: the poem "enacts" its meanings. The reviewer could have cited other instances in this final stanza that perform equal service. The repetition of "on edge, / Always on edge" and "fear tells / It tells," for example, reflects the emotional experiences to which the lines refer, the persistent quality of being on edge and of fearing. By breaking each repeated phrase in two, Kennedy further coalesces form and meaning: structural disjunction becomes inseparable from emotional dysfunction. This phenomenon further creates the subtle paradox: unity of meaning emerges from structural and emotional separation and turmoil. The reviewer could also have mentioned the way Kennedy uses language to lend a choral emphasis to the meaning created, in part, by the structure. Throughout "Mining Town" Kennedy contrasts the generative element of the natural order with deterioration of the manmade world: "Clapboard houses lose / Gray clapboards the way a dying oak sheds bark" (ll. 2–3), for instance. The oak will regenerate as the houses will not—they will "lose" with a finality reflected in the word's placement at the end of the line; they will lose the way the line loses its connection with the line following it, connected yet disconnected. The miners and their machines merge with the earth as the language merges the animate and inanimate: "Sheds for machines that lower tons of men / Hug dirt for dear life" (ll. 1–2). By placing "men" and "Hug" together in the same sentence but in different lines and by using language that personifies the sheds and dehumanizes the men (in the phrase "tons of men"), Kennedy directs the reader to see an interchange of the two, and a merging of sheds and men. The poem's final line expresses a final judgment of this coalescence: the landscape formed by man and nature is rickety, and the balance of the two is uncertain. The *Times* reviewer has discovered a central feature of Kennedy's poetry, what makes it "beautiful": design is inherent in the creation of meaning. Design and meaning in a Kennedy poem are the same.[42]

"Leave of Absence" illustrates Kennedy's use of imagery to create a web of meanings that lie close to Kennedy's personal commitment to poetry. The instructor's academic predicament—growing old while trying to write a book and teach at the same time—is woven into images of autumn, the suggestion being that both the year and the man are in their season of decay. The poem overlays these two realms by means of puns and images:

> Now the full pear inclines its shape to fall,
> The wind persuasive in the looselimbed trees
> Meets with each traverse less resistance.
> Now twitched loose from your academic bough,
> You swirl to earth. They call it leave of absence.
>
> (ll. 1–5)

The "looselimbed trees" in the second line are transformed into the "looseleaves of the themes" in the last line of the poem—one of the subtitles of Kennedy's ironic web is that trees are actually transformed into writing paper. The professor, now "twitched loose" from the "academic bough," cannot free himself of the memories of a life spent reading the "Drab prose of pretty girls" and essays "on the nonconformity of Thoreau . . ." (ll. 11, 14). The poem's final set of images brings together the implicit violence of the season and the professor's frustration and anger that his memories arouse in him:

> Cars crash through leaves: a sound of shuffled papers
> Batters my sleep, routs to the wind my dreams—
> Some scrape, others cartwheel with dry twicks of stems
> While slow as frost through boughs, moves your veined hand
> Scoring with red the looseleaves of the themes.
>
> (ll. 16–20)

In addition to imagery, Kennedy often combines language, rhythm, and theme in a single design that reaches far beyond its particular subject. The four-line poem "Two Lovers Proceed to Love, Despite Their Sunburns," for example, depicts two lovers doing what the title says:

> With motion slow and gingerly they place
> Their outward forms, broiled bright as carapace,

> Like linesmen handling bared high-tension wires
> Dreading the surges of abrupt desires.

The poem itself illustrates Kennedy's belief that the rhythms of metric poetry reflect the rhythms of the heart, and of sexual activity. The rhythms of the lines suggest a "motion slow and gingerly" that the lovers are performing, and the subject is also reinforced by a simile: "Like linesmen handling bared high-tension wires / Dreading the surges of abrupt desires." Associating emotional tension with wires carrying high-voltage is clever enough, but the cleverness pervades all of the poem, including the language. The phrase "handling bared" suggests the lovers' hands touching bare flesh, and the pun on "surges" brings together the electrical and emotional worlds with which the poem is concerned, creating a harmony that is reflected as well in the rhythm of the final line: "Dreading the surges of abrupt desires." The language of the poem also suggests a subtle allusion to the art of making poetry itself: "motion," "forms," "linesmen," the tension in "high-tension," and others, for example. As he does in many of his poems, "First Confession," for example, and "One A.M. with Voices," Kennedy appears to be speaking to the reader about the art of making poetry as well.

In "Woman in Rain" Kennedy again uses grammatical structures to parallel and reinforce meaning. Stanzas two and three are linked by an irregular grammatical series, two verbs joined to a complete clause by the conjunction "And":

> She dodges sheets of water, steps
> Past handbills (DEEP MASSAGE –TRY SHEP'S)
>
> And, twained by her determined stride . . .
> She parts its danglings, steps on through.
>
> (ll. 7–9, 12)

The poem's syntax is crowded with sentence units that, like these, are not grammatically coordinated. The sentence units are as grammatically disconnected as the woman is from us and as disconnected as the elements of this street scene are from one another. Even when lines enjamb, they suggest the nonstop flow of traffic and humans. The central figure in the poem, referred to only as "she," is a stranger who is briefly glimpsed, like the street scene itself, and the distance that remains between her and the reader is part of the poem's implicit statement: this street scene symbolizes modern existence, crowded with humans and a woman who attracts momentary attention but remains distant and unknown. The image of "the bole / Of a young tree uprooted whole" (ll. 1–2) by association, suggests the young woman, herself uprooted. The lack of grammatical connectors reflects the impersonal quality of city life that is also somewhat threatening, as the language and imagery suggest: "breakneck," "flesh and blood," and "Sleek taxis on the prowl."

Kennedy correlates the spacing of the lines with the meaning conveyed by the words, thus making structure into a visual, fluid symbol. The final line of the third stanza, "She parts its danglings, steps on through," continues into the final stanza, "To farther rooms." This design suggests that the final stanza itself is one of the "farther rooms" into which the woman steps. The space between these two "rooms" represents a blankness between two visible realities and provides a visual counterpart to the narrative, which concludes in an existential poise between two possible existences: she "Might grace a page or fill a frame" (l. 15). The language in this line brings together two realms, the printed poem and the poem's imagery, which creates a picture of the woman as though she were in a painting. Tension is generated by interaction between the static representation of the woman—the tableau element—and the motion described by the narrative and imagery. The poem composes these two elements into a rhetorical question: "But then, what planet knows its name?" (l. 16). It transmutes into a statement rhetorically, as the woman transmutes into a heavenly body in the final image:

> And, twained by her determined stride,
> The strings of rain to strands divide,
> A beaded curtain, thin and blue.
> She parts its danglings, steps on through
>
> To farther rooms, still unaware
> That she as we behold her there
> Might grace a page or fill a frame.
> But then, what planet knows its name?
>
> (ll. 9–16)

The poem thus demonstrates the tenuous nature of reality, the impermanence of the visual world whose meaning shifts, becoming an optical illusion or an enigma. This poem extends the portrait of the woman that Kennedy began in "Nude Descending a Staircase," defining in motion, or creating a form in which motion defines, something elusive in the nature of woman that the eye may capture and the hand transmute into a poem.

Stanzaic structuring is used to enclose a darker picture of an urban scene in "On the Square," which opens with two male birds "Competing for one kernel" and attacking each other:

> Neither will acquiesce.
> Blue beak-tipped arrow, one dives for the other,
> Grasps and removes some neck-fluff. Whorls of feather
> Phosphoresce.
>
> Slowly as if in dream,
> A dealer in crack unjacknifes from a bench,
> Twitches numb muscles, makes stiff fingers clench,
> A switchblade gleam. . . .
>
> (ll. 5–12)

The rhymes and the balanced lines, emphasized by their placement and length, send a message of harmony, balance, and tightly knit enclosures. The elements of this urban scene are as knit together, balanced, and harmonious as the poem's structural features—one concludes as much from Kennedy's design. The murderer needs a victim; such an environment is not complete without those elements that degrade—and define—it. All is balanced: murderer and victim, motion and color, human and bird. The images of the birds brace the poem's meaning the way Kennedy braces the middle two lines of his stanzas with two shorter lines that rhyme:

> Meanwhile, at one remove,
> From the cool eaves of the urinal
> Plump hens with throats of umber, breasts of coral,
> Flute and approve.
>
> (ll. 29–32)

The hens close the poem on a positive note, which balances the opening scene, where two "he-males" perch on "rusty benches" and attack each other. The male birds are of the same breed as the drug dealer who murders the boy. The hens add beautiful colors and a cool, approving, peaceful presence. Like deities perched in judgment, the hens "Flute and approve," suggesting that death, squalor, and cold indifference are the deserved lot of humanity, while they perch above it like the last line in the stanza above.

Kennedy repeats this picture somewhat in a poem late in *Dark Horses*, "Tableau Intime," which suggests that the image of animals suffering human deprivation with dignity and patience is compelling to him. In this poem Kennedy displays another of his talents: the ability to intensify meaning and effect by contrasting a uniform, attractive structure with images of disorder and ugliness. The "intimate picture" of the ironic title is a sordid slice-of-life in the lives of three people, a "large mother"; her daughter, Cora; and the mother's "live-in" lover, Fritz. All three are unattractive individuals behaving in an unattractive manner. In the opening scene, the lover is vomiting into a toilet; Cora is refusing to practice the violin; and the mother, in addition to urging the daughter to practice, referees the hostile exchanges between Cora and Fritz by bringing the daughter her "pills" and the lover his bottle of liquor. Kennedy then shifts the perspective: "Stunned by a bounding shoe, in its waterless bowl / The old paint-mottled pet turtle collects its wits." The turtle is superior to the humans in this scene. Victim of neglect and abuse, it still manages to remain free of the ugly behavior and thus to retain its innocence and dignity. The poem's five stanzas keep regular rhythms, and the rhymes are exact, if somewhat irregular; that is, Kennedy rhymes all of the lines in the second and fourth stanzas but does not do so in the other three, and he uses rhyme to emphasize the ugliness:

> Curls in a heap on the couch, limp from the rebuke
> Of her large mother who stands imploring, "Practice,
> Damn you, practice your violin." A stream of puke
>
> Pours from her mother's live-in lover's lips. . . .
>
> (ll. 2–5)

The repetition of *l*'s in that final line gives the image additional emphasis, suggesting sensuality in a mess of vomit. The man and woman are bound together by parallel acts, spewing, but what they spew defines their character as well as the quality of their outpouring. Visuals for Kennedy are an essential poetic device, whether they are reflected in the outline of the poem itself or its images.

The use of spacing and placement of words on a page to represent meaning is a common practice among poets. A poet writing free verse might visually represent rain by placing the letters vertically so that they appear to "fall" down the page. Kennedy himself will resort to this visual device, as he does in "Two Views of Rhyme and Meter" and "Alternatives." In "Fall Song," a translation of Paul Verlaine's "Chanson d'Automne," Kennedy closely follows the original poem in using word placement to create an emblem of the subject. The lines are broken into short ones of two and three stresses each that rhyme in all three stanzas. In the first stanza especially, this structural feature, combined with the sound patterns of long and short *o* sounds, reflects the subject of the lines, the fall season, whose characteristic sound is a moaning wind:

> Low notes drawn long,
> Fall's fiddlesong
>   Makes moan,
> Lets heart loll
> In its dull
>   Monotone.
>
> (ll. 1–6)

Each stanza, discrete and short, is shaped almost like a leaf, and as the three stanzas advance down the page they suggests leaves falling. Kennedy makes subtle use of this device in so many poems that it becomes characteristic. In "In Faith of Rising" the lines, thirteen of them, are centered on the page and reflects the speaker's "alignment" with God.

In another poem on a religious theme, "Great Chain of Being,"[43] the structure gives the appearance of a chain, befitting the poem's subject. Each of the five stanzas forms a link in the chain of poetic statements that corresponds to the links in the natural descent from "Lord God at the top" to the "dumb mud at the bottom rung," as the first stanza says. A two-line refrain at the end of each stanza throughout the poem—for example, "*Great Chain of Being, / Great Chain of Being*" and "*All its spokes busted, / All its spokes busted*"—serves as the point where each stanza links subject and structure.

Some traditional forms, such as the sonnet and couplet, possess features that allow, even invite, the use of contrast and the interplay of order and disorder, regularity and irregularity, to create certain effects. Kennedy frequently and imaginatively uses these advantages, making the poem's design emblematic of his meaning in more complex ways, as he demonstrates in "Nothing in Heaven Functions as It Ought." He uses the traditional sonnet structure to contrast heaven and hell, devoting the octave to heaven, the sestet to hell, and double spacing between the two parts, emphasizing their separation. Heaven is a disorderly place, and the rhythm and sounds reflect the lack of harmony: "Peter's bifocals, blindly sat on, crack; / His gates lurch wide with the cackle of a cock. . . ." The slant–rhyme of *crack* with *cock* together with the word *cackle* and the image, "gates lurch wide," reinforces this meaning. Harsh, heavy sounds reinforce the cacophony: "crack . . . cackle . . . cock . . . choir . . . keep breaking up, coughing." In hell, where machinery dominates, on the other hand, the rhythms are regular and the rhymes are true. The irony of the poem is that heaven is a place where events happen by accident, but the order in hell is grim by comparison. Kennedy suggests that order and harmony are antithetical to freedom, and though muddle may result without a strict adherence to them, it is preferable to the mechanical, monotonous misery of hell. To this irony Kennedy adds that of structure, using a very order-demanding sonnet form to argue in favor of a certain kind of disorder and freedom. He thus demonstrates a paradox that is fundamental to his poetics: the poet must submit to the restrictions of a demanding form to gain a measure of freedom. A slavish adherence to form produces a hellish monotony; disorder, however, produces a divine comedy, or can. This poem offers the ideal picture: both monotony and chaos are avoided.

Reviewing "Nothing in Heaven Functions as It Ought," Robert E. Bjork says that the "malfunctioning sonnet becomes the perfect vehicle for the poet's message" as Kennedy "manipulates meter" and rhyme to establish and defeat expectations in the poem, both formal and cultural: "Whereas iambic pentameter, with occasional trochaic or spondaic substitutions, usually characterizes the sonnet, the meter here is chaotic in the octave, regular in the sestet, once more coinciding with the meaning of each."[44] These skillful effects, Bjork asserts, include Kennedy's using "imagery and diction, like form and meter, to underscore meaning and intensify the markedly ironic, Shavian tone of his ostensibly simple poem."[45] Marden Clark also looks closely at this sonnet, seeing in it essentially what Bjork does, a masterful use of diction, rhythm, rhyme, and other elements that convey the poem's vision of heaven and hell. To Clark, the sonnet creates an impressive "energy" and demonstrates by its formal achievements a literary paradox: restricting form "has been the means of releasing the energy in the poem."[46] In this case, Kennedy's Catholicism provides the concepts and experience that give the poem its power and meaning.

David Shapiro sees a similar use of form in *Celebrations after the Death of John Brennan,* an elegy written in memory of a former student of Kennedy's. The poem's rhythms reflect the poet's emotional state, for the poem is "full of rigorous metrical struggle with itself." For Shapiro, too, Kennedy's attention to form seems to be as important as the subject in the poem: "Its conscientiousness is also a topic of the elegy. . . ." Kennedy seems to find solace in complications of form, weaving into his own words quotations from the student's own writing. In this way, Kennedy creates the effect of "carrying on a last painful dialogue with the dead" and at the same time "contrives a discontinuous unity." Intellectualizing emotion does not drain it of its power, however; nor does the act of making an artifact of one's experience diffuse emotion or make it artificial; rather, the process is transformed into emotional experience and revelation. Structure becomes an objective correlative of the poet's emotional struggle, so that any disarray in form may be seen as the poet's disquietude. This may be what Shapiro means when he says of *Celebrations,* "A fine enjambment reminds one of the disorderly vitality of didactic decorums."[47]

The structural features of "On a Child Who Lived One Minute" reflect a disorder of another kind, one that does not let newborns live. The poem's framework appears at first glance regular: all the lines are of even length; all three stanzas contain five lines each and are closed. Within this neat package, however, the lines are fragmented by internal stops; enjambment pulls phrases apart, and slant rhyme suggests that something is not quite right, that the world is imperfect. The poet himself seems emotionally pulled apart, caught up in the give-and-take of life and death: "Her first breath drew a fragrance from the air / And put it back." (ll. 6–7). He is also caught up in the demands of his elegy, having to keep the lines regular and having to rhyme and make sense, yet something in him rebels: "Oh, let us do away with elegiac / Drivel!" (ll. 11–12). The slant rhymes reflect his loss of control and his impatience with form. In light of the child's death, they seem mere "jingle." Yet at the end, he hints at a restored faith as the mystery of life and death causes him to "marvel," and having come back to that center, he makes his final rhyme true:

Who can restore a thing so brittle,
So new in any jingle? Still I marvel
That, making light of mountainloads of logic,
So much could stay a moment in so little.

(ll. 12–15)

As he often does, Kennedy makes the poem itself a statement about making poetry. In the context of his final stanza, in which he expresses doubts about the efficacy of poetry, the final two lines take on added meaning. The two phrases "So much" and "so little" refer to the child's life and her brief time on earth. At the same time, the two phrases also refer to the poem itself, so much meaning being expressed in so little space. In this context, the phrase "I marvel" suggests a renewed faith in the power of poetry to express feeling and to contain somehow "mountainloads of logic."

A much later poem, "Separated Banks," shows that Kennedy's sophisticated use of design to create the image of the poem's meaning remains an essential feature in his poetry. The separated banks of the river symbolize the separation of a man and wife:

It seems as if both sides await
Some last division of estate
Or kind winds from a civil court
To shake one down for nonsupport.

(ll. 9–12)

The fallen bridge represents their failed marriage and consequent separation. The winds that felled the bridge are depicted as the actions of "a civil court" that might "shake one down for nonsupport." The poem becomes almost playful in the fourth stanza in portraying a "go-between" in the image of "one wan oak leaf at loose ends," passing from one bank to the other. Nature, imagistically, is thus enlisted in the poem's effort to answer the question, Can this marriage be mended? The wind aptly characterizes the unbridled, unpredictable, and impetuous nature of human emotions. In the effort to "make amends," all that nature can offer is a solitary oak leaf, no match for the violence of human emotions.

By casting the poem's meaning in imagery of natural objects, wind, oak leaf, and river (representing time and the shifts in human events and emotions), Kennedy further suggests that great forces are behind human affairs and that humans are subject to those forces and are helpless to change them. In the final stanza the poem drops the natural imagery, as if stripping away the metaphoric guise—and reminding the reader that the imagery is only a guise—to reveal the human element underneath:

> And where's true compromise in such
> A slight attempt to keep in touch?
> Neither owns up to being wrong
> And so they stand and stand and long.
>
> (ll. 17–20)

The last line suggests that a "true compromise" is possible, if only both sides would admit to being wrong. Such an admission would break the stalemate that separates them. Though a mutual attraction holds the couple together, they are fixed in everlasting separation by and in the image.[48] Those who think Kennedy's penchant for punning diminishes his stature as a "serious" poet ought to ponder the final line of this poem. The pun on "long" heightens the seriousness of the poem's message, that pride causes unnecessary and lasting pain. Rather than making light of a serious subject or diminishing the force by resorting to a "shallow" device, Kennedy demonstrates the power a pun can have, when used by one who appreciates its potential and has the skill to mine its depths.

Kennedy achieves another small triumph in "Similes," whose title draws attention to the poem's formal design before the poem's subject is introduced. The poem's ostensible purpose seems to be to exercise Kennedy's skill in making similes, but in reading the poem one realizes that Kennedy's far more serious goal is to draw a connection between a kind of human experience and certain aspects of nature. The simile is a literary device used to reveal correspondences that the simile itself symbolizes. Kennedy is suggesting that the simile is more than a device; it symbolizes the relation of humans to nature: what happens in the one sphere has its correspondence in the other. The poem's first simile establishes the relationship between the outdoors and indoors and between the man and the woman:

> As fallen snow, allowed to take firm hold
>   While all inside draw solace from the fire,
> Revolving brandy in balloons of gold,
>   No shoveler at the doorbell seeking hire,
> Exerts its weight in silence, and slow rain
>   Seals and defines the content of each drift,

So our misunderstanding, settling in,
  Hardened to ice impossible to lift.

(ll. 1–8)

The pun on "drift" in the sixth line underscores the connection between the outdoors and the couple's misunderstanding, which has "Hardened to ice impossible to lift." In the next stanza, the speaker dismisses his companion—"Go catch your death of absence"—thinking she will miss him, but he discovers otherwise: "the world he'd quit withstands / The downfall he so yearns for"; in fact, it even "exudes / Top popsong hits, diurnal tax demands" (ll. 12–14). The final stanza, and final simile, compares the speaker and the woman he is addressing to humans who destroy one another: "As killers who'd accelerate decay" by pouring "on an upturned face a cloud of lime. . . ." This simile, like the one in the opening lines, mingles a natural element, a cloud, with humans; the word, *decay*, and the mocking reference to earth taking "her own sweet time" bring the two realms even closer by combining their functions or characteristics into the same word, just as the word *diurnal* does in a line from the previous stanza: the world "exudes / Top popsong hits, diurnal tax demands" (ll. 13–14). The final phrase in this line is part of a pattern of images that fuses into a single linguistic unit the natural and human realms. In the first stanza, for example, a similar coalescence takes place in the line "the slow rain / Seals and defines the content of each drift," in which the words "Seals," "content," and "drift" refer both to the rain and the snow and to human affairs: in their exchanges, their words seal, the conversations have content, and their meaning has a "drift." Kennedy's apparent playfulness with words and word sounds, as in the phrases "her own sweet time" and "Top popsong," cannot be separated from his primary purpose in a poem such as this, which is fundamentally about disjunction, decay, discordance, and death; were it only playfulness, he might well be accused of flippancy or superficiality, but he is too serious about disjunction for discrepancies between sound and sense to be anything but keen insight; or he is equally concerned about what words ordinarily mean and what they mean in a context in which the human realm opposes—and ultimately decomposes—nature. The simile, as this poem demonstrates, is the structure of profound insight.

Kennedy achieves a similar triumph in "Overnight Pass," a poem from *Dark Horses*. In this poem, he shows his skill in developing two very disparate ideas simultaneously with the same image. A soldier's trek through terrain at the battle front is turned into the soldier's spending the night with a prostitute. Her wrinkled demeanor has the "rutted look" of the battlefield, and when the soldier traversed her terrains, the experience was akin to fording streams and mounting "hills thick / And dark with tufted firs" (ll. 3–4). Her roads are "in disrepair," too, and regiments have passed "scatheless" over her terrain:

> Up from her body's stony trench
> Where many a private crept,
> Ducked for a while the kiss of shell
> And caught his breath and slept.
>
> (ll. 9–12)

This final image of the woman makes her an impersonal, anonymous "trench" that gives temporary safety to fighting men. More than being a witty extended comparison that evokes a knowing grin, however, the poem loses the grin as it inverts the comparison, suggesting that the battlefield is a prostitute through which hordes of soldiers have passed, found brief refuge, and died.

Still exploring the permutations of dislocated love with the power and wit of parallel meanings—one world mirroring the other in telling reflection—Kennedy turns to the disillusioned woman in another poem collected in *Dark Horses.* "Speculating Woman" develops as a conceit that compares the male-female relationship to investing money. The poem's speaker explains that as a result of being "Left in the lurch," she takes revenge by investing her monetary resources instead of her emotional resources. This shift has brought her a surer profit: "A constant eight per cent more fond / I grew in that new marriage bond . . ." (ll. 5–6). Several other puns rise from this principal conceit: she beds down "with a dollar bill" and finds herself "In Grover Cleveland's rustling arms." Turning away from men has been a profitable move for the woman, saving her from emotional loss while bringing her monetary gains. She has replaced unsecured investments with more reliable returns: "Unlike grown daughters, dividends / Make no pretense to be your friends . . ." (ll. 9–10). Although the woman boasts a more profitable bond with investments and savors the revenge she has taken, her victory rings hollow: "What mortal husband do you know / Whose interest each month will grow?" (ll. 13–14). Kennedy has developed a marvelously effective portrait of a woman who has succeeded in reducing her love relationships to profit and loss. The irony is that she cannot see how reduced she has become; thinking that she has grown because her stocks have accrued greater value, she measures her successes monetarily. Her financial sheet is balanced but her mind is not.

Kennedy continues to demonstrate his interest in natural forces and their relation to human existence in "Twelve Dead, Hundreds Homeless." As in other poems, the forces of nature are the protagonists, and as they are personified, they seem to take on superhuman dimensions and strength. To heighten the wind's destructive power, Kennedy contrasts it to the soothing nature of song, using the poem's rhythms to suggest the wind's motions and imagery to reinforce the connection between design and meaning:

> The wind last night kept breaking into song—
> Not a song, though, to comfort children by.
> It picked up houses, flung them down awry,
> Upended bridges, drove slow trees along
> To walls.
>
> (ll. 1–5)

The poem's first line moves smoothly from beginning to end, the rhythm and mellifluous sound slightly interrupted by *kept* and *breaking*, which forecast the abrupt halt and staccato movement in the second line's single-syllable language: "Not a song, though. . . ." When he wants the sensation of flinging and wants to suggest the violence of the windstorm, Kennedy resorts to single-syllable words and harder *d* sounds, as in "Upended bridges, drove. . . ." The image of the wind driving trees along leads into the second abrupt stop in the fourth line: "To walls." Ironically, these auditory effects underscore Kennedy's meaning: the sound of the wind was "Beautiful only if you heard it wrong" (l. 12). The poem gains tension by repeating the line "The wind last night kept breaking into song" (l. 11) and contrasting it with images of destruction. The human tendency to see beauty in natural events is viewed here as a dangerous delusion. Though succumbing to the beautiful sounds in this poem is not a dangerous delusion, Kennedy uses sound and rhythm to demonstrate how powerful such lures can be and how easily one can come under their spell. He casts a spell to dispel mistaken notions.

In "On the Liquidation of the Mustang Ranch by the Internal Revenue Service," Kennedy again uses structural features to construct a vivid image of the poem's subject. The poem's theme is suggested in the rhythm of the first line of the second stanza: "A hibernating snake / . . . Lies not more still. Beneath the auctioneer's / Gavel. . . ." The halting rhythm of the phrase "Lies not more still" contrasts with the image of the "hibernating snake" in the previous line. The absence of formal regularity, suggesting a sprung logic, is evident in the rhyme patterns as well. The first stanza divides into two quatrains, each rhyming *abba.* The second stanza, however, scarcely rhymes at all. Only the third and fifth lines rhyme, leaving an odd pattern: *abcdce.* The scantiest of assonance may be noted in the end words of the first and second lines, *auctioneer's* and *lingerie.* It is as though Kennedy purposefully abandoned rhyme in the first part of the second stanza so as to avoid writing a sonnet, although the poem's fourteen lines and division into a stanza of eight lines followed by one of six lines indicate otherwise. This "deviant" structure suggests that something is out of focus, maladjusted, and awry.

The poem further uses imagery to weave together meanings that are conveyed both structurally and semantically. At the division of the two stanza, the poem thus split apart, Kennedy places the image of a snake: "A hibernating snake / Lies not more still." He is writing of the Mustang Ranch, suggesting that, although it "lies here slain," the ranch will, like the snake, awaken. Human lust, as natural and predictable as the snake's waking from hibernation, forecasts the revival of this house of sin. The statement about the snake is split in two, yet, semantically, it bridges the gap between the two stanzas. By implication and by design, this disheveled sonnet is in the same state as the Mustang Ranch. Reader interest will keep the poem alive, just as lust will save the ranch. Once again, Kennedy demonstrates a sexual link between making poetry and making love.

In *Landscapes with Set-Screws,* which is divided into two parts, "The Autumn in Norfolk Shipyard" and "Airport in the Grass," Kennedy again uses structural features to create a visual replica of his subject. The poem's complex framework hints at the structured look of a naval yard, with its cranes and cables, girders and ships, as seemingly haphazard as the unrhymed lines themselves:

The Autumn in Norfolk Shipyard

Is a secret one infers
From camouflage. Scrap steel

Betrays no color of season,
Corrosion works year-round.
But in sandblasted stubble
Lurks change: parched thistle burr,
Blown milkweed hull—dried potholes
After tides reassume their foam.

(ll. 1–8)

The scene could not be more arid and devoid of life, and in the second stanza, the clutter continues to pile up: "Destroyers mast to mast . . . Moored tankers . . . Under a power crane . . . In drydock ripened tugs," and so on. The first two stanzas are shaped like a steel plate. Their form is open, unrhymed lines without regular end-stops unfolding like prose and stopping almost haphazardly through nineteen lines. In the first stanza above, a predominance of *s* and *b* sounds underscores the harsh, heavy qualities of this wasteland. Paramount in the build-up of this scene is the ironic interplay between what man has done with his machines and what nature has done, an interplay of two forces, that of humans and that of nature. Nature "corrodes" the green leaf, turning it in autumn to brown, whereas human corrosions only destroy and are not in a natural cycle that leads to rebirth. The more the poem identifies the elements of the shipyard in natural terms, the more emphatic grows the ironic contrast between nature and machine, concluding the first section with a pun that joins manmade junk with nature's autumnal shedding: "Green seas spill last year's needles." The by-product of nature's autumn is recyclable; the by-product of human creation is ugly, hazardous waste that destroys the environment.

Section two shifts scene as well as stanzaic form:

Airport in the Grass

Grasshopper copters whir
Blue blurs
Traverse dry air,

Cicadas beam a whine
On which to zero in flights
Of turbojet termites,

A red ant carts
From the fuselage of the wren that crashed
Usable parts

And edging the landingstrip,
Heavier than air the river
The river
The rustbucket river
Revs up her motors forever.

(ll. 1–14)

The shift is dramatic: the poem seems to come alive with living creatures—grasshoppers, cicadas, termites, red ants—all bringing life to this scrap heap and making life in it and from it. Kennedy intertwines nature and junk syntactically to reflect their physical merging. The grassy world of the live creatures becomes an "airport" where "Grasshopper copters whir" and "turbojet termites" land. The theme of environmental depredation continues through the final stanza, in which rhyme, rhythm, and repetition are used to drive home the final point: "the river / The river / The rustbucket river / Revs up her motors forever."

Kennedy uses also the visual character of the poem to focus attention, placing the single phrase, "The river," in the middle of the final stanza, as though the phrase is a fulcrum that balances yet joins two opposites: man's world and nature's. It marks a turning point in the thought, and the final two lines, with their emphasis on the *r* sound and the unstressed syllable at the end of the lines, give the appearance of being run-on and of running on like the river. Kennedy's skill at having the form of his poem reflect what the words are saying is quite evident here, and the use of irony to make his point is too: though man has turned the river into a polluted rustbucket, it shall flow on forever. Nature's engine, in the end, is more powerful, more sustaining and sustained, than any of those found in a shipyard or airport. The underlying absurdity, if not hubris, of equating human endeavor with machines is underscored in this final section, where grasshoppers are viewed as helicopters, and the lowly termite becomes a turbojet. Given the ultimate triumph of natural forces, however, the termite "becomes" a turbojet and the turbojet "becomes" a termite. Human mechanical prowess has inverted nature, and this thesis is reflected in the way Kennedy inverts with the use of language and imagines his own point of view as he shifts from the shipyard scene to that of the airport.

Although deeply committed to poetry, traditional forms in particular, Kennedy has throughout his career questioned the value of this commitment. He ends his first collection of poems, *Nude Descending a Staircase,* with "One A.M. with Voices," a dialogue that seems to look back not only on the previous thirty-three poems in the collection, but more generally on what the poet does and intends to do. The scene is that of a man and woman in bed at one A.M., a subtle suggestion that the midnight hour of the poet's day has passed. The man "rimes" and is a tomcat; the woman, a mouse—he addresses her as "sweet mouse." She wants him to quit wasting his time "coupling on a page"; instead, he should couple with her in bed. She says that the mice he chases in his verse are "dream-mice," and she asks what motivates him, "Is it love or rage?" Not for love, he answers—that would be "rape indeed." The "old creeping tom," when awake, chases phantoms in his mind. The woman believes the result is not worth the effort: "When did you ever catch a mouse / But lean ones, wide awake?" (ll. 23–24). She suggests he "Put cat and light out" and grope elsewhere for a mouse. Although she has the final word, the implication is that the poet is compelled to perform otherwise; awake, he will have the mouse holes that are in his mind to keep an eye on, mice to hunt, and rhymes to peruse in a room where "shapes twitch." The lure of the flesh, representing the need to function in a physical, practical, and demanding world, is strong, but the poet's urge to rhyme is as strong and persistent, as is the feline instinct to prowl in search of mice.

The poem suggests that the poet must keep his eye fixed on his true task, his real journey. By casting the poet's progress in terms of a tomcat chasing mice, Kennedy acknowledges the point made by those who doubt the value and efficacy of writing poetry, even going so far as to concede that the effort is impractical, perhaps even foolish, misguided. Nevertheless, "old creeping tom" must prowl. He must stay on course if he is to reach home. As the concluding poem in his first collection, "One A.M. with Voices" represents a confirmation of what Kennedy implies in "First Confession," that his independent spirit shall find expression in a secular tradition, that of poetry. The poet's conflict in "One A.M. with Voices" is again expressed in sexual terms, and again his independence is maintained. Yet the woman expresses doubts concerning the value of the creative effort that continues to occupy Kennedy's mind. These doubts return in various guises in a number of Kennedy's poems, both serious and playful.

Perhaps his final statement on the matter may be found in *Cross Ties*, which contains, he once said, most of the poems written before 1985 that he cares to preserve. The opening poem in that important volume, "On a Child Who Lived One Minute," has already been discussed in terms of its implicit commentary of the value of making poetry in general. Again, Kennedy seems to be having fun with the reader, suggesting that this "child" of his, this poem, lives but a moment, like the child in the poem. After all, is it not mere "jingle"? Despite that possibility, Kennedy comes to "marvel" that the child could contain "So much." Though this little child of his could stay but a moment, "making light of mountainloads of logic" (l. 14), it nevertheless wins his admiration, his dedication, and all his skill. By implication, he invites us to marvel too.

It is surprising, if one reads Kennedy's poetry carefully, that some critics and reviewers long considered Kennedy a poet of superficial ideas, whose chief skills were wit and wordplay, and whose poetry was best suited to an academic audience. The variety of designs he displayed from *Nude Descending a Staircase* onward, the range of subjects, and, above all, the skill and frequency with which he constructed poems of power, insight, and complex meanings laid a foundation of a career that would become increasingly better understood and appreciated. One might focus on any of Kennedy's skills—his wit, his use of rhyme and meter, or his imagery, to name but a few—and miss the total effect of them all. The subtlety with which he designs many poems could be missed by a reader who is distracted or dazzled by the puns, the playfulness, the sound effects, the clever rhymes, and other more obvious elements, but the more one reads, sees, and feels the total design of a particular poem, the more one understands and appreciates the craftsmanship and Kennedy's superb ability to craft poems in which the whole is always far greater than the parts considered by themselves.

Chapter 2
The Poetry Collections

LIKE OTHER POETS, KENNEDY PUBLISHED MANY OF HIS POEMS SEPARATELY in various magazines and periodicals before accumulating enough to put them into a single volume. In doing so, he was able to select only those he felt were worthy of reprinting and to make changes in some of them. On the whole, these changes are minor, but they do show a penchant for revising even work that has been published. He confesses that the temptation to revise finished work is dangerous. He has told the story of an early misjudgment in this regard. After one of his poems had been accepted by the prestigious *Poetry* magazine, Kennedy had second thoughts: "I began toying with the accepted poem, rewrote the last lines, loused them up, but took a notion that my later inspiration was superior. . . . I rushed the new draft to Mr. Rago [then editor of *Poetry*], begging him to substitute it. Another silence followed, and then a gentle letter explaining that he thought the original version much better, that he himself was often prone to second thoughts, but that in this case I had best leave well enough alone. . . . I now know that Henry Rago wasn't willful, but wise. (The poem, "Nude Descending a Staircase," unmuddied by my later worryings, appeared in *Poetry* in January 1960.)"[1]

By 1960, while still in graduate school, Kennedy had already published poetry in the *New Yorker, Poetry, Paris Review,* and other prestigious magazines, including *The Cornhill Magazine* in England. At the urging of Naomi Burton, a literary agent with Curtis Brown Limited, Kennedy assembled thirty-four poems into a book and called it *Nude Descending a Staircase,* which appeared in 1961 and promptly won the Lamont Award from Academy of American Poets, which only first books by American poets may receive. This was an impressive beginning for the young poet. The book's title recalls a series of photographs with the same name created by Gustaf Marley in the 1880s. The series depicts a nude woman walking down stairs. This visual representation does with photography what Kennedy aimed to do in his own poems with language and poetic form. Kennedy would also have in mind the famous painting by Marcel Duchamps that caused some stir when exhibited in 1913. The painting transforms Marley's photographic idea into a Cubist vision that looks like, as one critic put it, an explosion of shingles. Both the photographs and the painting express the idea of sequence and introduce motion into a static form, suggesting to Kennedy that what was done in film and paint could be done in language on paper. He may also have wanted to associate his first book of poems with works of art that looked at experience in a new and sensational way. He therefore designed his first book to suggest that poetry is performance, a visual, musical potpourri that takes the reader through individual "acts" or scenes, the poet performing in various ways and creating various meanings, both serious and playful. Like the nude descending a staircase, the book would offer frames of static meaning set in motion by reading, and the result would be provocative, daring, and inviting. Performance is the key feature of the book's design, reflecting Kennedy's desire for the reader to see that poetry is both an aural and a visual experience, a desire that has fueled his career-long involvement in public readings of his work. This first book of poems also marked Kennedy as a traditionalist of impressive technical skill, represented by the ballad, elegy, sonnet, epigram, with a heavy emphasis on the quatrain, and some verse for children. His mastery of form drew immediate praise and serious attention from many reviewers.

Clearly, Kennedy wanted to present the range of his poetic interests. His subjects in his first collection include the classical past, religious authority, and the modern condition. "Leave of Absence" reflects his academic experience, and several poems indicate an interest in and knowledge of French poetry ("Rondeau," "Ladies Looking for Lice," "Where Are the Snows of Yesteryear?"). All the poems together set the tone of Kennedy's whole career: irreverent, impatient with authority yet obedient to it, wayward, recalcitrant, witty, playful, yet profoundly serious. As a first collection, it shows remarkable maturity and polish in the handling of form and tone.[2] Though the product of a relatively young poet, it bears few marks of youth and inexperience. As his worldly experience grew and his mind sifted it, his attention would dwell more often on human types, human relationships, and human conditions. Children would receive greater attention; death would become a larger presence; and thoughts regarding the future, or fate, of humankind would invade his mind. Kennedy's development in his first collection was so sophisticated, however, that only the retrospect of nearly forty years would highlight these changes.

Among the critics, *Nude Descending a Staircase* established Kennedy as a poet of considerable skill in the use of conventional forms. His impressive weapons included metaphysical wit and Augustan satire, although his achievements in this area did not impress some critics favorably. John Simon saw Kennedy as "a curious cross between the *boulevardier* and the Metaphysical: he believes in the well-made, witty but significant poem, donning its top hat and its Donne. When this blend comes off . . . the effect is rousing. But when the wit fizzles or the elegance gets creased, things look sorry indeed. Even a relatively successful poem like "Solitary Confinement" can leave us ill at ease, because so serious a subject is handled with a facetiousness under which one looks in vain for a deeper humanity or profounder pessimism."[3] Nor did Forrest Read have much patience with Kennedy in this regard. He admired "the quick and clever wit for which Kennedy has been properly singled out," but he regretted that Kennedy "allows himself to become bedazzled by his own virtuosity."[4] Nevertheless, others saw much to be praised. Theodore Holmes noted some of Kennedy's trademark skills, an "incomparable mastery of pun" and an eye for the "fragmentation, impersonality unto death, and the disintegration of human values."[5] This laudatory assessment is remarkable for a young poet's first slim collection.

Because of his persistent use of rhyme, meter, and stanzaic regularity, Kennedy was regarded by many critics as an anachronism and was set upon by those who took offense at his use of traditional forms. More than one critic saw Kennedy's use of rhyme and meter as a weakness. One of them asserted: "He relies heavily on end rhyme and the four-stressed line, a form that lends itself to recitation rather than reading. The jaunty sound often carries the verse; that is, the sentiment or image may be nothing more than a commonplace dignified by rhyme . . . many of Kennedy's poems are funny, rhythmic, and interesting, but they are often superficial."[6] This same critic thought he had found the key to Kennedy's art, saying that "The clue to reading Kennedy comes as early as the table of contents in *Nude Descending a Staircase,* where readers find the book divided into three parts and an 'Intermission with Peanuts.' Kennedy's metaphor is a good one; his poems are usually entertaining sidelights or intermissions."[7] Forrest Read thought Kennedy's ballads had "only shaky voices. They remain too close to untransmuted jargon and sometimes descend nearly to doggerel." Read cannot praise Kennedy without heavy qualification: "In his poems on remembered subjects (a partial list: Jonson, Donne, Lewis Carroll, Waller, Rimbaud, Villon), he is far better than in the songs and ballad. But even there he is best at wry, oblique comment on the established and traditional, as by a witty and sharply perceptive scholar; he misses the note of compelling currency, of insight into modernity which would make even the traditional come alive. He looks back at the images of the past, and doesn't often enough live now, in this place, with them."[8] Read is impressed by Kennedy's "great skill with charged words, unexpected and surprising phrases, juxtapositions and overlays," and his "brilliant phrasing . . . has light, but it lacks fire."[9] Despite these snipes and misreadings, this first collection introduced several of Kennedy's most praised and enduring poems, including the title poem, "B Negative," "In a Prominent Bar in Secaucus One Day," "The Man in the Manmade Moon," and others, particularly "Solitary Confinement," about which Theodore Holmes said, "For its size, what more could anyone expect of poetry . . . ?"[10]

In the same year that *Nude Descending a Staircase* was published, 1961, poems by Kennedy and several of his friends—Donald Hall, Keith Waldrop, and W. D. Snodgrass, were collected in a chapbook titled *The Wolgamot Interstice.*[11] Of Kennedy's five poems, four were taken from *Nude Descending a Staircase.* His selection shows that he wanted a variety of moods. "Little Elegy," written "for a child who skipped rope" and in whose play Kennedy discovers circles of significance, added poignancy. Critic David Harsent objected to "Little Elegy" for its "woefully inadequate language" that produces a "stultifying cuteness," but he admired Kennedy's "economical, near vernacular line: by turns acerbic, lilting, or racy. . . ."[12] The boisterous "Satori," not in *Nude* and not in later collections, mocks beatniks and their lifestyle. "In a Prominent Bar in Secaucus One Day" showcases his interest in the musical aspects of poetry, especially in combination with bawdy humor and raucous goings-on in low places. The two-line "Overheard in the Louvre" again illustrates his gift for aphorism: "Said the Victory of Samothrace, / What winning's worth this loss of face?" He had already demonstrated this quality in *Nude* with "Ars Poetica," one of his most well-known and most appreciated poems:[13]

The goose that laid the golden egg
Died looking up its crotch
To find out how its sphincter worked.

Would you lay well? Don't watch.

The poem also serves as a testament to Kennedy's conviction that rhyme and meter have a place in modern poetry. The message in this succinct statement is timeless, as is all good poetry, Kennedy would say. "Ars Poetica" encapsulates Kennedy's acerbic wit and epitomizes his gift for combining serious and playful expression to the advantage of each. Kennedy ends his contribution to *The Wolgamot Interstice*, however, on a more serious note with "Leave of Absence," whose academic subject would suit this college production. In all, the five poems reflect Kennedy's conviction that poetry can be playfully wicked as well as serious.

In 1965 Anchor Books included five poems by Kennedy in its volume of poems *A Controversy of Poets: An Anthology of Contemporary American Poetry*, edited by Paris Leary and Robert Kelly. Though Kennedy's work shared space with the poems of Denise Levertov, Robert Lowell, Galway Kinnell, and other distinguished poets, it received little critical attention. Nevertheless, the poems again showcase the range of his subjects and moods, a range that includes serious intent and social consciousness as well as an irrepressible comic spirit. "A Water Glass of Whisky" depicts a slice of the American landscape where the inhabitants are connected to the outside world only by television. "Song to the Tune of 'Somebody Stole My Gal'" is a comical lament bemoaning the absence of classical myths in modern times. "Down in Dallas," already published in a collection devoted to the death of John F. Kennedy, transforms the assassination into an image of the Crucifixion and works toward a sense of harmony, balance, and compensation.[14] "Hearthside Story" treats of a young man's visit to a prostitute and his attempt to put the experience into perspective. The last poem, "Cross Ties," shows a remarkable sophistication and maturity early in Kennedy's career. Kennedy thought well enough of this poem to include it in all his major collections and to use its title for his award-winning collection.

In 1969 Kennedy again collected several years' worth of poems and published *Growing into Love*, his second major collection, this one published in hardcover. More substantial in terms of number of poems than *Nude Descending a Staircase*, it contains fifty-three poems, divided into three sections. Fifty of the poems are newly collected, and forty-two of them would find their way into later collections. Unlike *Nude Descending a Staircase*, the book contains no ballads or songs and lacks an "Intermission" containing light verse and epigrams. The poems, particularly in the first two sections, "Experiences" and "Countrymen," offer images of a modern American landscape blighted by industrialism or tourism. Unheroic people, trapped by materialism and greed and alienated from one another and from heaven, fall into madness or retreat into an alcoholic blur. In this world, men are lost and women are contemptuous of the failure of men to find enrichment and fulfillment. The middle section closes with the gloomy image of an army of modern men, all failures, twitching in death. One reviewer, Steven Tudor, understating the case, saw the poems of the first two sections as "rather negative," adding that "While art itself is an affirmation, the occasions for these poems seem bitter, even petulant."[15] The third section, "Growing into Love," injects a note of hope, however. Tudor believed the poems in this part of the book "mainly celebrate various dimensions of love."[16] The dozen poems in this section speak of man's rescue from his worst conditions and qualities. Though salvation is not attained, endurance is noted. In their journey, humans may be improving. "Growing into Love," for Kennedy at least, suggests emotional growth and reflects a broader understanding of his personal experience and public vision.

Not surprisingly, reviewers of this collection spoke of Kennedy's characteristic intellectual intensity, inventiveness, and laughter.[17] Peter Simpson saw in the new collection an "ability to see oneself grappling sheepishly—yet with a kind of sustained grace—with the large and the small challenges of the human condition. . . ." He regarded this ability as one of Kennedy's "most engaging qualities. . . ."[18] John Leggett noted these same qualities and found "a pair of triumphs in the collection," the poems "Cross Ties" and "Ant Trap." [19] On the other hand, reviewer John Demos echoed earlier complaints, that Kennedy's word play and "sophisticated wit" and "metaphors under glass mar what otherwise would have been straight but good poems." When "wit and passion meet, this poet can be brilliantly wonderful." Demos also finds Kennedy's language "verbally sensuous," particularly in lines such as "O Lukewarm spew, you, stir yourself and boil," from "West Somerville, Mass."[20] This poem represents the volume's serious elements, which critic Alan Brownjohn singled out for comment, saying that "under the confident surfaces lurk numerous worries about sin, war, religion . . ." Recalling Kennedy's first collection, Brownjohn said that *Growing into Love* is "less overtly humorous"; it seemed that Kennedy "really wants to do something grave and substantial with this flair for polished, elaborate, zanily conceited writing." To Brownjohn, Kennedy is "one of a diminishing band of American academic poets who are still fettering these topics in punctilious metrics," but Brownjohn thinks that Kennedy is improving: "he is beginning to turn to a kind of eloquent irony that is all his own, especially where the social detail succeeds ('Poets' and 'Pottery Class'), or where he goes in for grim, pointless narrative. 'Artificer,' a poem of insolent, ingenious extravagance, succeeds beautifully."[21] Knute Skinner also believed that this collection "shows a deepening seriousness of purpose. The comic poems turn serious and the serious poems reflect a mind grappling with aspiration and doubt at one and the same time."[22]

Growing into Love further established Kennedy as a practitioner of traditional forms. In a review of this collection, Skinner refers to Kennedy as "a marvelous, if unfashionable, poet," then sets out to defend his use of rhyme and meter by instancing "Reading Trip," which Skinner considered "a tour de force narrative in heroic sestets. . . ."[23] Thomas Tessier began his review of the collection by saying that "Kennedy's techniques are conventional—his rhymes and stanza forms date back centuries—but he is always in control and never uses the forms for mere convenience."[24] Though Kennedy was still considered "academic" for his efforts, at least one critic was able to see that traditional forms were a source of his excellence:[25] "His adherence to stricter forms never hampers the verve and forcefulness of his writing, nor the acuteness of his irony. On the contrary, his poems demonstrate the great value of traditional devices in giving shape and muscle to imaginative vision. While it is all the rage these days to make poems discontinuous and open-ended, Kennedy's work can stand as a sturdy reminder of what can be accomplished by order and unity. His new book is refreshing and delightful."[26] Tessier agrees that Kennedy's "rhythms are often subtle and clever, and would . . . sound very musical if the poems were to be read aloud." Tessier also senses "powerful and potentially explosive passions smoldering beneath the surface" of the book's final poem, "The Shorter View."[27]

In his review of *Growing into Love,* James Carroll saw Kennedy's use of form in a positive light, saying Kennedy "takes form seriously and bothers to work hard at it. He is master of an un-self-conscious rhyme," and his "disciplined expression allows him to achieve control and flexibility." Carroll believed that this volume would establish Kennedy "as one of our country's formidable poets."[28] This prediction has proven correct. Reviewer Henry Taylor appreciated Kennedy's skills with light verse, "which he is able to raise above the usual level." Taylor was especially impressed by Kennedy's "astonishing ability to absorb and revivify the flat rhythms and colloquialisms of contemporary American speech."[29] He cites the language of "O'Riley's Late-Bloomed Little Son," a poem on the death of a child who had been frostbitten and then died from croup: "in their arms he just went stiff" (l. 6). The bland finality of this statement and the sorrow inherent in its meaning poignantly balance ordinary speech and fresh poetic insight and expression. Perhaps it is in instances like this one that a critic like Louis Martz sees Kennedy's "admirable taciturnity"[30] as well as the revivication of ordinary speech.

Thomas Tessier refers to one of the few very personal poems Kennedy has written. In "The Shorter View," the final poem in *Growing into Love,* Kennedy returns to the theme that is developed in the book's first poem, "Cross Ties," the theme of procreation and generation and of futurity. Kennedy develops "The Shorter View" on two levels, in literal and metaphorical terms: the wife and husband are in bed, and she falls asleep reading while he is thinking of birth, death, and the future of their family. He imagines she is seeing them both in their old age: "seeing how in space / Stars in old age will stagger, drop, and burst, / throwing out far their darknesses and dust." Kennedy's ambivalence is evident in the contrasting meanings of these lines: they are stars, but they shall become decrepit and die; they will have offspring, but their children are "darknesses and dust." His ambivalence extends to what his wife thinks of him, or will think of him, when he is old. When the wife "lets her book fall with stricken face," stricken because she has not thought of dying: "She'd thought tomorrow set and rooted here, / And people" (ll. 5–6). She also sees "through me to an earth / Littered with ashes, too dried-up to bear" (ll. 9–10). The vision, in which the old husband and the earth are one and the same, causes her to see little point in giving birth, and her despair casts a shadow over their marriage bed and over the future. Making children takes place in "our dark bed," and giving birth is a growing burden, more so in light of these dark thoughts. The wife, "Her arms drawn shut," appears to retreat from her husband, his love making, his lack of concern: "What the Hell," he tells her, "we won't be there" (l.

11). She knows their descendant will be, and this conviction makes her obstinate in the face of his indifference: "this night will not give / One inch of ground for any shorter view" (ll. 15–16). The poem returns full circle—even the language makes it so, "Her eyes" opening the poem and "view" closing it—back to the wife's vision, only by the close of the poem, her arms are closed, contrasting with her "outstretched" eyes at the beginning, and his ambivalence turns into her obduracy.

At the time he was having doubts about parental responsibility, Kennedy looked at the issue from a different perspective in "One-Night Homecoming." Though not collected in *Growing into Love,* the poem grew out of the same stage of his poetic development and shows that he had more than a passing interest in this theme.[31] The poem records the disillusionment that occurs when one returns to the parental home and discovers change. Parents get old: the father cannot quite lift the son's suitcase, "Breathes hard, mounting stairs," and the mother "doesn't notice yolk stuck to the dishes / Nailheads arising from the kitchen chairs" (ll. 2–4). The son cannot endure his mother's "persistent needling," which "hurts without intending to, like sleet" (ll. 7–8). The parents' physical deterioration is reflected in images of deterioration in the house itself, symbol of the child's world:

> From childhood's bed I follow in the ceiling
> The latest progress of each crack I know,
> But still the general cave-in hangs suspended,
> Its capillary action running slow,
>
> And the huge roof I used to think unchanging
> Gives with each wind.
>
> (ll. 9–14)

Kennedy sees the speaker's discovery as part of a generational sequence: "It's my turn now to fall / Over strewn blocks, stuffed animals on staircases, / My turn to read the writing crayoned on the wall" (ll. 14–16). The decline runs through the generations, perhaps all the way from Eden—the use of the word "fall" suggests this idea. The poem's tone is pessimistic; children are viewed as clutterers whose crayon markings on the wall forecast decline and symbolize destruction. Parents are seen as deteriorated beings, and with advancement into adulthood comes sight enough to see the human predicament, which is dismal.

Growing into Love showed Kennedy at his most personal. Many critics again focused on his use of traditional forms, overlooking the many poems in which he turns the light directly onto his own experience. "Cross Ties" opens the collection, as if to signal to the reader that the book's focus shall be on aspects of the poet's life. This poem is immediately followed by "Snapshots," which includes two parts, "Birth Report" and "The Nineteen-thirties," both of which deal with Kennedy's first days of infancy. The first poem, "Birth Report," likens the poet's conception to a foot race: "When blam! My father's gun began the dash / Of fifty thousand tadpoles for one egg . . ." (ll. 1–2). From the start, Kennedy sees his life as a struggle, and it did not get any better: "And then my mother in a nest my aunt / Had paid for let me down" (ll. 5–6). Although the baby's delivery is a "letting down," Kennedy's primary meaning here is that his mother disappointed him somehow, perhaps by simply bringing him into this world. The second poem of this pair, "The Nineteen-thirties," reinforces the idea that the poet was brought into a horrible place: "Wall Street swallowed brokers whole," in the Midwest "dust clouds chased their tails like dogs" (ll. 1–2), and the Holocaust raged while the infant, "Not knowing who'd been let to live / Or who'd been herded in and gassed" (ll. 5–6), slept. The pair of memories ends on another catastrophe: "The sky's bough broke. Down fell / The Hindenburg's big blue hornet's nest" (ll. 7–8). Kennedy saw himself brought into the world of unspeakable horrors for which he was not responsible. By placing these two "snapshots" together, Kennedy suggests that the larger context follows from and creates a context for the smaller one and that somehow they cannot be disconnected from each other, only from heaven. Both are the result of a separation: the poet was let down, the world fell down. Together, they go down.

In "The Shorter View," in addition to its picture of marriage, Kennedy offers a vision of his own child's future that reminds one of his view of his own infancy: his child shall inherit "an earth / Littered with ashes, too dried-up to bear." It is undoubtedly these images that trouble his mind whenever he considers his role in continuing the generations, as he does in "Cross Ties" and in later poems, such as "Last Child" and "One-Night Homecoming" (all three collected in *Cross Ties*). In "Cross Ties" he senses something "Bearing down Hell-bent from behind my back" (l. 4), and he believes the world might be ruled by both God and the devil. In "Last Child" he has begun to see that the babies themselves may be part of the problem: "Your fingers writhe: inane anemones / A decent ocean ought to starve" (ll. 9–10).

The last section of *Growing into Love* contains poems that reveal perhaps more than any other group of poems Kennedy's ambivalent attitude toward not only his own children but his wife. They are among his most personal poems and probably the last ones of this kind he would publish. Several poems in the collection show that he views his own infancy with mixed feelings, mainly negative. "First Confession," in *Nude Descending a Staircase,* is the first poem that deals with Kennedy's troubled relations with the church. In "At the Stoplight by the Paupers' Graves," another poem from *Nude,* the poem's protagonist is stopped at a traffic light thinking of the dead in a nearby cemetery. He wants to have faith, but he has "no heart to wait with them all night / That would be long to tense here for a leap. . . ." (ll. 10–11). Kennedy uses the same image in "Cross Ties" to characterize a similar feeling, this one associated with his own parenthood: "I go safe, / Walk on, tensed for a leap, unreconciled / To a dark void all kindness" (ll. 12–14). The later poems in *Growing into Love* cannot let go of his ambivalence. "Transparency" begins with conflict: "Love was the woman I loved, / A grave, inhuman woman . . . ," (ll. 1–2), and it ends with mixed feelings about his wife:

> She'd turn to me dim lips
> Held next my lips by will—
> Yet, as we thinned to sleep,
> Even through gorged eyes,
> I could see through her skull.
>
> (ll. 11–15)

The central image of "Mean Gnome Day" (so far collected only in *Growing into Love*) is that of a dwarf-like creature who lives underground and guards treasure. Both the tone and theme of the poem are established in a definition placed at the head of the poem: "LOST MOTION: Looseness / which allows movement / between mating parts / supposed to turn in unison / *The Machinist Dictionary.*" The poem opens with unattractive images of the husband and wife and their day:

> The day comes limping in as though a hump
> Stood on its back and bowed it. As we fall
> Apart in bed, each to a separate lump,
> We do not speak. Our thoughts are shrunk to dwarfs

> Whose piggish eyeballs glitter as they curl
> About to stoke their privates.
>
> (ll. 1–6)

In this life, "There is small remedy, no, none in gin" (l. 7). At dinner, the turkey pies reflect the couple themselves, who are "Frozen" and "deformed." As night approaches, "Something in us begins to yield" (l. 20), but the two are likened to the "matted form of some Neanderthal" frozen in a glacier. They are chipped free and "boated south, / There to be thawed, there to bestir numb arms, / To try ripe fruit with unfamiliar mouth" (ll. 25–27). Their lives have so deformed them physically and emotionally that they can scarcely manage physical contact. Kennedy suggests that a marriage can come to this, a frigid confinement in which warmth and love have vanished and which turns husband and wife into lumps, "blurred but alive."

"Two Apparitions," which is placed right after "Mean Gnome Day" in *Growing into Love,* returns to the worry Kennedy has at this point in his marriage: growing old in a way that turns the couple into monsters. Lying beside his wife in bed, he sees the two of them misshapen by old age, and Kennedy transforms the moon-June cliché into an image of fairy-tale magic that casts a haunting glow over the frightened pair:

> Another man's hand, not mine,
>
> A scaled hand, a lizard's blotched over with bile,
> Every knuckle a knot on a stick,
> And in her cheek, dug there, a crone's wan smile.
> I shuddered. Wild-eyed she woke,
>
> Then in the next moment, the moon's white rise
> Cast the two of us smooth once more
> And we fell to each other with timid cries,
> Backs turned on what lay in store.

In the second part of this poem, the moon itself is drained of spirit, "Having had to look on / In diseased old age" (ll. 7–8). The prospect of a diseased, impotent old age and parenthood darkens these two poems, but the volume as a whole is rescued from pessimism not only by the few poems in it that express genuine love and appreciation for the child and the wife but by the understanding that the poet is a young man looking ahead, expressing doubt about his ability to measure up. As the title of this section and of the whole volume suggests, the future entails a growing, which represents for Kennedy a promise and a challenge.

For critic Louis Martz, *Growing into Love* marked a shift in American poetry: the younger poets at the time tended to "work very close to the land or the city of our time. Mythology, the past, plays little part. The effort is, I think, to move out of the interior world and to place concretely before us the world we know. . . . If the past exists, even its crises stand as a witty memory of something that hardly touches the new consciousness."[32] If Martz sees in Kennedy's poetry an absence of the "confessional" impulse associated with the open-verse poetry of the recent past, his remarks certainly apply to Kennedy, and one does see that in his second major volume of poetry, Kennedy looks increasingly at the world around him, producing, in Martz's opinion, his best work to date. Nevertheless, Martz missed the mark widely if he means that Kennedy has begun to exclude the past from his repertoire of subjects or poetic consciousness. In *Growing into Love* the past in one form or another plays a part in many poems, including "The Korean Emergency," "Creation Morning," "Nothing in Heaven Functions as It Ought," and "Golgotha," not to mention elements of the past implicit in the formal aspects of the poems. Kennedy's later collections would continue to show that the past, expressed either in subject or form, is essential to understanding the present and to capturing its essential nature.

For Kennedy, the past offers a context in which the present is measured. As he shows in the final part of "Inscriptions After Fact," the theater of Dionysus is a stage for a young sailor to find his part. Kennedy elaborates the contrast between a heroic past and a diminished future in "The Korean Emergency," which he placed in the first part of *Growing into Love*. His tour of duty in the Mediterranean provided him with a number of opportunities to contrast the bookish world of epic characters and events with modern reality. "The Korean Emergency" elaborates the experiences of a young sailor on liberty, this time in Sicily. Most of the poem's forty-five lines are taken up with vivid description of what the young sailor experiences ashore:

Let loose,
The lira leaking out of your dress blues,
You'd wander, up for grabs,
Through droves of boys who'd feel you up and pluck,
Or, if it were your will

> Down on the beach or under some dark arch,
> Nurse or give suck.
>
> (ll. 33–39)

In lines such as these, Kennedy derives from language extraordinary descriptive power. The phrase "Let loose," in light of the sexual implications of the whole passage, suggests not only pent-up desire, but pent-up animals wild with the desire for freedom and other stimulants. The image in the next line describes both the way money flows from sailors on liberty and the consequence of unbridled sexual indulgence, this idea reinforced by the rhyming of *crab's* and *grabs* in the same stanza. In such a rich context, words and phrases take on meaning that, in a more innocent, more wholesome place, would not occur to the reader, "Down on the beach" among them. Another rhyme in this group of lines, *pluck* and *suck,* is especially well placed to capture the young sailor's sensual sense of the experience, and the final line suggests in its brevity and lack of qualification neither approval nor condemnation.

The poem contrasts three environments, each unattractive. The ship's world is replete with foul language, impatient officers, and ponderous duty; it is set in a sickly sea: "Swelling a moment only to subside, / Hesitant as breath from an injured lung" (ll. 10–11). Disease mingles with animal energy. The final five lines capture the sailor's perspective with marvelous force and precision:

> Who'd hate a thirst that held him in its sway
> When the deep wine dish of the Mediterranean lay
> Within his hands? Once more
> We steamed back home. To meet us on the dock
> Sat Gene's Dry Cleans.
> Emergency, not war.
>
> (ll. 40–45)

Reflecting on his shoreside experiences, the young sailor is reminded of Odysseus lured by the Sirens, who held the men in their sway, and the line "the deep wine dish of the Mediterranean lay / Within his hands" recalls the epic metaphors of Homer, even as it combines the sailor's sexual memories. "We steamed back home" forecasts the dry cleaning the sailors will get back home and suggests their angry state of mind, angry for having been plucked from Sicilian pleasures. Although the Roman theater in Syracuse is "some crab's / Picked gutted shell," at home the sterile cleanliness of "Gene's Dry Cleans" is just as repellant to the young sailor. Given a choice, he would clearly choose the unwholesome to the wholesome, for this is an "Emergency, not war."

Two years after *Growing into Love* appeared, Kennedy brought out his third major collection of poems, *Breaking and Entering* (1971), published in England by Oxford University Press. On its title page appears a quotation from T. S. Eliot:

> The chief use of the 'meaning' of a poem,
> in the ordinary sense, may be . . . to satisfy
> one habit of the reader, to keep his mind
> diverted and quiet, while the poem
> does its work upon him . . . [.]

Kennedy said that Eliot's metaphor gave him his title. In his explanation, he reveals one of his artistic motives: "A remark of Eliot's has stuck with me: his comparison of the meaning of a poem—the prose sense of it—to the burglar's bit of meat. There in the darkened house sits the mind of the reader, a house-dog given a kidney to keep him quiet, while the rest of the poem stalks about its business: making off with the first editions and the silver gravy-boat."[33] Perhaps because he was having difficulty with the creative process, only eight of the forty-five poems in this collection are new.[34] Fifteen are reprinted from *Nude Descending a Staircase* and twenty-two from *Growing into Love.* He rearranged some of the poems, as he would continue doing through his most recent collection, and he added lighter poems, including the seriocomic *Bulsh* and more than a dozen epigrams, one of his favorite forms. The epigrams make fun of such subjects as the Teutonic scholar, the literary anthologist, marriage, death, and a young poet. These light, satirical pieces help to dissipate the somber mood that dominated *Growing into Love,* though several poems show that Kennedy continued to be interested in religious subjects and the grimmer aspects of the modern American scene. Modern domestic relationships received attention, including his own in "Cross Ties" and "Last Child" (dedicated to his son Daniel).

The new volume brought increased attention to Kennedy, this time from England as well as America, and his work won praise on both sides of the Atlantic. A reviewer for the *Times Literary Supplement* noted the "humour, wit, elaborate figures and technical mastery [that were] demonstrated by his first book," features that by now had become widely accepted as Kennedy's best and most characteristic. In this third collection, however, the reviewer found that "Mr[.] Kennedy has steadily infused a moral energy independent of religion and dark with ambivalence. His art and articulateness, the evidence of his control over his rhetoric, add power to the wry insights."[35] Alan Brownjohn, as he had done with *Growing into Love,* mingles praise with criticism. Calling Kennedy "a fantastic" and "one of the most bizarrely resourceful practitioners of the earlier style," meaning traditional forms, Brownjohn considers Kennedy's wit "uneasy, abrasive. Archaic phraseology is made to bite with energetic technical accomplishment, and irony"; Kennedy's performance is "skillful and alarming, if not often moving," but the "extraordinary wit and energy startles and hurts rather than touches."[36] The new poems showed Kennedy experimenting with formal features in new ways, with the refrain in "Drivers of Diaper-Service Trucks Are Sad" and with tag lines in "Song: Great Chain of Being."[37] On the whole, he wanted to give the reader a taste of the full range of his poetic skills—he said that this collection "offers the gist of me,"[38] though absent are poems for children.

In 1974 Kennedy's fourth collection, *Emily Dickinson in Southern California,* appeared. It contained fifteen poems and two series of epigrams, comprising fifteen couplets. Fourteen of the poems had not been collected before, and three were from *Breaking and Entering.*[39] Twelve of the poems, with revisions, would be reprinted in *Cross Ties.* Five of the poems appear in only this collection. Kennedy's interest in form is given prominence in one of his longer poems, "Emily Dickinson in Southern California," which is sustained for one hundred and four lines. It is unusual for Kennedy to write poems of this length; only a handful exceed fifty lines. In this collection, for example, only one other poem reaches thirty lines, and most of the poems are under twenty lines, with several under ten.

The volume received very little critical notice, although it was, in the words of one reviewer, a "charming book, made even more attractive as the first volume in David R. Godine's new, beautifully printed and handsomely bound Chapbook series."[40] The book's principal poem, "Emily Dickinson in Southern California," is remarkable for reasons more important than length, of course; it brings together Kennedy's skill in infusing a new vision in an established form, his skill in imitating the idiosyncratic style of another poet, his interest in the modern condition in America, and his skill in sustaining a narrative through many lines. Ignoring the poem's subject, one reviewer thought this poem "skillfully done" but "not much more than high pastiche—nine Dickinsonian essays in the cryptic-ecstatic. . . ."[41]

In this collection of poems, Kennedy's interest in the past remains in evidence, both as an ideal of wit and polish and, in the four-line "At Colonus," as a context for suggesting that in ancient Greece, mankind has been abandoned by the gods of antiquity. The idea of abandonment turns into a sense of futility in a two-line poem, "Protest," that ends the book: "On marble stairs under the bloated dome of time / Everyone living sets himself on fire." Such a sentiment is offset by Kennedy's continued interest, and seeming faith, in parenthood, the family, and the flow of generations. A degree of skepticism is evident in his treatment of poetry and poets and in the value of writing. His relations with church authority are replete with disillusionment, disapproval, even contempt—*Bulsh* may be fun to read, but it has a sharp edge of bitterness. In his personal remarks, Kennedy has said that his religious faith weakened early in his life and that he abandoned it soon after.[42] His poems dealing with church authority reflect this personal shift, and his faith in literary pursuits seems to be strong but ambivalent. Meanwhile, he is increasingly interested in the family, children in particular, including his own. In this collection he reprints "Last Child," and would reprint it again in *Cross Ties.* The poem shows a father filled with disgust and loathing as he looks upon this "Small vampire" and wonders whether he and his generation will be the ones to break "earth's back." Joseph Parisi sees a "curious mixture of resentment and tenderness"[43] in the father's attitude, but it is difficult to find the tenderness.

In this same year as *Emily Dickinson in Southern California,* Kennedy published *Celebrations after the Death of John Brennan* in a limited edition of 326.[44] As a student of Kennedy's, Brennan had made a deep impression on his professor. The young man's suicide inspired this poem, one of Kennedy's most personal expressions, which throughout is somber, dignified, and restrained. Despite Kennedy's growing popularity, the book received little critical notice. David Shapiro reviewed it along with three other collections in *Poetry* two years after the poem appeared, and though he admired the poem, Shapiro spends more space on its alleged flaws than on its genuine merits. He objects to some overwriting, slang, "archaic diction" (as in Kennedy's phrase, "fugitive songs"), and some "clotted melodrama." Shapiro was also "appalled" by the "abstract genitive" in the line "Churned by the wind, the iceberg of his death / Slowly revolves. . . ."[45] On the positive side, Shapiro found that Kennedy's use of "interpolated quotes from the student's own poetry enhance this book and give it a formally interesting dramatic structure."[46]

As a deeply personal and intensely felt poem, it bears close scrutiny and deserves more attention than it has received. The poem begins with Kennedy approaching the place where the public celebration of John Brennan is to be held, and at the end of the poem, Kennedy brings the reader back to the celebration as it is ending. Between these two points, Kennedy recalls moments from Brennan's life along with some of their encounters, all arranged in chronological order, taking Brennan through his college days. Kennedy broadens the scope of the elegy by drawing a parallel between his relationship with Brennan and his relationship with his own sons and father. In the middle part of the poem, Kennedy wrestles with powerful, entangled feelings that have been exposed by the younger man's death:

> I'd not aspire to be your father, John.
> I meant only to copyread your words.
> Hard enough now—four blood sons of my own
> Trussing me too
> In dried umbilical cords.
>
> (7:ll. 7-11)

Kennedy's characteristic wit and playfulness are absent here; he is entirely serious, relying almost exclusively on the sound effects and rhythms to convey the depth of his emotions. The effect is to amplify both. The *I*s in the first two lines sound like cries of anguish, and the alliteration in the fourth and fifth lines is aided by the imagery "blood sons" opposed by "dried umbilical cords." In the next stanza, part 8, the thought shifts to Kennedy's father:

> "Well, most of me's still here," my old man said
> After the surgeon pared him, hospitaled. . . .
> Still hanging on. John gone.
>
> (ll. 1–2, 5)

The poem, reprinted in *Cross Ties,* reveals more about Kennedy himself than Brennan and represents an important step in Kennedy's psychological and artistic development. It demonstrates clearly the breadth of his poetic skills, which are capable of the most sensitive expressions of feeling and subtleties of thought in forms exceedingly suitable to both. The poem's candor is as striking as its depth of feeling and maturity.

In 1975 Kennedy teamed with James Camp and Keith Waldrop to publish *Three Tenors, One Vehicle: A Book of Songs.* Twelve poems by Kennedy are listed in the table of contents, although the last poem in the list, "If You Got a Notion," is not wholly Kennedy's.[47] Of the eleven that are entirely his, three are set to tunes. One of them, "Ultimate Motel," is a "hymn in common meter," and two are in dialect. Kennedy's characteristic playfulness is predominant in three of the poems, in which he mocks the individual who mourns the loss of mythical beliefs ("Song to the Tune of 'Somebody Stole My Gal' "), the poet who gives up poetry for booze ("Uncle Ool's Song against the Ill-Paid Life of Poetry"), and the masochist ("Flagellant's Song"). Several poems deal with a familiar subject, the loss of some ideal, whether it be classical myth or biblical tradition, or the loss of a past that gave the individual a certain order, beauty, and certitude. When Kennedy looks at the world around him, as he does in several of the poems, he sees a loss of order and faith, an ugly landscape peopled by disenchanted, confused lost souls who appear to have given up the struggle for truth and beauty. The poems also show a variety of forms, including some poems in which elements of the folk ballad are used. The poems in dialect explore the possibilities inherent in adopting a variety of voices, and the structural diversity evident in all of the poems suggests that Kennedy is experimenting. In "Great Chain of Being," for example, each stanza ends with a repeated refrain:

> Drinking smooth wine in a castle or digging potatoes knee-
>   deep in dung,
> Everybody in creation knew just how high or how low he hung
> On that ladder with Lord god at the top and dumb mud at the
>   bottom rung,
>   *Great Chain of Being,*
>   *Great Chain of Being.*[48]
>
> (ll. 1–5)

"Sentimentalist's Song, or Answers for Everything," set to the tune of "Deutschland über Alles," represents an ironic commentary on present-day existence; its short rhymed lines mock the poem's subject:

> Strife-torn city?
> What a pity!

Tint it pretty,
  Pop rose pills.
Air pollution?
Quick solution!
Evolution,
  Smog-breathing gills.

(ll. 1–8)

Throughout the series of poems, entire stanzas are italicized, and although rhyme occurs in all the poems, the lines vary widely in length within several of the poems and from poem to poem. It seems as though Kennedy is as interested in how his poems look and sound as in what they are saying. Technical exploration is the theme of his contributions to this slim volume as he skips from the serious to the playful, from heaven to earth in locale, from the ironic and mocking to the more serious and reflective.

For several years after this publication, Kennedy continued to explore different ways to express his ideas, even turning from his own ideas to those of others, thereby relinquishing self-expression for the benefits of trying new forms. In 1983, eight years after the publication of *Three Tenors, One Vehicle,* he published *French Leave,* a volume of twelve translations from the works of eight French poets, whose dates range from the sixteenth to the twentieth century. Kennedy's attraction to these French authors may be due to their anger, their cynicism mingled with a weariness of the world, their *doleur,* their interest in male-female relationships, and their sophistication and intellectuality. Formally, they offered him a chance to manipulate language into tight structures and to use language under the pressure of formal demands, including the challenge of capturing from another language such difficult elements as tone and image.

"Sonnet for Hélène" by Pierre de Ronsard is a poignant expression by the poet who complains to his mistress for having rejected him. He exhorts her to read his lines when she is old, when her beauty is "long gone by." With that prospect in mind, he pleads, "delay no longer. Gather ye / From this day forth the roses of To Be" (ll. 13–14). The sentiments of this graceful sonnet no longer suit the modern sensibility, but Kennedy expresses the ideas in such subtle, fresh ways that the old seems new. How he manages may be seen in the use of the rose, a traditional symbol both of woman's beauty and romantic love, in the poem's final line: "From this day forth the roses of To Be." By giving the image an existential twist, Kennedy saves the symbol from being simply a cliché and fuses the old with the new, tossing in a clever reference to Hamlet's soliloquy as well.

Kennedy translated three poems by Charles Baudelaire. "Epigraph for a Banned Book" tells the reader to "Throw down this book, it's steeped in bile, / Cocked for an orgy, melancholic" (ll. 3–4). The pun on "Cocked" cleverly illustrates the kind of material the reader will find in "this book." In the final two lines, the poet imagines the self-righteous would-be reader, and scornfully tells him to "Run along. Chase your perfect whole" (l. 13). The parting pun is classic Kennedy, in the vein of "Ars Poetica." The second poem, "Abyss," is a dolorous, self-absorbed expression of the poet's feeling of emptiness. The chasm within himself is "seductive space," a "gaping pit / Oozing with spooks . . ." (ll. 9–10). The human intellect is suspended above this fathomless chasm. The third poem, "Conformity," is a four-line satirical attack on the Belgians for being conformists and for drinking "to drench / Their drawers." The sardonic wit of the final line appeals to Kennedy's affection for the sting and brevity of aphorism: when the Belgians catch syphilis, "They'll double-dose, to be twice French."

"Pierrot's Soliloquy" by Jules LaForgue laments the famous clown's desire for immortality in a quatrain as graceful as it is succinct:

> All I am is a clown in the moon
> Plunking pebbles in fountain pools with
> No particular hope, no design
> Except one: to make myself myth.
>
> (ll. 1–4)

Paul Verlaine's "Fall Song" continues the melancholic mood. The poem's short lines suggest the speaker's enervation, and Kennedy's use of image and sound plays fully to the speaker's mood:

> I go away
> Any old way
> Ill winds drive—
> Here, there—off
> Like a leaf
> Once alive.
>
> (ll. 13–15)

Thinking of the "Olden days" he cries, envisioning himself driven like a leaf by autumn's ill winds, and, like the leaf, he will die.

In the translation of "Pont Mirabeau"[49] by Guillaume Apollinaire, Kennedy returns to the theme of the lover and his beloved, symbolized by the Seine and the bridge on which the lover stands, reminiscing about the past and the "flow" of time. The poem is a marvelous creative effort on Kennedy's part that bears close scrutiny.[50] Kennedy uses wide spaces and other structural and grammatical features to express the disjunction the lover feels between himself and his beloved and between the past and present:

> Under Pont Mirabeau glides the Seine
>   And loves of ours
>   Must I think back to when
> Joy always followed in the wake of pain
>
>   Sound the hour   night draw near
>   The days go running   I stay here.[51]

The final line of the first stanza begins with "Joy" and ends with "pain," balanced at opposite ends by the opposite states of the poet's remembered love. Contrast, too, is evident in the opposition of movement and stasis, which the refrain expresses in a balanced line: "Sound the hour [space] night draw near." This refrain seems to freeze time on a stroke of the clock, an impression reinforced by the heavy stresses on *Sound* and *hour*. After the wide medial caesura, suggestive of the poet's meditative pause and of the wide and long separation of the lovers and of the poet's present and past times, the line continues: "night draw near." The image here is of motion, a contrast to the abrupt sound of the hour. Grammatically, the line suggests that the poet is addressing night, asking it to "draw near," to bring to the poet forgetfulness, death, sorrow, the inability to see. The second line of the refrain continues the idea of motion: "The days go running." The poet's sense of time's quick passage contrasts with the first line, which ends with a spondee that emphasizes movement toward closure and finality. But this motion is brought to an abrupt halt by the second half of the line: "I stay here." These contrasting ideas and images suggest the poet's painful dilemma: he wants to die, to forget, and to escape his painful memories and sense of loss, but he is mindful too of the fact that time swiftly distances him from his "loves." Paradoxically, ever in the moment, he finds that he does not move, however; he is always in sorrow and pain, for he is always in the moment. Every sounding of the hour reminds him that he is fixed in the moment. Time passes swiftly but he does not move: "I stay here." By not closing this line with a period, Kennedy suggests that his dilemma and sorrow are endless; ironically, he is fixed in endless time and is ever moving with it, but is ever fixed in the moment.

The second quatrain continues the poet's recollection of his time with his beloved by the Seine, under Pont Mirabeau. The image is of the lovers embracing, hand in hand, face to face, but the poet is looking for support too: "Hand in my hand stand by me face to face" (l. 7). The Seine lends counterpoint to the freshness of the lovers' joy: "Weary of everlasting looks the slow wave passes" (l. 10). Again, contrast expresses the poet's dilemma: to the river, the lovers are a wearisome sight, but for the lovers, the experience is fresh and joyful. The third quatrain returns to the idea that time passes swiftly by, like the river, only now the poet connects time and the river to love in an image, "Love flows away as running water went" (l. 13), and his sense of fixedness and entrapment returns in the next line: "As life is indolent" (l. 15). Contrast plagues his mind, for life is "indolent," yet "Hope is violent." The violence is caused by the poet's emotions as he hopes for a return of his love, yet he knows that time at every moment distances him from his loves, and, fixed in the moment, he can only suffer violent emotions, sorrow, and a sense of entrapment and helplessness. The final stanza states the poet's dilemma emphatically, repeating in the first line the sense of movement in time, "Though days run on [space] though days and weeks run on . . ." (l. 19). He knows, however, that "No time gone by / No love comes back again . . ." (ll. 20–21). Like the river, what flows away is gone forever. The final refrain, "The days go running [space] I stay here . . . ," (l. 24), underscores the poet's sorrow and the painful dilemma that, like the line that lacks a period, continues without end.

"Pont Mirabeau" appealed to Kennedy for several reasons. Through it, he could express the kind of sorrow that his own experience probably lacked, and the poem's expression of love-sick suffering offered emotional, if vicarious, fulfillment. The poem also represented an artistic challenge beyond the difficulties of translation. The quatrain, one of Kennedy's favorite forms, is in this poem often "sprung" by spacing, and the lines vary in length. He was also challenged to capture not only the mood of the original poem but the imagery, which expresses complex feelings and paradoxical ideas about time. The poem is ostensibly about romantic love, but underneath the surface, as it were,

Kennedy addresses the concept of flowing, structurally, emotionally, and philosophically. His success may be gauged by how he changed the opening line from the way it was printed in *French Leave.* His first attempt states the idea of the river's movement thus: "Underneath Pont Mirabeau flows the Seine." By the time he printed the poem in *Dark Horses,* he had honed his mastery of both form and idea to a point where he could with the slightest modification shift the emphasis from the preposition, *Underneath,* to the bridge, Pont Mirabeau, whose vowel sounds establish the poem's mood. Kennedy's impeccable ear for sound and exquisite taste told him also not to retain *flow,* which repeats the same vowels sounds as *Pont Mirabeau;* rather, he opened the sound somewhat with the word *glide,* which also suggests swift motion somewhat better than the original *flow* and shifts the sound from *o* sounds to the *s* sounds in *glides* and *Seine,* which suggest the idea of water slipping by. By shortening *Underneath,* he not only rids the line of the unnecessary sound and meaning of *neath* but also creates a better balance between the *n* sound in *Seine.* Thus altered, the new line reads: "Under Pont Mirabeau glides the Seine."

Kennedy next turned to Apollinaire's collection of animal portraits in *The Bestiary,* from which he translated six, each given four lines. This work resembles Kennedy's book for children, *Did Adam Name the Vinegarroon?* which was published a year before *French Leave* and which consists of portraits of natural and supernatural animals. The premise of the poems from Apollinaire's work is to draw parallels between the animal addressed and some aspect of humanity. In "Hare," for example, the animal offers an example for the human addressed by the poem's speaker of how to conduct himself in his love making. Instead of leaping for cover "Like buck hare shacking up with lover," one should let his mind "obscenely lie / Like fat doe hare and fructify." In "Grasshopper" a connection is drawn between the grasshopper, "The diet of Saint John," and the poet's verses, which are exhorted to be like the grasshopper, "What the best folk nibble on." In "Sirens" the poet sees in the "discontent" of the Sirens a reflection of his own. It is not much of a leap from Kennedy's own bestiary to these French poems.

Robert Desnos is represented by two short poems. The first one, "Sun," addresses the sunflower as the "Sun in the earth" and draws a parallel between the poet and the moon, "For round ourselves we go round / Like madmen in a pound." Desnos's "Last Poem" plays on the idea that the poet is a shade dreaming of the shade of his beloved. He is "A hundred times more shade than shade" (l. 7). In the final image the poet sees himself cast "into your sun-transfigured life" (l. 9). This final burst of poetic light demonstrates Kennedy's skill with imagery, even when he is bound by the ideas of another poet.

Kennedy's attraction to the poetry of despair in the French poets he admires drew him to Robert Sabatier's "Mortal Landscape," which is somber, despairing. The speaker opens with a sense of anticipation, and the prospect is dark: "The bird is flown, the monster not yet born," and the world is "demolished." He lies with someone "in position on our deaths, / . . . in decrepit light / Weary of walking to encounter dawns" (ll. 3–5). Life is also brief, "A hairsbreadth crack"; even the stars "sink teeth in worlds," while he plants "the stolen dagger of my cry / Into that breast where Godhead walks its rounds" (ll. 7–10). The final stanza repeats the statement that opens the poem, "The bird is flown," and the poet seeks "a dirt hole where [he] can sleep." Death seems attractive to him, but that prospect disquiets him, too, for "so many bodies dreamless lie / That what in man is man has had to die / And even words at last make meals on lips" (ll. 18–20).[52] In the end, the speaker remains suspended in a bleak world with few options, none of them inviting—murder or peace—or death, wherein none dream—and in that state, "what in man is man" dies.

The last poem in the series, "Central Heat" by Pierre Reverdy, develops through a series of impressionist images that express disillusionment in unrelenting expressions of despair:

> Utter nought
> Dead fire a man relights that goes back out
> I've had enough of the wind
> I've had enough of the sky
> Deep down whatever we look at is a lie
> Even your lips. . . .
>
> (ll. 10–15)

The poem's dominant metaphor is that of a furnace and its attendant features, principally light and heat. The speaker's problem is that he suffers a "Short circuit in the heart / Engine that won't start . . ." (ll. 6–7). By the middle of the final stanza, it becomes clear that the speaker is the light in the furnace who responds to the presence of the woman. The poem becomes a revelation of the meaning of the "central heat" of the title: it is the fire of sexual arousal, and for the male, the "Light's led here on a leash of copper wire," whereas her heart is "of the same stuff as the sun's fire" (ll. 24–25).

Kennedy's interest in translation did not begin, and would not end, with this small volume. He would go on to translate some German poems as well as, most recently, Aristophanes' *Lysistrata,* but early in his career, when French poetry was still fresh in his mind, *French Leave* offered him an opportunity to concentrate on those sentiments that reflected his own mood and offered him a rewarding challenge.[53]

In the same year that *French Leave* was published, 1983, the self-published chapbook *Missing Link* appeared, containing eighteen adult poems and four children's poems collected under a single title, "For Children, If They'll Take 'Em."[54] Kennedy sets the tone of this slim volume with an overblown subtitle: "*Being a Retrospective of Twenty-two Songs, Poems, Epigrams, and Verses That the Author Now Considers among his Least Unsuccessful and Contemptible, Including Several Long out of Print in This Country, and Offered as a Freeby to a Patient Listener, in Thankfulness, by X. J. Kennedy.*" In collecting his poems for *Cross Ties,* he omits seven of these poems. The front cover is illustrated by a drawing of a giant hairy paw wrapped around a young man dressed in eighteenth-century attire, including a wig. On the monster's wrist is a shackle with a broken link. Kennedy was having fun with this volume. Some of the poems appear to have been snipped out of previous books and simply pasted into this one. Some titles are typed above their respective poems, and different typewriters were used to type the poems, too. All of this informality is consistent with the poems Kennedy selected to reprint here, including a handful of his best serious poems— "First Confession," "Nude Descending a Staircase," "Cross Ties" (in its fourth collection so far), and a few others. Despite the presence of some serious poems, the emphasis is on playfulness and lightness of spirit.[55] He also advertises on the back cover five books of his poetry for children and his anthology, *Tygers of Wrath.* Perhaps the link that Kennedy felt had been missing was this lightness of spirit.

Hangover Mass, another chapbook, appeared in 1984. The collection included fourteen poems. All but "A Word from Hart Crane's Ghost"[56] are reprinted a year later in *Cross Ties.* The excellent quality of the printing of this volume, published by Bits Press, makes the book remarkably different from *Missing Link.* The text and paper are first-rate, and the pages are stitched between a soft cover. The selection of poems has a characteristic range. Five of the poems have religious elements or themes, and the first one, "Hangover Mass," combines a father, booze, a saloon atmosphere, and the Catholic religion, all in five quatrains. None has the rebellious spirit of "First Confession" and satirical attacks of *Bulsh,* yet Kennedy's attitude toward religion remains irreverent. Although the spirit is more often serious than lighthearted, the volume is never grim, and it contains none of Kennedy's satiric epigrammatic attacks on human types and conditions, his sense of futility, or his gloomy assessment of conditions in the modern world.

For all his efforts and continued publication, Kennedy's poetry did not attract much critical attention from *Breaking and Entering* (1971) to *Cross Ties* (1985). His collections consisted of skimpy chapbooks and shared space with other poets, and when he did produce a collection, many of the poems were taken from earlier collections and would appear in later ones. Perhaps Kennedy's heart and mind lay with the children's literature he was publishing in this interim, four volumes of verse and a novel.

Another contributing factor to the paucity of Kennedy's output and public notice during these years may be discerned in the public notice of the publication of *Hangover Mass,* in which Peter Wild declares that "Writing in meter and rhyme leads to sure artistic disaster, if not psychic disorder,"[57] for "The more hidebound proponents [of open forms] would have all measured poetry swept into the dustbin." Kennedy, however, has "stuck with the poetry world despite the uneasy ride, writing all the while and iconoclastically in metered, rhymed verse." According to Wild, the evidence that Kennedy has survived is *Hangover Mass,* "an elegantly printed offering of a mere fourteen pieces, but its length serves as a testimony to Kennedy's demands of the quality of what he prints."[58] The reason for Kennedy's slight public showing over the previous fifteen years has been, it seems, his insistence on quality, on not releasing a poem until it has matured in his mind. Whatever the reason, Kennedy's next collection brought his poetry once again to the attention of a host of critics, who recognized him as a poet of the first rank and effectively answered those critics who seemed unable to see beyond Kennedy's puns, playfulness, and technical virtuosity.

Cross Ties: Selected Poems was published in 1985 and promptly won the Los Angeles Times Book Award.[59] It represented Kennedy's most important collection to date. The book's back cover says the book contains "every poem that the poet cares to save . . . ," although Kennedy has revised this claim. In the book's notes he explains the arrangement of the poems: "For a reader who might care to trace the progress of my work, or its deterioration, I have sorted these poems into five sections; then, within each section, arranged things from early to late, following the order in which they first appeared. In between these five acts, each section called an Intermission offers light refreshment. Like each act, each intermission also follows a chronology—one that begins as early as 1955 and ends as late as 1984, since it displays the kind of verse I have been writing off and on all this while." Curiously, Kennedy had earlier given a different opinion of arrangements. "Me, when I read a book, I don't give a hoot about how the poems are arranged; all that counts is: are there a few good poems in it? Auden once twitted this fallacy by arranging his *Collected Poems* by titles, in alphabetical order."[60] In any case, the book's design follows that of his three major previous collections, *Nude Descending a Staircase* (1961), *Growing into Love* (1969), and *Breaking and Entering* (1971). Of the one hundred twenty-two poems in *Cross Ties,* twenty-eight had not been collected before, and, like *Nude Descending a Staircase* and *Missing Link,* the book contains light verse, serious poetry, and verse for children. As in *Nude,* the sections of light verse are titled "Intermissions," giving the whole collection a theatrical connection. Though this framework remains more abstract than felt as one reads, it nevertheless illustrates how Kennedy sees his poetry and his relationship with readers.

Cross Ties shows clearly that throughout his career Kennedy is aware of the diversity of his literary heritage, seeing in it an opportunity to weave new patterns, richer for the diversity. His skill in journeying into hazardous waters is remarkably present in poems that find in traditional subjects and forms new directions. He is so astute in his handling of subjects that the old or familiar comes forth entirely fresh, freshened not only by his imagery and form but also by the meaning that emerges from his choices. Without the appearance of great compression, lines can express a great deal, both seen and felt, because the poems work on many levels simultaneously. What appears first in the collection is a series of poems whose subjects reflect Kennedy's early interest in what other poets have done, from medieval ("Faces from a Bestiary") to modern ("Ladies Looking for Lice/after Rimbaud"). Kennedy's interest in popular (or folk) subjects and rhythms is evident in "Song to the Tune of 'Somebody Stole My Gal'" and "In a Prominent Bar in Secaucus One Day." These serio-comic exercises prominently display the importance to Kennedy of rhythm and playful wit and suggest that he is exploring the relation of ideas to rhythms that have that "swing." This interest leads in two directions: into poetry for children and into the serious poems. The more one reads these latter poems, the more one sees that play is basic to Kennedy's poetic craft, most evident in his many puns, in his recurrent ambivalence, and in his irrepressible humor and irony, all complementary expressions of his creative impulses and vision.

Although *Cross Ties* is laid out like a five-act play, the poet journeying, not unlike Odysseus, from one time period, or act, to the next, the poems may be viewed also as discrete expressions strung on a different string, depending on which thematic trail one follows.[61] When asked whether there is "a single thematic thread running through *Cross Ties*," Kennedy replied, "Ex-Catholicism,"[62] but many themes tie the poems together, actually. The theme found in "The Sirens," for instance, surfaces again in "Two Views of Rhyme and Meter." The sound Odysseus hears "in his loins" echoes in the later poem's definition of meter as "the thrust rest thrust of loins." Many of the poems explore the creative process. Kennedy mocks the writer's self-scrutiny in a reprint of his famous epigram—"Would you lay well? Don't watch"—but elsewhere he is serious about the origin of the creative impulse. In "Creation Morning" he likens God's impulse to that of boys wanting to leave their mark in wet cement and to the bridegroom's urge to make something grow from effort (sexual). In his final poem Kennedy resorts to the poet's traditional "Envoi," sending his book into the world with a hope that it enjoys good fortune. Typically, though, Kennedy's version ends on self-effacement. Addressing his "slothful book," he tells it to go forth and sing to the one who "will care / Should words with a rhythm align" (ll. 6–7) and to sing to lovers. They will soon have other interests, however, and will abandon his book, which then "Crash-lands."

In several poems the advance of generations plays a major role. The interweaving of generations is especially pronounced in Kennedy's old companion, "Cross Ties," in which the speaker sees his child as the recipient of his own entwined loyalties. "Last Child" and "The Shorter View" also deal with generational sequence from the perspective of Kennedy's personal experience. Seeing lineage in "Dirty English Potatoes" makes the poet realize how far the new world has taken him from the land: "I want / Unreal meals risen from sheer mist." Kennedy is not despairing, however. Perhaps his faith in the benefits of artful play and in regeneration keeps him balanced between the light of blind faith and the darkness of despair. The individual may reach the end of the line, but the generations advance.

Kennedy's interest in people is also a main feature in the collection. His songs capture the spirit and comical character of the raucous denizens of saloons; his epigrams skewer ignorance and pretense; and several poems portray the aged, the isolated, and the disturbed. Some early and middle poems address the despoliation of the American landscape by industry and neglect.

"No Neutral Stone" takes a pessimistic view of human worth and the value of beauty and love. Summer passion generally turns into "Starved sod . . . and ashen / Leaves . . . ," symbols of decline of flesh and spirit and of death. John Keats used the stars and planets to characterize human love and beauty, he reminds us, but today "Venus thus invoked / Scrapes dog dung from her soles and comes indoors." The world consists of "debris," which "Sprawls formless" until a passing poet, using "an electromagnet of emotion," collects material from this formless heap of debris to create a "whole mess." The junk parts that the poet misses in his sweep meanwhile lie "in the rejected world's trash heap," pelted by incessant rain. One of these rejected parts, a "rusting wheel or gearshift lever," asks, "Am I not what Hardy must have felt, / Alone, after Tryphena slammed her thighs?"[63] This closing image, reminiscent of the talkative earthen jars in the *Rubaiyat of Omar Khayyám,* suggests that the poet's depiction of human love and beauty leaves something out, the aftermath of passion, the "junk" that would show what the lover feels after the act of sex, passion, or love. The poem suggests that human passion, love, and beauty occur in a world where frost holds sway, a world that is a junkyard, which provides poets the material for creating images of beauty, love, and passion. The poem also suggests that "No Neutral Stone" exists, this stone being a magnet that draws from the junk heap random pieces to form its own vision, or version, of the "truth." Inevitably, though, pieces are left out; no one perspective, not even the poet's, is wholly true.

This is Kennedy at his bitterest, and he seems convinced that nature and humans are too often at odds, nature being the universal spirit that runs through all things as well as the visible parts of our existence that are not made by humans. He seems also convinced that humans lack the ability to understand how nature works. He makes this point in "Categories," which focuses on the puzzles found in nature and in man's condition. "Nothing stays put" is the opening statement; today "Species collide like fast tailgating cars . . . ," (l. 3), and the century "Collapses through the mind's pained hourglass" (l. 11). These changes are illogical and beyond human comprehension; they are also unpredictable. Understanding natural phenomena challenges the human intellect almost beyond limit: "Was it Rimbaud, that trader of tusks, who said / You don't begin to understand / Till through the tip of your tongue you hear bright red?" (ll. 12–14). The poem ends on a story about "that master in Kyoto who began / 'To seize on what had been left out before'. . ." (ll. 15–16). This bit of wisdom is counterpointed by a novice monk's demonstration that "you can / If you have hatched from names, or lack clean plates, / Serve cake on a shut fan" (ll. 18–20). If one can understand the monk's demonstration, one can perhaps understand nature and man's condition. The inability to understand is proof that one lacks the insight or wisdom needed to understand the puzzle of nature and human behavior. The poem puts the reader in the poet's place, faced with a conundrum that leaves one stymied.

Kennedy believes that as long as humans assault the environment, it will retaliate, and that in the end nature will prevail. Its great trump card, of course, is death, and throughout his career Kennedy shows an interest in death, increasingly in his own. One of the intermissions in this volume, in fact, is subtitled, "Epigrams and Epitaphs."[64]

The changes in Kennedy's thoughts regarding mortality and other abiding concerns may be attributed in part to his maturing. Early poems argue that the ancient gods abandoned humankind, and in later poems nature seems to have taken their place. Religion offers Kennedy no solace or hope, but nature does, in close, personal ways. The accumulation of snow, the falling of a leaf, the fresh earth, all seem to comfort Kennedy. "Epiphany," the book's penultimate poem, helps to explain a profound shift in his vision of the world. Lying on the floor one day, he regards a simple chair: "For days I'd gone on trudging, too far dulled / To take mere things in" (ll. 5–6). Astounded, he finally sees "how they joined—the legs and rungs of chairs." His position is symbolic: he is "Floored now, freed from airs / Of uprightness. . . ." (ll. 6–7). He could be speaking of his entire career, during which he has been "too far dulled / To take mere things in."[65] He also could be speaking of humans in general: when they are "freed from airs / Of uprightness . . . ," they can see that focusing on what is near and basic can bring an understanding of their relation to the Everything.

Five years after *Cross Ties* was published, Kennedy came out with another chapbook, *Winter Thunder* (1990), consisting of fifteen poems, though two poems, "City Churchyard" and "Epigrams," contain individual poems under their titles. Six of the poems were originally intended for another collection.[66] The poems are often negative in their treatment of parenthood, the writer's lot, and death. The two longest poems add considerable weight to the darker mood of the selection. "Pileup," which is reprinted in *The Lords of Misrule,* depicts in forty-one lines the scene of a traffic accident on a modern freeway, littered with wrecks and mangled bodies. In seventeen quatrains, "Invitations to the Dance" shows a nursing home where the dying inhabitants fight despair. Someone shouts, "'For what in God's name do we cling to living?'" Mabel offers a grim alternative to passivity and futility: "'Why, I'm dancing,' said Mabel, 'to keep from dying'" (l. 61). Ironically, Mabel's desperate effort to coax some liveliness out of her peers takes place on Easter morning. The final poem, "Ambition," shows another protagonist frustrated by forces out of his control. In the poem's concluding quatrain, the entanglements that impede human effort are expressed in images that depict nature as the human's antagonist:[67]

> I'd be glad to go out on a limb with those
> Who can live with whatever a wind bestows
> Were it not for these roots, dug in deep to bear
> Never being done grasping for light and air.
>
> (ll. 9–12)

Two years later, in 1992, Kennedy published another major collection, *Dark Horses,* containing forty-three poems in three sections. Despite the "New Poems" printed on the book's cover, nine of the poems had already appeared in *Winter Thunder,* and "Pont Mirabeau," here heavily revised, had been printed in *French Leave.* The title, *Dark Horses,* suggests that each of the poems in the collection is a "dark horse," an unlikely success, expressing Kennedy's characteristic modesty in presenting his own poetry. The title also has an apocalyptic sound, suggesting that Kennedy intended a significance beyond the individual meanings of each poem. In this sense the book contains Kennedy's vision of the times, and of the future. The implication is that the human race is in for a rough ride.[68]

One of the fundamental qualities of the poetry in *Dark Horses* is Kennedy's particular brand of wit, which was quickly noted by one of the book's reviewers, who appreciated its importance: "Although some of the New Formalists have published amusing formal epigrams, wit in the Jacobean or Augustan sense is not central to the work of most of them. For Kennedy, an older formalist, it is; every poem he writes is at least touched and sometimes profoundly shaped by it. As a feature of style his wit manifests itself in verbal sleight-of-hand, often in the interest of satire. As a quality of thought it brings notice, as Doctor Johnson said of Metaphysical poetry, to 'occult resemblances' between apparently disparate things, yielding a complex overview of existence."[69]

By placing "Woman in Rain" at the beginning of *Dark Horses*, Kennedy establishes a connection between it and "Nude Descending a Staircase," the title poem in his first collection. It is no coincidence that both poems employ structure to depict the literal and metaphorical motions of a woman. Both poems suggest how much and in what ways Kennedy has and has not changed in the intervening thirty years. He has developed a clearer focus on the relationship of humankind to nature and remains concerned mainly with contemporary scenes and figures, often in a context reminiscent of prior ages—the epigraph of "The Woodpile Skull" is a line from *Hamlet*, for example, and Hamlet is alluded to in the poem itself. Though his range is wide, Kennedy looks deeply at the world we live in, keenly aware, as Robert Frost was, of the menacing aspects of man's physical environment. This theme runs throughout *Dark Horses*: "The wind last night kept breaking into song / Beautiful only if you heard it wrong," he writes in "Twelve Dead, Hundreds Homeless." The wind can be a weapon, delivering "A note so high / Removed an ear that listened."

Kennedy believes that the future depends on a synthesis of what has been and what is. In "The Woodpile Skull," for instance, we find the speaker confronted by "a black ant's severed head." Remembering a similar scene in Robert Burns's "To a Field Mouse," the reader is intrigued: what will the poet do with this familiar theme? Kennedy brings a modern perception, of course:

> Wind wedges through my woodpile. But this chill
> Comes from a sense that, blindly, I can kill
> And can be killed. Bemused and metaphoric,
> I stand, ham Hamlet to a formic Yorick.
>
> (ll. 29–30)

The speaker's dilemma is contemporary. The past gives him cause to ruminate anew on his relationship to higher forces. Though he may feel like a "ham Hamlet," the playfulness of the expression suggests that he is not entirely uncomfortable in his predicament, chilled, perhaps, but finally bemused because he can be metaphoric, and formic. Poetry may be a means to keep the chill off. The final stanza of "The Woodpile Skull," like the entire collection, reflects a view of the human condition that is neither bleak nor sentimental. It is often just commonsensical, as he says in "Christmas Abrupted," where he explains the "common sense in stripping bare" the tree that fixes children in fantasy.

Still, many poems take a gloomy view of the human condition, and Kennedy ends the volume with a series of them. In "Staring into a River Till Moved by It," a bridge breaks from its supports and sweeps two people away. They barely make it back to land. The title suggests that the couple would be emotionally "Moved" by the river, but the poem gives an ironic twist, turning the river into a hazard barely survived. In another poem, the speaker nearly drowns; in another, a leopard in a painting is "crouched to leap / Upon a bathing beauty sound asleep." This poem, "Black Velvet Art," claims that the stars "at the final dawn" will vanish, and God—in a rare poetic appearance—will command "Even the last black hole, *Get off My Hands.*" In "Winter Thunder" cell mates hear "the widening crack of thunder" and their "jailblock breaks and falls." Finally, the speaker in "Ambition" wonders whether he has wasted his summer indoors. Speaking perhaps for Kennedy himself, he suggests that he is rooted in earth, and though these roots provide an anchor in "whatever the wind bestows," they also leave him "grasping for light and air." If Kennedy late in his career feels the heaviness of years accumulating in an indifferent universe, poetry gives him a means for recording his predicament. Poetry may not promise happy times ahead, but it offers an activity that has long sustained him. Both *Winter Thunder* and *Dark Horses* end with the same two poems, "Winter Thunder" and "Ambition," suggesting that Kennedy wants to leave readers with a dark view of the modern predicament. He does not reprint in *Dark Horses* the more boisterous "Invitation to the Dance," although this poem's rollicking spirit underlies many of his poems.[70] When one thinks of Kennedy's poetry, the voice that rises above all others, it is hoped, is Mabel's, and she is shouting, "This world is the worse for too little dancing."

In recent collections, Kennedy has focused on epigrams.[71] The all-Kennedy number of *The Epigrammatist*, published in 1994, collects forty-six poems of various lengths, none more than eight lines and most only two or four lines long. The dedication to Donald Hall, "master of the art of making each word matter," befits the ensuing series of epigrams, in which each word matters and which features the best of Kennedy's epigrammatic skills: wit, grace, and verbal dexterity. The ironic voice gives Kennedy a distance from his subject that suits his poetic temperament, and the formal brevity of the epigram allows him to deflate, deride, and denounce and have fun doing so. The poems include Kennedy's favorite targets in his epigrams: hypocrisy, pretense, and folly. Three of the four sections are titled "Literati," "Sexual Combat," and "Epitaphs," and one section lacks a title.

The Minimus Poems (1996) continues in the same vein as *The Epigrammatist*, offering satirical epigrams on favorite subjects. It differs from all of Kennedy's publications, however, in its format. Each epigram is printed on a separate card, each is about the size of a postcard, and each is printed in a different typeface. Some are illustrated with graphics or simple drawings. None is numbered, so readers may arrange the poems in whatever order they wish, even use them as greeting cards, sending them to friends. The title of this little production may be a playful poke at Charles Olson, the poet-guru who inspired legions of free-verse writers and who titled his poetry collection of 1960 *Maximus Poems*. If so, Kennedy's epigrams contain features that would be anathema to Olson—rhyme, meter, regularity, balance—and the expectations and demands of preconceived form. The effectiveness with which Kennedy uses these elements makes his twitting of the opposition all the more fun.

The Minimus Poems represents one of Kennedy's main features: a willingness and ability to remain fluid. His maturity as a poet is reflected in his treatment of such subjects as mankind's relation to the world at large, and if he has grown pessimistic about the fate of mankind and if he remains less than rosy about the role good poetry will play in the future, he seems unable to sustain a bitter attitude for long. Perhaps the epigram helps him to diffuse the pessimism. In any case, he can continue to experiment, to be challenged, and to see the past not as a burden but as a kind of anchor. Perhaps, he would say, the past is almost all we have left, and writing about it and learning from it may be the best we can do for our future.

Kennedy has remarked that he seems to come out with a new

collection about every ten years. If we scan the list of his major publications, we find that he is not far off the mark. *Nude Descending a Staircase* appeared in 1961, *Breaking and Entering,* in 1971, *Growing into Love,* in 1969, *Cross Ties,* in 1985, *Dark Horses,* in 1992, and *The Lords of Misrule,* in 2002. He sends poems first to magazines, where they incubate until a collection is offered or until he feels ready to give them another burnishing, and out they come. Each collection represents not only the accumulation of a decade of thinking and maturing but a fresh opportunity to stage a new presentation, to put on a new show. *Nude Descending a Staircase* was designed both as a confession and as an introduction, Kennedy the poet descending the staircase and baring all in tantalizing artfulness. *Breaking and Entering* was an attempt to burglarize the reader's mind; *Growing into Love* offered a mature poet's exploration of love's emotions and commitments, and in *Cross Ties,* Kennedy tied together twenty years of writing poetry for adults and gave it all a dramatic structure. He was not altogether pleased with *Dark Horses,* for it lacked his characteristic light verse and epigrammatic sorties into contemporary manners, morals, and moronic behavior. He made up for the omission partly by publishing a series of epigrams in *The Epigrammatist* and *The Minimus Poems,* just prior to *The Lords of Misrule,* which contains only one epigram ("Epitaph Proposed for the Headstone of S. R. Quiett") but several comic poems.[72] The book's title also calls attention to the book's premise: traditional forms control the riotous spirits of poetic creativity.[73] Kennedy may have intended a sly dig at the free-verse poets by casting his "Invocation" in unrhymed stanzas of irregular length and, in that same invocation, by giving some of the elements of traditional poetry a living presence: "Come then, sweet Meter, / Come, strict-lipped Stanza, / Regulate the revels / Of these half-crocked lines" (ll. 16–19). These spirits overlook the "revels" that follow, and the poems themselves are a blend of celebration and reflection.

In the absence of stinging satire, Kennedy has turned his mind to reflecting and recollecting scenes and people from his own past. The first two poems set the tone of the whole book, a somewhat bemused, somewhat nostalgic, looking back. Time is on the poet's mind first. " 'The Purpose of Time Is to Prevent Everything from Happening at Once' " conflates into a sonnet a series of remembered moments: "Suppose you crash / Your car, your marriage—toddler laying waste / A field of daisies, schoolkid, zit-faced teen / With lover zipping up your pants in haste / Hearing your parents' tread downstairs—all one" (ll. 4–8). The next poem, and several after it, turns to a childhood memory in portraying a relative who died of cancer, still presesnt in a series of images: "But here you are with your invented toy, / This empty cup suspended in midair, / Arms uplifted, sunlight drifting through your hair, / Your upturned face still wreathed with utter joy" (ll. 13–16). The quatrains condense into vivid images years of life and intense emotion. In portraits of Jimmy Harlow and Naomi Trimmer, Kennedy recalls former companions in fond detail, and the ten quatrains of "Five-and-Dime, Late Thirties" offer images that remind one of a Norman Rockwell painting, the youth savoring the aroma of "frying franks' / Salt pungent odor" and giving thanks "For shreds of turkey strung / On a mound of stuffing doled / With icecream scoop, lone spoon / Of gray canned peas, one cold / Roll, cranberry half-moon" (ll. 4–8). The painter, however, gives way to the poet who has seen what the youth cannot or will not see and what the poet cannot forget:

> nightly, hordes of rats
> Shat in the licorice lace
>
> Until one day the Board
> Of Health padlocked the door.
> As sure as FDR
> Had kept us out of war,
>
> Brown Shirts were just a show,
> Hitler a comic wraith
> Far off. What you don't know
> Won't hurt had been our faith.
>
> (ll. 27–36)

The following poem, "Sailors with the Clap," captures a theme that runs through all Kennedy's collections, that revelry has a sharp edge to it. The sailors' venereal disease is symbolic punishment for the sins of the flesh: "each man smokes thoughtfully, / Counting his shots, those daily penances, like beads told on a cast-iron rosary" (ll. 6–8). Kennedy the ex-Catholic recalls his navy days with the poet's ironic perspective shaping the memory in a sonnet as smoothly made as the sailors' rosary bead.

The underlying pattern in these early poems in *The Lords of Misrule* reflects one of the reasons Kennedy turns to the sonnet, the epigram, and the rhymed stanza: each is shaped by opposition, point and counterpoint. The yin-yang of his vision provides the swing he looks for in poetry: as he has said, "it don't mean a thing if it ain't got that swing," the swing from bright hope to gloom, from resplendence to tawdriness, from one perspective to another, which often undermines the previous idea or qualifies it in some way. This pattern is seen in "Salute Sweet Deceptions." This eight-line unrhymed poem, like the epigram and the sonnet, establishes a thought, and an image: "At break of morning / How the brick firehouse / Seems carved from amber . . ." (ll. 3–6). The image stays in the mind across the space that separates the two stanzas and comes to rest on another image that contrasts sharply with the previous one: "Beer cans in river / Mime stars dissolving / A seedpearl necklace / Of rain wears phonewires" (ll. 5–8). Like the collagist, Kennedy creates an arresting beauty out of details that in themselves are unattractive or unremarkable. His poem unfolds in layers of meaning and effect, one thought or image opposed by another, yet together they form an attractive whole. Without the second image, the first would be unredeemed ugliness or commonplace; without the first, the second would be sight without insight. Together, for Kennedy, they form a striking vision that comes out of his experience.

Kennedy has spoken of the tension derived from working with traditional forms, such as the sonnet or couplet, and the poems in his latest collection are rife with this kind of tension, as "Salute Sweet Deceptions" demonstrates. He favors, too, the quatrain, which allows him to vary the rhyme scheme and, in that way, vary the tension and the poem's yin-yang swing. Two dozen of these poems employ the quatrain, which are unrhymed, or have varying rhymes, *abba, abab,* or *aabb.* The sonnets, of course, are made up of two quatrains in the octave and another in the sestet, and five of the poems use the sonnet form. The metric base of the lines, too, can vary from five stresses in each line to an alternate pattern of three and two. The "Epitaph Proposed for the Headstone of S. R. Quiett," for example, consists of one quatrain, each line having five accents:

> Born with loud cries but carried off in quiet,
> I lie, the stillest of the Quiett boys.
> Death sang a song so sweet I had to try it.
> I might have known. It's only empty noise.

Subjects characteristic of Kennedy's earlier collections are represented here as well. He especially likes to portray tourists confronted by unsettling places, as he does in "Fat Cats in Egypt," where "One thin barefoot girl / Nibbles from empty fingers. Given cash, / She yells—and we're surrounded in a flash . . ." (ll. 16–18). A street scene is revisited in "Street Moths," where "Grown boys at night before the games arcade / Wearing tattoos that wash off in the sink / Accelerate vain efforts to get laid" (ll. 2–4). An airport lounge, a bus station where "People lip cupfuls of coffee," a police court, a motel, or a "funky pizza parlor," all remind us that Kennedy has kept a keen eye on humans shuffling about. What people have made of themselves and their world is the subject of many of these poems, a pileup on the freeway and commuter's experience symbolizing the loss of roots in the earth. The television screen, for Kennedy, symbolizes another shift in the human condition, which fixes the individual in front of a "beaming face" that "for a moment . . . obscures / The stares of unforgiving stars" ("Covering the Massacre"). It all makes the poet occasionally long for the good old days, as he does in "Then and Now," which opens with a forthright statement: "I half long for those crappy days again, / When babies used to be produced by sex. . . ." Sometimes he is simply tired: "I'm sick of old perplexities. Sweet Jaysus, / Give us a patch of clarity instead" ("Perplexities").

For Kennedy, who is fond of singing "In a Prominent Bar in Secaucus One Day" and other rollicking ballads to audiences and friends, song has offered a way of enduring whatever in a fallen world blocks out the stars, and he restates his credo—and this book's major theme—in a brief poem that also acknowledges the loss of an audience for poetry these days:

> How odd that verse that's song
> Should so displease the young.
> They are so serious.
> They hate all artifice
> As standing in the way
> Of mind's insistent say.
> But to my mind what counts
> Is language that surmounts
> The message it must bear,
> Steps back without a care
> And, stone blind, yields the day
> To bloodstream's reckless play.

Old people, children, death, these subjects, too, are given ample space in thse poems, and all leave images that represent Kennedy at his best, where all the elements of his art combine, and where sound and sight form music and insight. Two poems that best illustrate this kind of poetic moment deal with very different experiences, but each is exceedingly private and intensely felt. Together they place Kennedy at the peak of his achievement and show how he finds stability in a world that has lost its center. "Close Call" stops time for an instant as the poet catches a sudden insight:

> How suddenly she roused my ardor,
> That woman with wide-open car door
> Who, with a certain languid Sapphic
> Grace into brisk rush-hour traffic
> Stepped casually. I tromped the brake.
> Her lips shaped softly, "My mistake."
> Then for a moment as I glided
> By, our glances coincided
> And I drove off, whole rib cage filled
> With joy at having not quite killed.

The joy of this moment is generated, partly, by the realization that this near collision has brought together two strangers into an intimacy that would not have occurred otherwise. The poem becomes a paradigm of the experience itself, for it brings together sound and sense in a momentary coincidence, fixing disparate elements forever in a single unity—"ardor" and "car door," for example, or "Sapphic" and "traffic"—in a flawless, surprising intimacy. The humor of the expression is as light as the moment and their relationship are fleeting. We realize the exchange is sexual when we read, "Her lips shaped softly, 'My mistake,' but their encounter is too accidental, brief, and unphysical to be other than innocent.

A different world is evoked in the book's final poem, "September Twelfth, 2001," which eschews words of outrage and does not attempt to describe the horror of a terrorist attack in photographic detail; rather, Kennedy has condensed both outrage and horror into an image that expresses more than a thousand pictures could: "Two caught on film who hurtle / From the eighty-second floor, / Choosing between a fireball / And to jump holding hands . . ." (ll. 1–4). The absence of rhyme in this quatrain strips the moment down to its bare elements, floor, fireball, hands. Kennedy, with exquisite taste, lets the image carry the unbearable lightness of his being still alive:

Alive, we open eyelids
On our pitiful share of time,
We bubbles rising and bursting
In a boiling pot.

He shows how imagery can make the heart burst. His latest collection shows how strong are his principles, how keen his mind, how sharp his eye, and how honed are his skills.

Chapter 3
Subjects and Themes

The Creative Process and Literary Context

Some of Kennedy's own early literary development may be seen in "Poets,"[1] which is in part a response to a couple of epigraphs: "These people are . . . quenched. I mean the natives. / *D. H. Lawrence, letter of 14 August 1923 / from Dover, New Jersey. / Le vierge, le vivace, et le bel aujourd'hui. . . .*"[2] Lawrence's negative characterization of the "natives" of Dover would apply to many of the very people Kennedy knew, was related to, and grew up with, since he was born in Dover, New Jersey, six years and a week after Lawrence made this statement.[3] The French quotation appears to be a reply to Lawrence. Together, they seem to be saying that the people are suppressed and stifled in a world where vivacity and the beautiful day await them. The poem begins with a question: "What were they like as schoolboys?" They "squirmed / At hurt cats, shrank from touching cracked-up birds" (ll. 5–6). They were, like Kennedy himself, Catholic boys, whose sexual feelings were perhaps quenched: "Quenchers of their own wicks. . . ." The poem associates these timid youths with "swans in ice . . . so beautiful, so dumb . . . ," so dreamy and helpless as to need rescue by "real" men: "A fireman with a blowtorch had to come / Thaw the dopes loose" (ll. 16–17). These little boys had wicks, men have blowtorches. Poets may suffer as little boys do.

The poem's final stanza looks upon the geese and the boys with nostalgia, becoming itself dreamy and, like the youths, brought up short by reality: "getting bit, / Numb to the bone, enduring all their crap" (ll. 19–20). The ambivalence of the poet's attitude derives from his nostalgic sympathy for those boys; he even suggests that, if he was not one of them,[4] he shared their appreciation of beautiful things. Yet he stands apart from them, observing them as he does the swans: "Birds of their quill," finally impatient with them, having to endure "all their crap." The last word of this line, the poem's final, plays on both the sound and sense of *crap,* whose flat, abrupt, emphatic sound works like the slap of reality and dispels the dreamy affection for beautiful things that are also troublesome. The title of the poem, "Poets," broadens the meanings within the poem, making them applicable not only to a certain kind of Dover schoolboy but also to poets in general, especially budding poets, as Kennedy himself was. The poem suggests that poets, like swans, are beautiful and dumb, dreamy types who do not live in the "real" world as others do, "Crawling along a ladder, getting bit. . . ." Lawrence's statement and the French quotation describe two types of people in Dover: those who were quenched, and those who longed for, even sought, beauty, life, love, the beautiful day. The swans symbolize the beauty and those who live a life of beauty, who are themselves beautiful. The practical ones, who must rescue the dreamers, have a blowtorch and get the work done.[5] Life as a poet was both a social and an artistic challenge to Kennedy and to all who would dare.

In other poems early in his career, Kennedy explores the nature of the creative process and the poet's occupation. "First Confession" suggests that making poetry is a form of confessing, but it has a broader function as well. Poetry serves as a bridge between the best of the past and the future. Well aware of its lofty lineage, Kennedy would naturally turn to antiquity for models that would characterize the creative process as he understood it. The story of Pygmalion and Galatea becomes, in "To Break a Marble Block," a premise for exploring the artist's relation to what he creates. Although Kennedy has never reprinted this poem after *Nude Descending a Staircase,* it nevertheless offers an intriguing interpretation of how a creative artist, in this poem the sculptor Pygmalion, is made a captive of his creation. In the poem's last five lines, the word *stone,* repeated nine times, hammers the point home:

> Then shall you rut in stone.
> Shall stone give birth to stone
> And stone swing cradled in stone arms,
> To cold bald stone stone croon
> And stone to ravenous stone give suck.
>
> (LL. 12–16)

All Pygmalion will have when his work is completed is a relationship with "cold bald stone." The poem's language suggests a relationship between artist and creation like that between lovers and between mother and child: "And stone swing cradled in stone arms / . . . And stone to ravenous stone give suck." The nature of the creative act is, on the one hand, sterile—the artist gives "birth to stone"; on the other, it is nurturing and generative. The language throughout the poem indicates a scornful attitude toward both artist and his creation, if not toward the creative process itself and the relation of the artist to his creation. Pygmalion (his name is only implied) is to "Croon," his hand is "dense," the stone falls "with bumbling clatter," and Galatea is but a thing of stone. Like a beast, the artist will "rut" with his creation, who has "concessive loins." Yet, however beastly the relationship, or stonelike the artist and his creation, the poem gives them a life or life-giving powers: "stone to ravenous stone give suck." The symbiotic nature of this relationship is clear. They are bound by a process that each needs if life is to be created and sustained.

The relation of the artist to his production is again explored in "Girl Sketching Me into Her Landscape," in which the speaker observes a young female artist sketching him. In an imaginary conversation with her, he advises her to learn more about her subject: "Better bone up on such anatomy / At first hand . . ." (ll. 10–11). The poem's imagery blends painting, courting, and sexuality: "On scaffoldings of gesture let you rise / Into the fixed from of your lover's eyes" (ll. 14–15). In the second stanza, the speaker says that if she wishes to create a man with her art and give the creation permanence, she should "from the mold the good Lord gave you, cast / Your children, that a trace of you may last" (ll. 19–20). Making children is better than making poems: "Bones bloom again though anapests grow old" (l. 22). But because she continues to paint instead of mating with him, his likeness will not be given birth. Art is not a substitute for procreation; in fact, if pursued too single-mindedly, art prevents birth altogether. Kennedy did not reprint this poem, either, though it expresses a view of the artistic effort that continued to interest him. He had already broached this subject in "One A.M. with Voices," in which the woman wants the man to quit wasting his time "coupling on a page" and couple in bed with her. In that poem, Kennedy suggests that writing poetry is impractical, perhaps foolish and misguided. He takes up this theme again in "Scholar's Wife," in which the woman is neglected by a husband lost in scholarship.

The element of play informs virtually all of Kennedy's poems, and the seriousness of his ideas and intent, if not the subject, combines with the playful spirit to create a number of effects, among them ambivalence toward the poet's subject, his craft, and the enterprise of writing itself. This ambivalence forms an ironic context within which the poet develops his ideas. Kennedy continued viewing the creative process with ambivalence, in many ways confining and futile, yet also life-giving. His ambivalence has already been noted in "On a Child Who Lived One Minute." Throughout the poem he expresses a bitter disappointment in the efficacy of the healing arts, including poetry. This theme is explored also in "Artificer," reprinted in *Cross Ties.* In this poem, the artist, or artificer, insists on populating his world with creations of his own imagination. Pride in his workmanship separates him from the world outside his own: "Blessing his handiwork, his drawbridge closed . . ." (l. 1). He creates replicas of real things, "stainless steel chrysanthemums . . . / Little gold bees with twist-keys in their backs" (ll. 3–4). Proud of the intricacies of his creations, he seeks perfection: "So, he shaped a wife . . . / Begat sons by excisions of a knife" and "warned them not to die" (ll. 9, 11–12). His creative power cannot, however, keep out the real world, which invades this artificial, static world: "Tarnish kept ripening," and rust grows; while he sleeps, the world outside sends "newborn rats under his door" (ll. 17, 20). However much the artist wishes to create his own world, perfect it, control it, and make it provide him with all his needs, he is doomed to fail, like Pygmalion, for his creations are, after all, only assembled materials. However intricate and "perfect," they cannot reproduce or live. The poem suggests that not only is the artist here deluded and doomed to fail—the tarnish and rust will ultimate prevail—but art itself is disconnected from the procreative spirit of the world, and as long as it is, the artist's creations will be only intricate curiosities. By opposing the artist's world and his creations with tarnish, rust, and rats, the poem suggests that artistic effort, as long as it is concerned merely with artifice and is kept apart from the real world, will allow only degraded life forms to creep in under the door. Life will prevail in the artist's world; he cannot keep it out. But in trying to, he destroys any chance of connecting with anything more than tarnish, rust, and rats.[6]

Turning again to antiquity for a model, Kennedy characterizes the futility of writing in "Sisyphus: A Parable of the Writer's Lot," a poem from *Winter Thunder* that likens the writer to the mythic figure doomed to perform the same task day in and day out. The second stanza asks the writer why he works "so hard." Because he "makes tracks and / Remains his own boss. . . ." The poem ends by applying a popular saying to the writer's activity: "So what if stonerolling / Gathers no moss?" (ll. 10–13). The poem's central image—Sisyphus pushing the stone up the mountain, beginning anew each day—suggests futility, true enough, but it also suggests the writer's endless labor in the end may be his salvation, for at least it gives purpose and focus. Though Kennedy offers the writer hard choices, he ends by giving the writer's life some validity.[7]

Despite these early expressions of his misgivings, however, Kennedy's faith in the value of writing poems may be glimpsed in brief instances and indirect ways. "Veterinarian," from *Dark Horses*, hints that Kennedy yet holds his profession in high regard. Cast in three neatly molded stanzas of seven lines each, the poem begins with a series of favorable images depicting the work of the veterinarian, "a carpenter of flesh," as she tends to ailing animals. In stanzas two and three the language hints that the veterinarian and poet perform similar offices: "She murmurs words to soothe the languageless. / / Leaves like a plowman order in her wake" (ll. 14–15). Kennedy may not have intended this poem to express his later views of the poet's work, but such a reading is compelling, especially in light the poem's imagery, which depicts the woman's healing activity in terms of constructing, ordering, and putting ideas into words for those who cannot do so themselves. The simile, "like a plowman," also associates her work with renewal, creativity, and fertility. Her activity offers an attractive parallel to the poet's labors.

"None but the Spirit," which ends *Missing Link* and appears again in *Cross Ties*, gives artistic effort an exalted origin, claiming in its two lines that the human spirit, "moving and igniting, / Deserves the credit in creative writing." Kennedy is somewhat more forthcoming in a companion epigram (in *Cross Ties*), "Sappho to a Mummy Wrapped in Papyrus." These four lines address the "Dull Pharaoh" through the voice of Sappho, whose speech opposes the "pride" of the ruler to the poet's poetry. Sappho asserts that "Each stately line" of the Pharaoh's "strict form lies packed in one of mine," punning on the words "form" and "stately line." The Pharaoh's form is mummified, and Sappho's lines contain the Pharaoh by virtue of her addressing him in her poetry. Though "priests regaled" the ruler, "scarabs ravaged" his remains. Sappho ends with a challenge: "sleep / Till time decide whose leftovers will keep." The derisive image distinguishes the physical remains of the Pharaoh from the poet's. The ruler leaves a mummified body; the poet leaves poetry, making clear that the better "leftovers" are those of the literary artist, not the mummified remains of the proud ruler.

Yet Kennedy does not rest with such a rosy view of the future of the poet's output. While reveling with his companions in "Dancing with the Poets at Piggy's," he notes the gathering darkness and senses fathomless depths beyond the noisy barroom, in the sea. He tries to dance with the others as snow begins to fall, and he seems to hear intimations of something beyond the music and gyrating bodies. His question, "why hasten?" echoes questions in earlier poems (both in *Winter Thunder*): why does the Sisyphean writer work so hard? And why does Mabel dance ("Invitation to the Dance")? Kennedy knows that creative endeavor is short-lived, but he can take little satisfaction in knowing that a poem outlasts an erection, for in the end, the great tide rising beyond the door will engulf him and his words.

Even when the writer succeeds in achieving something, the satisfaction is brief and shallow. "Giving In to You" is about the experience of having written a book. The speaker confesses self-deprecatory feelings about himself and his achievement. To accomplish the task, he withdrew from the world. Comparing himself to the lord of a castle, he mocks himself and his creative labor: "Laird of my makeshift castle, / Drawbridge trussed up tight" (ll. 1–2). The language suggests stuffiness, restriction, anal-retentiveness, ineptitude, and ignorance: "I sat supplanting light," he confesses. The second stanza satirizes the writer who prides himself too much on his achievements. He wrote a book and it "dried / I stood it on my shelf / And fed, my pride / A mouth swallowing the body from around itself" (ll. 5–8). This image of self-consumption suggests the extent to which the vain writer is absorbed by himself. In the final stanza, the speaker sees himself as the lord of the county. Now that his great opus is finished (and ingested), he is prepared to "give in to you," as the "Gauze curtains do" in the house of the county poor "To the luxurious wind . . ." (ll. 9–12). Like the wind that "overflows all outdoors," he knows "how to be kind . . . ,"[8] but the comparison suggests that his kindness is, like the wind, fleeting and impersonal.

"In a Dry Season" compares the artist's effort to taking flight, but the picture of the writer's life is unappealing. Ironically, this comic poem develops the notion that the writer is "that early would-be astronaut . . ." (l. 2). His problem is that he is "Willing to rise" yet is "weighed down with thought," and instead of being an astronaut capable of flying into outerspace, he "only walks, / Flapping upholstered arms, emitting squawks" (ll. 3–4). The second stanza develops the contrast further: the speaker yearns "to straddle stars" and asks himself why he toys "with drained steins in unswept singles' bars?" (ll. 5–6). He does so, the implication is, because he cannot write, cannot, in this sense, straddle stars. The final two lines attack the Muse as an "ungracious slattern," who is, like an airliner, "circling Boston in a holding pattern" (ll. 7–8). He is idle, helpless to create, or to fly, and all he can do is toy with drained beer mugs and pray the Muse will descend. The creative impulse again has sexual implications, and the writer's impotence leaves him physically disabled, too.

The writer in "To the Writers Forbidden to Write" suffers another kind of restriction. The dominant metaphor of the first stanza is that of clothing, which confines the writer:

> In shadowland you learn to wear
> A doublebreasted shadow suit,
> A mask for when you venture out.
> You sleep, flesh draped across a chair.
>
> (ll. 1–4)

Clothing symbolizes entrapment in the business world, which is antithetical to the writer's creative urges. We are not told why the writer lives in this world, probably from economic necessity, although the title suggests the possibility of other repressive forces, such as political repression. In any case, the writer lives behind that mask, retreated or forcibly enclosed. The second stanza begins with a paradox: to "stand up straight" the writer must "bend." That is, he must defer to the powers that control him if he is to stand. The image is that of a contorted human, upright but bent over. In addition to this difficult and humiliating condition, he is at the mercy of small but besetting elements, startled by a cat crossing his path, by the clang of a telephone in the flat above his own. The third stanza continues the idea that the writer lives hidden, his creative life repressed and controlled by the clock. His life is, however, only one among many others: "While in a thousand basement rooms / Your thoughts explode like fire alarms" (ll. 11–12). Nevertheless, Kennedy suggests, the creative urge persists despite repression.

Another serious poem in *Dark Horses* affirms the value of art. "On Being Accused of Wit" opens with the poet's complaining that he is "witless." Part of the writing process for him is writing and throwing most of the work away, ruled by "Blind chance" and luck. "The rest is taking pride / In daily labor. This and only this" (ll. 6–7). At least his Sisyphean drudgery brings him a measure of satisfaction. The second stanza shifts to other examples of accomplishments: the juggler, "rich in discipline / Who brought the Christchild all he had for gift" (ll. 9–10), and La Tour, "that painter none too bright," who measured "how a lantern stages light . . ." (ll. 13, 15).[9] Both artists are triumphant and "Witless," too, and in that way are like the poet himself.

At some point in his career, Kennedy became convinced that, however important or personally satisfying writing poetry is, it is in many ways an unlucky profession. More often than not, he takes a humorous, satirical approach to this subject that is nevertheless tinged with a fearful poignancy. "Reading Trip," one of Kennedy's longest poems (ninety-six lines), depicts a poetry reading at a college given by the poem's speaker, whom Kennedy places among people with such names as Mister Nutt and Miss Cone. The poem's speaker passes through this academic sea like the "unancient Mariner." Part of the humor comes from combining formal and informal elements. The eleventh stanza, for instance, begins with "A drag, man," advances from "the varlet dies" to "Get with it, baby," and finishes, with "Screw prosody." Reviewer Henry Taylor singled this poem out as an example of Kennedy's ability to tune "the music of his forms precisely to the various attitudes of his speakers. . . . Even within the same poem, Kennedy can make successful shifts of tone by increasing or decreasing his dependence on light-verse techniques."[10] The poem's opening, for example, is as dignified as the campus groves the speaker first encounters on his visit:

> Just past a grove where roots in overthrow
>   Work air for nothing and boughs lie, still clung
> With oranges stopped short, the towers show,
>   Slim exhalations from a plastic lung,
>   Shimmering distinctly: knowledge reared with pride.
>   Whose Hell is here? Nutt's letter for my guide. . . .
>
> (ll. 1–6)

The clue that something is awry in academia is evident in the language and imagery: roots overthrow, roots work air for nothing (whereas no human on campus works for nothing), boughs lie (with a pun on "lie"), and so on, the stanza closing on the abrupt shift in tone from "knowledge reared with pride" to the irascible question, "Whose Hell is here?" This is Hell? the reader may ask, wondering at the speaker's impatience and getting a further clue in the rest of the line, "Nutt's letter for my guide. . . ." The light-verse turn here is in the use of Nutt for a college official's name. It is playful, but its import is not: the campus is populated by nuts; it is an institution for the mentally unbalanced, perhaps. Kennedy rides these two horses throughout the poem, poking fun at the situation, academics fawning over and posturing for a visiting poet. Seeing the poem as "wildly playful in spots," Henry Taylor also sees that "the playfulness is part of a serious vision."[11] Stephen Tudor recommends this poem "to every poet who has ever been on" a reading trip,[12] presumably because he thinks Kennedy has successfully captured the essence of such an experience. Nevertheless, the poem rises above this individual experience to offer a vision of Everyman confronted by the ages, ending with a sense of imminent doom as the speaker edges "out into the dusk to claim my slot / . . . less and less / The bard on fire, more one now with the blot / That hoods the stars above Los Angeles . . ." (ll. 91–94).

Ignored by most of their contemporaries, many poets are driven to drink. Though in reality this idea may be supported by many sad examples, Kennedy prefers to make comic light of it, as he does in "Dancing with the Poets at Piggy's" and in other poems. The only recourse the neglected writer has, or at least the easiest and most satisfying, is to have a beer and cry in it. Such is the premise of "Uncle Ool's Song against the Ill-Paid Life of Poetry." Ool finds "hard drinking sweeter" than beating the "pate / Against stone walls of meter." The poem continues, in hyperbolic strains, to contrast writing poetry to drinking beer. The effort is thankless, and the writer is eaten by wolves, so he suggests that we drink "Till the toothless mutts lap mush!" The ancient bard at least died in an attempt to charm with his poetry.

Many of Kennedy's salvos aimed at literary types and the literary life are delivered in his epigrams. In his series in *The Epigrammatist* alone, he attacks poor translations, postmodernist poetry, book reviewers, literary movements, writers of book blurbs and epics, poetry anthologies, the lust for fame and winning literary prizes, meager book sales, and a writer who sent him a book manuscript and "Decrees That I Criticize It, Edit It, Retype It, and Find It a Publisher." Contemporary writers are also ridiculed for the dull uniformity of their verse. Kennedy does not withhold his barbs from even writers of traditional forms. A writer of sonnets is attacked for cramming dull words into the sonnet, "Like socks packed in a hurry for a trip."

Kennedy is particularly concerned that many writers are motivated by vanity and greed. "Vision" satirizes the egotism of "our poets nowadays," saying, ironically, that they do have vision, but it is focused inward. "To an Unpopular Novelist" ironically advises the unpopular novelist to improve his chances of success by catering to the popular taste for horror and cheap sensations, adding a bit of sex. The poet pretends to favor those writers who pander to readers, since having money is certainly more practical than pursuing literary merit. To be read by many people may in the end be better than to be praised by critics. In "The Devil's Advice to Poets," the devil himself advises poets who seek popularity and acceptance to adapt to audiences. Echoing "Ol' Man River," he exhorts the poet to "Molt that skin! lift that face! . . . / Only minors remain who they are." In another epigram Kennedy says the writer who writes "for none but friendly eyes— / . . . is wise." In "An Editor" the editor's name, Peter Pitter, is sardonically rhymed with "Litter," and another epigram attacks the literary critic comparing him to "A puking dog to rotten meat returning."

Were Kennedy asked whether any good poets exist in the contemporary scene, his answer would be "Terse Elegy for J. V. Cunningham," which not only praises Cunningham's poetry but draws an ideal portrait of one kind of poet. In his poetry Cunningham wielded a "weaponed wit," which Kennedy emulates in lines that are skillfully balanced, exactly rhymed, and smoothly rhythmed. In the first four lines the poem praises Cunningham for his economy of language, "So loath to gush," and for his sensitivity, kept behind a "a protective crust." The next few lines praise Cunningham's various qualities, "patient skill and lore immense / Prodigious mind, keen ear, rare common sense" (ll. 7–8). Cunningham would write "Only those words he could crush down no more / Like matter pressured to a dwarf star's core" (ll. 9–10). This is an elaborate compliment to Cunningham's poetic power. The final four lines look ahead, hoping that future generations will esteem Cunningham for his "steady, baleful, solitary gleam." The celestial imagery is continued, and Cunningham is given the demeanor of a god with a "baleful" look, a celestial figure so stellar, so rare, that he resides, or presides, as a "solitary gleam." Though other poets may come whose work inspires love more quickly than Cunningham's, a poet with his qualities will never be seen again.

When Kennedy focuses on specific writers, such as J. V. Cunningham, one can see evidence of a wide interest.[13] Often the evidence is subtle, as in the title of Inscriptions After Fact, which echoes the "Inscriptions" in *Leaves of Grass.*[14]

Interest in other writers is shown in more obvious references. "On a Child Who Lived One Minute" develops the theme found in Ben Jonson's "Epitaph on Elizabeth, Lady H——," which opens, "Underneath this stone doth lie / As much beauty as could die." Elsewhere Kennedy references Robert Herrick, or his epigrammatic mentor, Alexander Pope, as he does in, appropriately, a heroic couplet, whose witty word play might have impressed Pope himself:

> Leaden, my thoughts. For saving grace they grope,
> Lightness their God the Father, Pope their pope.

A line from Omar Khayyám or a reference to Thomas Hardy or William Wordsworth gives a literary reference point, and in some, something more substantial.[15] "Lewis Carroll," for example, makes a serious point about this important writer of nonsense literature, whose *Alice in Wonderland* and *Through the Looking-Glass* are models of serious playfulness and meaningful nonsense. "To the One-Eyed Poets" pays a compliment to three contemporary poets Robert Creeley, Robert Penn Warren, and James Seay, who "might well be kings / In this country of the blind."

William Wordsworth is more than an echo in Kennedy's "Invasion and Retreat," a poem that follows the speaker from a Manhattan ferryboat to his home. Kennedy's title recalls Wordsworth's "Resolution and Independence," a poem in which the speaker recalls a chance meeting with an old leech-gatherer whose wisdom lifts the poet's spirits. Kennedy's epigraph to his poem reminds one, too, of Wordsworth's definition of good poetry as emotion recollected in tranquility: "a recollection of a voyage / to and from Manhattan by Barclay Street ferry." Kennedy's poem falls into two parts, as the title suggests: an "invasion" of Manhattan by the poem's speaker that ends in his retreat, and a recollection of that experience:

> My plan to storm New York died in midcharge—
> I cruised home. In reflection still repose
> Swayed waters, that intensity of rose
> With which the sun, transforming tug and barge,
> Captured Hoboken's archipelagoes.
>
> (ll. 6–10)

As if to contrast New York with Wordsworth's field of golden daffodils, Kennedy describes the city's seamier aspects: torn posters on "scabrous" walls, gulls, and fishmongers "who swore in Portuguese." On reflection, however, the speaker remembers the sight as an example of nature's power to turn daunting ugliness to beauty, to capture it with roseate beams and to transform it, visually, into a South Pacific island. Kennedy gives the power of transformation not to his own imagination or to a Wordsworthian overflow of powerful feelings, but to the sun, to forces in nature outside and beyond himself. By casting the experience in the language of warfare and placing the final image in the South Seas, Kennedy further removes the experience from the tranquility of an English Romantic poet, underscoring the distance between himself and Wordsworth in circumstance and belief.

Kennedy has said that the poetry of William Butler Yeats, his favorite poet, is inimitable, but he does use Yeats's "Among School Children" as a point of reference in his own "Among Stool Pigeons," which is very different from Yeats's sober, reflective poem. Kennedy's schoolroom is thrown into disorder by a drunken teacher who falls between two stools and imagines the school board charging him with moral turpitude and advising him to quit teaching. He also has Yeats in mind in "The Medium Is the Message," which suggests that Yeats's vision of the Second Coming may have already been realized: "The rude beast slouches," he says. In some poems, another poet will be the subject of the entire poem. In the eight lines of "A Word from Hart Crane's Ghost," Kennedy ponders the reason Hart Crane took his own life.[16] Kennedy speculates that the effort of a certain kind of building became too great for Crane: "sleep / With a woman and you build a bridge / Across two minds, two bodies, inch by inch . . ." (ll. 2–4). Having taken on too much, trying to join himself with someone: "The whole steeled cognizance swung round and / Backfired" (ll. 6–7). By comparison, "The sucking Gulf seemed, oh, / A deep green cinch" (ll. 7–8).

"At the Stoplight by the Paupers' Graves" reminds one of Robert Frost's "Stopping by Woods on a Snowy Evening," especially in reading the line that begins the third, final stanza, "My engine shudders as if about to stall" (bringing to mind, "My little horse must think it queer"). Another poem, "Robert Frost Discovers Another Road Not Taken," mocks the seriousness of Frost's poem (and Frost himself) by having the traveler explain,

I had to keep going on one
To get to the end of a scent
That a nostril had begun,
But I picked out the no good.

(ll. 3–6)

The mockery is heightened and the tone of the poem is lowered, with a pun on the word "picked." This poem, from the 1970s and reprinted in *Cross Ties*, represents Kennedy in a confident moment. Not only will he pick his nose in the face of potentially momentous decisions (and America's most revered poet), but he is sure of his direction:

Still I'm bound to put up with Fate
Despite that aftermath.
I'd hold out for some kind of path
Under a body's feet.

(ll. 9–12)

Twenty years later, in "The Waterbury Cross," Kennedy portrays a poet whose spiritual independence is less than confident. Seeing a cross on a hill while driving through Connecticut, the speaker is reminded of Wallace Stevens, and he wonders whether "even Wallace Stevens" turned to Mother Church "at the last." Stevens here symbolizes the poet who, "Having sown all his philosophe's wild oats" (l. 10), at last seeks comfort and support in the "swaddling petticoats" of Mother Church. Feeling a kinship to that spirit, the speaker wonders, "Is there / Still a pale Christ who clings to hope for me, / Who bides time in a cloud?" (ll. 13–15).

No poet receives as much overt attention as Emily Dickinson, whose style, voice, and stanzaic pattern Kennedy makes the vehicle of two of his poems. She may have typified the questing, unpretentious, withdrawn spirit whose keen intelligence and incisive wit matched Kennedy's and who was insouciant or diffident enough to eschew publication of her more than seventeen hundred poems. In her poetic style, Kennedy must also have found an apt vehicle for his talents, mood, and ideas. "Emily Dickinson in Southern California," published in the collection with the same title, is one of Kennedy's longest and most elaborately styled poems—it contains twenty-four stanzas of four lines each and one eight-line stanza. The poem places Dickinson on a Southern California beach in search of Eden. On her journey to California, her Spirit, a "scabbed thing," disappears in a "thick black Lily pond," and the Dark leaps up and clenches her till she nearly dies. Continuing to the ocean's edge, she still has not found what she is searching for—Truth? Beauty? Enlightenment?—though she bears "Hope's candle." Waiting for a sign, she hears "Asia's rumor of despair / Behind a wall of Salt—" (8: ll. 3–4).[17]

One of the few critics who have commented on this poem, Joseph Parisi, sees it as Kennedy's way of debunking "current follies" with "impish glee. . . . [His] Insistent little pecks—measured in short phrases separated by dashes—chip away at the bronzed and brazen images of our modern Lotus Land."[18] One might disagree with Parisi's characterization of Kennedy's manner and mood in this poem. Parisi may have in mind the early stanzas, mainly, from which he takes two to illustrate his point, and Kennedy is indeed somewhat "impish" when he says that the surfboarders are "Archangels of the Foam," or when he has Dickinson trip over "Browned couples—in cahoots— / No more than Tides need shells to fill / did they need—bathing suits—" (ll. 6–8). But soon after, the poem's mood darkens considerably, and when it ends, the reader is left with an image of Dickinson holding Hope's candle, staring at a bleak ocean wall. What Parisi says of the rest of the poems in this collection applies as well to this poem: "In other poems Kennedy abandons the gentle mockery for disquieting realism."[19]

"Emily Dickinson Leaves a Message to the World, Now That Her Homestead in Amherst Has an Answering Machine," published in *Dark Horses,* also uses Dickinson's characteristic punctuation and structural patterns and even some of her wit: "Speak quickly—or I'll intercept / Your Message with—a Beep" (ll. 7–8). Kennedy mocks the modern use of answering devices by creating an anachronistic situation in which Dickinson, unable to stop "for Breath" in her journey "Past Altitudes—of Earth . . ." (ll. 1–2), leaves a recorded message. The metaphor of the answering machine is continued to the end of the poem. Dickinson, too, had often "dialed and rung / The Bastion of the Bee—" (ll. 9–10), but the "Answer," she found, "Was seldom Home—to me—." Her failure to find the "Answer" parallels the modern caller's failure to get any "Answer" from such a machine.

Kennedy's interest in the poetry of other nations is evident in his translations of both German and French poems, in his recent recasting of *Lysistrata,* and in poems based on the work of other authors, including "At Brown Crane Pavilion," which is based on a poem by Ts'ui Hao. He is most interested in French writers, however, and many of his poems reflect his knowledge of French literature, history, and setting. On the whole, Kennedy has regarded French authors with affectionate respect, continuing to reprint his translations of their poetry in his later collections. *French Leave: Translations* contains twelve poems translated from the works of eight French poets, whose dates range from the sixteenth to the twentieth century. Several of his early poems, some of the reprinted in *Cross Ties* and *Dark Horses,* show that his memories of France and French poetry remain fresh in his mind. Kennedy's "Where Are the Snows of Yesteryear?" alludes to François Villon's famous poem, "Ballade des dames du temps jadis," and Kennedy has written several other poems based on the work of French writers. "Fall Song" is "after Verlaine," "Rondel" is a "Violation on a theme by Charles d'Orléans," and "Ladies Looking for Lice" is "after Rimbaud." As if to show that his affection for French writers is not unqualified, Kennedy, in "Palefaces," paints an unflattering portrait of the great French writer Marcel Proust, who in Kennedy's poem symbolizes a man "Walled like wine with cork for stopper," writing "reams about *temps perdu,*" not actually going to the moon himself or even going West. Apollinaire is also remembered in "Churchbells," "Crawfish," and "Pont Mirabeau." These poems offer Kennedy an opportunity to reminisce and revisit the work of favorite poets, and they also offer him subjects, moods, and imagery that appealed to his own interests and probably expressed some of his own feelings.

Church Authority and Religion

Many of Kennedy's poems are devoted to a kind of quest to understand the nature of the cosmos and how it bears on the human condition and the future of mankind. This interest often is expressed in poems whose subjects are biblical characters and events and in poems that question church authority. Kennedy once told an interviewer that the theme running through *Cross Ties* is ex-Catholicism, yet the same could be said of Kennedy's whole poetic career. He admits to having lost his Catholic faith in his early teens, but that statement could be true only in a narrow sense. From the very first poems to the most recent, in dozens of poems, he addresses the religious question and heaven's role in human affairs from the perspective of one who continues to respect Catholic doctrine.[20] He often attacks the church bitterly because it has failed to relieve suffering or to bring light into darkened lives, and he often treats it with humor, but always he believes in a higher power, however inscrutable it may be, that is defined largely in Christian terms, often in terms that are specific to Catholic orthodoxy.

Many of Kennedy's poems express the shifting nature of his belief. "First Confession" portrays a young man who has little liking for Catholic ritual and is impatient to be free of it. Much later, in "Dancing with the Poets at Piggy's," Kennedy sees a great tide rising to engulf his world, with no hint of salvation in the darkness that "gathers force and climbs. . . ." What he says at the end of "Emily Dickinson Leaves a Message to the World" again seems to reflect his own feelings. Like the Dickinson in this poem, he has often "dialed" Heaven hoping for an "Answer," but for him, too, it was "seldom Home." In "The Waterbury Cross" his protagonist clings to the hope of redemption, asking plaintively as he drives through the countryside, "Is there / Still a pale Christ who clings to hope for me . . . ?" Kennedy may have left the church, but the church has never left him, and what he says of the young man in "First Confession" may have been an unconscious admission of his own fear that he is "A fresh roost for the Holy Ghost." So far, he seems not to have decided whether faith is a curse or a blessing or whether he, and the rest of us, is doomed or on probation until the final verdict comes in. What is clear, however, is that he has never let go of these issues.

Kennedy included "In Faith of Rising" in *Nude Descending a Staircase* but never reprinted it. Though the poem is a skillful display of religious faith, he may not have wanted to reprint it because it was too distant from the "ex-Catholicism" of his later years. Nevertheless, the poem merits attention because it offers another of Kennedy's virtuoso performances in using structural design to reflect meanings that unfold before the reader's eyes. The poem's structure is as central to the meaning as the language itself:

When all my dust lies strewn
Over the roundbrinked ramparts of the world,
I can be gathered, sinew and bone
Out of the past hurled
Delaylessly as I
Flick thoughts back that replace
Lash to dropped lid, lid to eye,
Eye to disbanded face.

No task to His strength, for He
Is my Head—Him I trust
To stray the presence of His mind to me
Then cast down again
Or recollect my dust.

Kennedy gives line length, stanzaic form, pauses and stops, and other elements as much significance as imagery, sound, and statement. The stanza is rhymed *ababcdcdefegf*, the penultimate unrhymed line itself suggesting the straying of God's presence, mentioned in the previous line, and interrupting the rhyme pattern at a point in the poem that suggests the dislocation of one's being "cast down again." Structural irregularity reflects the disruption that human disobedience and punishment cause, but by the end of the poem, one discovers symmetry, too: three stresses in the first and last lines and two long lines at the head and foot, the second looking as though it rests on a pedestal. All the while, the lines are centered with respect to each other, giving the appearance of something being erected, part by part, as the speaker imagines himself to be, until, by the end of the poem, the entire mortal framework stands before the reader, resting imaginatively and linguistically on a stable base. The repetition of the pronouns—"His, "He," "Him," and "His," all capitalized in the presence of "my," "me, "my"—emphasizes the speaker's submission to God, which comes to a climactic merging of syntax, grammar, punctuation, and meaning in the tenth line: "for He / Is my Head—Him I trust . . . ," which is followed in the next line by the seeming contradiction, "To stray," which is resolved by the rest of the line in deft metaphysical fashion: "To stray the presence of His mind to me. . . ." Aptly, the poem ends on the pun: God shall remember his dust or regather it; either way, the speaker shall be reclaimed.

"Song: Great Chain of Being" also shows Kennedy exploring his religious feelings, though his focus has shifted somewhat. The poem claims that humankind has suffered a demotion. Before, "man was top dog on mother earth . . ." (l. 5), and "Everybody in creation knew just how high or low he hung . . ." (l. 2). The irreverent language and casual tone—"Well, I wonder who's been sitting in the Good Lord's old arm chair" (l. 17)—reflect the speaker's lowered condition, and the disorder in the outer world reflects disorder in his own mind. He sees "every creature . . . rattling around, come loose from that golden chain," and he feels aimless: "I'm fixing to let myself play out in the pouring rain, /

Snapped off and dangling . . ." (ll. 13, 15–16). The poem suggests that mortals lost their ability to see beyond the physical world when science demolished faith in the old order. The import of the final refrain, "Is seeing believing?" is that if people believe what they see, they will find themselves in a world without Heaven or Hell, a world overshadowed by bland bureaucracies and spiritless voids. The search for scientific proof, whatever benefits it has brought to humankind—the poem names none—has left the modern individual "Snapped off and dangling." Although the poem defends religious faith, the argument is rational, its language and tone very different from the same elements in "In Faith of Rising" and from a trio of poems Kennedy grouped together and reprinted in *Cross Ties.*

That group of poems treats religion in different ways, but together they represent a strong commitment to religious faith, and their emotional intensity is focused on Christian lore. "Creation Morning" argues that in spirit, God's or man's, there exists a fundamental urge to cause motion, to leave a mark, or to start something. The poem's second line asks a question: "Why should He have let there be light?" Because God, like man, is "unsettled" by the face of placidity and takes up a stone to shatter it, or, seeing a "new-laid sidewalk / That for empty blocks extends" (ll. 8–9), wants to mark it with chalk. God is like the husband who "beholds in his bride / Only her willingness" (ll. 13–14), which draws him to unite with her. The final stanza compares the impulse to "start growth rings" to "the toss of a seed like a stone" (ll. 19, 21), each a generative event.

The next poem, "A Footpath Near Gethsemane," combines a child's innocent nursery rhyme with a religious theme to heighten the emotional intensity of the poem's subject. Consisting of only four lines, it opens with a question from a child, a variation of the familiar nursery rhyme, "Mary, Mary, wan and weary, / What does your garden grow?" The mother (Mary) answers with a reference to the cross and to the woman who wiped Jesus' face as he passed on his way to Calvary: "Tenpenny nails and Veronica's veils / And three ruddy trees in a row."

This little nursery rhyme takes on a heightened intensity by being placed between two poems that treat religious faith in a form associated with adult poetry. It shows the importance of context and how placement can become a very effective device for a poet of Kennedy's skill and acumen. The brief exchange between the mother and child in "A Footpath Near Gethsemane" lends an almost musical, or choral, element to these three poems that elevates the sanctity of the poetry.

The third poem of the group, "The Atheist's Stigmata," is a stream-of-consciousness monologue in irregularly rhymed eleven lines and is delivered by one of the thieves crucified alongside Christ. The poem's graphic imagery creates intense seriousness that reminds one of the plaints of Christian martyrs: "The nail holes in my wrists / And ankles pop like bubbles" (ll. 1–2). People reach out to the thief, expecting him to heal their babies, but he cannot; he thinks of using drink to help him forget, but it fails him "—only the gradual rounding-out / Of buds in April warmth helps" (ll. 6–7). In the end, he is relieved not to be "the Middle Man" because "I'd be forsaken, thanks."

The fact that Kennedy reprinted these three poems in *Cross Ties* argues that his interest in religious subjects was still sufficiently strong in the mid 1980s to warrant their inclusion in his most thoughtfully constructed collection. The vivid imagery, emotional intensity, and religious content of these poems and others composed much later show that Kennedy's imagination was able to conjure up the spirit, the vision, and even the passion of the believer long after he became an "ex-Catholic." The sincerity of Kennedy's religious feelings may also be inferred from one of his most personal and impassioned poems, "Down in Dallas," which mourns the death of John F. Kennedy. A series of vivid images associates the details of the assassination with those of Christ's ordeal, this image concluding the first quatrain: "Little Oswald nailed Jack Kennedy up / With the nail of a rifle crack." The poet's emotion peaks in the last of the poem's five stanzas in a combination of repeated phrases, rhythmic force, imagery, and concordant sounds:

> Oh, down in Dallas, down in Dallas
> Where a desert wind walks by night,
> He stood and they bound him foot and hand
> To the cross of a rifle sight.
>
> (ll. 17–20)

The image of the desert wind and cross assimilates the assassination with the Crucifixion and Christ's sojourn in the wilderness. The calming effect of the wind, together with the final apotheosis, creates a sense of harmony, balance, and even compensation. The poem implies that the loss of the president has brought us closer to the forces of nature and to heaven—at the cost of a second Crucifixion. In this outpouring of personal feeling, Kennedy reveals that his Christian bearings have not been entirely lost. In a moment of national crisis, his religious feelings and Christian training seem to have offered him something to turn to for stability, direction, and order.[21]

Stephen Tudor considered Kennedy very daring in publishing "Down in Dallas," which "is either a very big flop or it is a tremendous success."[22] Tudor seems to be alluding to Kennedy's bold comparison of the president with Jesus Christ throughout the poem. On the other hand, Louis Martz seemed not at all bothered by the seeming deification of the president, reading the poem as folklore: "the death of Jack Kennedy [is] placed effectively in the form of a ballad. . . ."[23]

The spirit that impelled Kennedy to find his bearings in Christian imagery and tradition may have impelled him from time to time to explore certain biblical episodes as well. Searching the origins of human history enabled him to speculate about the causes of human misery and the apparent decline of civilization. "A Footpath near Gethsemane" and "The Atheist's Stigmata" are but two examples of this exploration. Kennedy's contentious spirit reappears in "Apocrypha,"[24] whose fourteen lines sweep from the creation of Eve to the murder of Abel, ending on a question: should not Cain have been "let to starve" rather than allowed to live in exile? The implicit answer is no.

"Carol," a Christmas poem from 1972, updates to modern times the story of Mary and Joseph in search of an inn and the subsequent birth of Christ. The story is told in a series of five balladlike quatrains, each having two refrains. The contrast between the biblical tale and the ballad rhythms and language creates an unusual mixture, as did the nursery rhyme quality of "Footpath near Gethsemane." Kennedy increases the effect of the odd blend in "Carol" by placing the bibilical events in a modern context, having the infant Christ swaddled in "the Sunday Herald," for instance, and having the Christmas message transmitted in scientific terms:

> Far quasars glittered. "Peace to all"
> *The barberry, holly, and ivy, O*
> Relayed a beeping basketball
> *Hold mistletoe over the lady, O*
>
> (ll. 13–16)

The final stanza shifts the scene to Saigon, where "a shell-shocked vet . . . / Cupped cold hands round a cigaret . . ." (ll. 17,

19). Like the vet, the world in which this child is born is shell-shocked, debased by blaring TV advertisements, and enmeshed in a sordid war. Kennedy heightens the point by juxtaposing the biblical tale with images of modern technology and the Asian conflict, placing the whole in the ironic context of a jolly ballad. The biblical story, idealized and sentimentalized to this day in standard Christmas versions, is given a setting that sends an implicit message: the modern world is a degraded, strife-ridden place that mocks the birth of the Prince of Peace. Kennedy may have also meant these five quatrains to say that the world has declined to this state despite Christ's birth and the centuries of the church's ministrations.

"Joshua," too, dramatizes a moment in biblical history when the conqueror of Canaan and leader of the tribes of Israel fought one of his great battles,[25] creating carnage so high that "all creation" was "Crushed like a sprig of heather in a book" (l. 12). Though strongly moved by the scene, Joshua cannot "feel commensurate remorse" with those who actually have suffered through the destruction. Kennedy connects the ancient scene with modern conditions in a single, vivid image that deflates any majesty the event may have: "The Holy City hit a mountain / As a tray of dishes meets a swinging door" (ll. 1–2). Despite the magnitude of this catastrophe, God remains "noncommittal" at the poem's close, and the sun "Rose in confusion and resumed its course" (l. 16). The poem, which Kennedy respected enough to reprint in *Cross Ties,* combines two perspectives on this ancient catastrophe: it was so tremendous that the "Sun and moon hung stone still, their axles stuck" (l. 8), yet in the end, heavenly and universal forces continue unaffected by it, regarding it perhaps as nothing more than a heap of broken dishes, a human catastrophe reduced to a trifle. The extent of the destruction and the magnitude of the "carnage" seem to explain why humankind is isolated from heaven and the cosmos and why, perhaps, heaven turns its back on the whole scene. As he does in several of his religious poems, Kennedy ends on the idea that higher powers—be they God, heaven, or the cosmos—stand back from human suffering, watching impassively as humankind slips toward annihilation.

In "Pileup," which is reprinted in *The Lords of Misrule,* Kennedy makes several clever shifts in language to create a modern version of a biblical episode. An accident on a modern freeway has gridlocked traffic, stranding motorists for "one long eight-nighted day" (l. 7), during which the lives of strangers are suddenly thrown into disorder and become temporarily entwined.

The poem's speaker hints that the accident is punishment for, or consequence of, their having fallen into a form of modern wickedness, isolation, and loss of direction: "It seemed we had elected to retreat / To separate Trappist walls. The Paraclete / Strode on the muddied rivers of our minds" (ll. 9–11). Like Noah, who released a dove that returned with an olive leaf, someone in this traffic jam lets loose a pigeon: it "Came back in a week, / An olive-loaf on rye clutched in its beak" (ll. 15–16). The shifts from dove to pigeon and olive leaf to olive-loaf suggest that these people are afloat on a modern deluge. The biblical overtones enlarge the significance of this familiar scene, and the language further implies that, like Noah and his animals, the motorists are given a second chance, for when the road is cleared, they are "salvaged" and they roar off "in second gear." Yet the entire episode is cast in a surreal blur, from which full recovery seems uncertain, and since the "thickening gloom" is not dispelled, we are left with the sense that their liberation is neither complete nor permanent.

The theme that runs through many of these recreations of biblical events is that heaven botched things at the start, and the modern scene is both evidence of that fact and a consequence of it. Religious subjects provided Kennedy with a standard by which to rate modern conditions and to indict Christianity at the same time. The more he finds wrong with the world, the more it seems that God has abandoned and punished the world after having pretty well fumbled Creation. Any attempt to romanticize or mask this grave truth is both futile and pathetic. "Christmas Abrupted" shows how wide the discrepancy can be between what Heaven promises, or represents, and what it delivers. In this household the traditional Christmas cheer has vanished under the pall of a death, that of the father. On the Christmas tree, Death has "hooked his stocking." To the children, the lights revolve like "carousels," the stars "needling through a sky / Of tensile boughs," and tin Santas sleigh "on and on, across the evergreen" (ll. 11–13). The celebration is cheering only to those unable to see its fakery. To the children, the future is evergreen. This view ironically contrasts with the father's death, and the unreality of this view is signalled by the tree ornaments: the Wise Men are made of plastic; the stars, "cool steel"; and the boughs, "tensile." The Santa figures are "Inhuman things that cast a silver sheen" (l. 14). All of the items are pretty to young eyes, but all are just things made of plastic, tin, tensile, and steel. In the end the children's fantasy creates a poignant contrast to the grim view of death that opens the poem. This religious ritual with its cheap decorations cannot mask the reality of death, which in ordinary lives is no occasion for celebration. The Christmas tradition in this poem, and in the larger world it represents, is offset by the reality that defines human existence.

Especially when Kennedy looks into the lives of people in the modern world, he sees betrayal and suffering and, in large part, blames formal religion, specifically the Catholic Church. "West Somerville, Mass.," a long poem in three parts, each part having its own stanzaic pattern, creates a dismal picture of an individual's life within a religious context. As in many other poems, Kennedy seems to be exploring his own religious feelings, and in doing so he reveals religious doubt.[26] Like Kennedy, who had been an academic and resided in Massachusetts himself, the protagonist of this poem is a professor and a poet. We journey through his mind on the Sabbath in a small town east of Boston in the present time. In the first section, "Day 7," the speaker is roused by the clatter of a newsboy's cart. The language and imagery emphasize the poem's religious theme. In addition to the pun on "Mass." in the title, the newspaper "comes in sections like a sacred robe" (l. 9). The imagery casts a gloom over this scene: and the newspaper boy's breath is "torn forth from his ribs," the man's children are "crowing in their cribs . . . " (ll. 11–12) and in the bathroom mirror, his eyes appear "Like windowpanes you'd see in blocks / Doomed to renewal. . ." (ll. 22–23).

The second section, titled "The Ascent," continues the religious theme through thirteen quatrains. The speaker recalls the Ascension of Christ, "The rock rolled back, the stained race hatched out new" (l. 1), as though the members of the redeemed race are insects. Struggle and defeat pervade his thoughts and the mood of the poem generally. Earlier, he could not even tie his shoelaces, and now a "half-baked villanelle" will not "rise." His faith, too, is "copped out." He feels unprepared to receive Christ as threatening ghosts loom: "One dark duenna screws up lips to slay / / Me with a word" (ll. 24–25). He conjures up a vision of Christ on the cross, the soldier piercing with his lance, laughing. In the final quatrain of this section, he sees himself as Christ: "At a loss / I stretch out arms, fix feet as on a cross / Till something says, *Come off it*" (ll. 50–52). The last section, "Golgotha," shifts to the site of the speaker's own crucifixion—not a mount, however; ironically, he descends to his basement office, a dark, musty, cold place where ashes mount behind a fragile door and "Mildew advances" down the spine of his "dogeared John Keats." One of the student papers he reads describes scenes in the Vietnam War, and another one is from a "John Bircher." As he takes the trash out, he is preoccupied with destruction, mayhem, and death, seeing them everywhere: "Torn gift wraps, Christmas-tree rain— / Lift can-cover on a white horde / Writhing . . ." (ll. 38–40). Earlier in this section, the broken, abbreviated sentences depict a mind in conflict and a world fragmented and besieged:

> Cramped handwriting, don't know his name
> *How Youth Is Shafted*
> *By Society*—now I've pegged him,
> They got him. Drafted.
>
> (ll. 25–28)

The speaker struggles to confront the day as he slogs through darkness, feeling alienated and inadequate. At the end the quickening rhythms suggest a growing desperation. He seems almost out of breath, frightened by his own thoughts. His final vision sees humans again as insects, "a white horde / Writhing," and he thinks everyone is a victim of the "mad in absolute power."

Because the Ascension was a failure, humankind has been doomed all along. Even nature has become threatening: the wind is "murderous," the rain "Has it in for you," and the snow is "gaining ground in the dark yard." Kennedy finally hints that humans have made such a mess of themselves and the world that civilization not only will be destroyed but deserves to be. This professor's world is but a microcosm of our world—the poem's first stanza begins, "Sundays we wake to tumbrils . . . ," before shifting to the more specific and personal "I quit my dozing wife. . . ." By the end the perspective shifts back to the reader, leaving us with the message that we all are together in the ensuing dissolution, both victim and perpetrator. Much of the fault is now within ourselves, and the outer world is a reflection of our wrongdoing as well as the means of our undoing.[27]

If this poem offers a vision of religious despair through the eyes of a literary and academic failure, other poems view religion from the perspective of the working man. "Hangover Mass," for example, is a poignant portrayal of old, lonely drunkards through a child's eyes: "Each knee I stared at cried out for a patch" (l. 16). The Sunday ritual depicted by the child, together with portraits of the drunkards, is presented with affection. The father is referred to as "that reprobate / my father," who has only one sin of the flesh, "and it had class: / To sip tea of a Sunday till so late /

We'd barely make it up to Drunkard's Mass" (ll. 2–4). The church, on the other hand, has become so ineffectual and routine that its ritual is a mockery of spiritual appeasement:

> After a sermon on the wiles of booze,
> The bread and wine transformed with decent haste,
> Quickly the priest would drive us forth to graze
> Where among churchyard flocks I'd get a taste
>
> Of chronic loneliness.
>
> (ll. 5–9)

Far from easing the suffering of these needy souls, the church provides a context in which human weakness and suffering continue unabated. "Requiem in Hoboken" also views the church from the perspective of working men, "Their wives and children, spiffed up fit to kill" (l. 1) as they attend mass. In this world, the men are "Suddenly cut to lengths befitting dust." The "Bird" that delivers the bread during mass becomes, in the second stanza, the Resurrection that hatches souls from their "patchwork shells." The poem asks whether "the grandest resurrection ever" has the power to redeem these men "Without their thirsting at the very throne / For Guinness's . . ." (ll. 16–17). The contrast between these men drinking beer in a bar and the communicants drinking wine at mass marks the discrepancy between faith and action and measures the distance between the lives of these people and the heaven they presumably strive to enter. Though the poem asks that "Peace drop upon these men / Of Hoboken . . . ," it suggests that this world and those in it are doomed because the Resurrection cannot "hatch" their degraded souls. Kennedy emphasizes Heaven's indifference by separating the last line of the poem from the previous two stanzas: "The Bird broods on a setting of brown stone" (l. 21). The double meaning of "setting" suggests that this world is declining into darkness, while the Bird impassively "broods" as the destruction takes place.

"Aunt Rectita's Good Friday" offers a moment in the life of "Aunt Rectita" (her name is derived from *rectitude*) when she is "Plate-scraping at the sink," thinking of Christ, to whom she "consecrates / . . . the misery in her legs." The contrast between heavenly and household concerns creates an ironic tension throughout the poem, a tension made all the more evident by the vivid details that define the aunt's misery and emphasize the unpleasant aspects of her condition:

Plate-scraping at her sink, she consecrates
To Christ her Lord the misery in her legs.
Tinges of spring engage the bulbous land.
Packets of dyestuff wait for Easter eggs.

(ll. 1–4)

Echoing Kennedy's own feelings, the question in the second stanza reveals the aunt's sense of injustice: "How can He die and how dare life go on?" She sees a contradiction between Christ's dying to save mankind and the reality that people suffer. Her dismay, bordering on despair, is unrelenting, and at one point she says that humans share some of the blame for the present state of affairs: "He died for all who do not give a damn . . ." (l. 9). In the final quatrain, her gloomy reflections are transformed into a macabre conjunction of food preparation and Crucifixion: "Brooding on sorrowful mysteries, she shoves / Into its clean white forehead-fat the ham's / Thorn crown of cloves" (ll. 10–12).[28] The poem's title becomes ironic, for nothing in the aunt's life indicates that her Friday is "good," and the old dam's way with the meat expresses anger, resentment, and frustration. The vividness of the poem's details makes her outrage seem just, and we come to admire her courageous ire. The poem casts a favorable light on the part of humanity that the old woman represents, the part that is unafraid to condemn human failing and to lay some of the blame of human misery at heaven's door. She stands for all the sufferers who do indeed "give a damn."

Heaven's indifference inspires another dark vision in "Black Velvet Art," whose subject is a collection of paintings for sale on a "rainriddled" corner in Maine:

Elvis with hairdo laced with bright gold nimbus,
Jesus with heart aflame, arms wide to bless
Your pickup truck, a leopard crouched to leap
Upon a bathing beauty sound asleep,
And all resplendent on a jet-deep back-
Ground of profoundly interstellar black,
Blacker than nearby space,
So that these cat-toothed hues spring to deface
Eyes disbelieving.

(ll. 3–11)

The poem's colorful details give clues of disapproval and disbelief—that final line serves as a commentary on all that has been described, and the eyes that disbelieve belong to those witnessing this scene: Jesus, the reader, anyone who dares look upon it. The paintings' velvet is "profoundly interstellar black, / Blacker than nearby space. . . ." The symbolic magnitude of their blackness is set in an unattractive, congested urban scene, a corner near the Androscoggin River, between whose banks "sprout work socks and cheap shoes. . . ." The final five lines of the poem shift to the next day when the speaker returns to the corner, only to find the artworks vanished, "The pavement gray and blank. . . ." To the speaker, the artworks seem like vanished stars on "that final dawn," when God rids himself of the burden of the entire universe in one final exasperated, weary command, "*Get off My Hands.*" The poem suggests that God is weary of all creation because it has spawned a race that creates "Two-for-fifteen-dollar art." Why? Because such vulgarity "Fulfills a need not known, for which we yearn / Unwittingly" (ll. 19–20).

Kennedy again addresses heaven's indifference to human suffering in "Invitation to the Dance." A relatively long poem of seventeen quatrains, it develops a poignant contrast between a festive Easter dance and death. A group of aged, ailing denizens of a nursing home, who are "stored . . . like bundles of kindling," are prodded by Mabel O'Lannihan to join in on a spirited waltz. Her spunk is engaging, and she does not mince words:

> "There's more than to sit here bitching
> In your motheaten sweater and catching chills.
> You've plenty of room for a second helping.
> Come dance with me now, you old bottle of pills."
>
> (ll. 29–32)

This burst of life amid decaying, decrepit patients represents a last gasp for some of them—old Katz drops dead of a heart attack during the dance. Amid the merriment, Mervin Finver declares, "'The nature of things goes from bad to worse,'" but Mabel believes "'This world is the worse for too little dancing.'" Easter is mimicked in her rousing call to resurrect and dance—rise and live, for dancing at least gives one the illusion, if not the hope, of not dying: "'I'm dancing,' says Mabel, 'to keep from dying. . . .'" This scene makes a rowdy, profane comment on the human condition: life is undercut by decrepitude and death, death mocking life and life—represented by Mabel's dominate presence and voice—bravely defying death. Christ's resurrection symbolizes the ultimate triumph of life over death, yet the final image of the savior staring unblinkingly at the revelers sobers the mood and reminds us that heaven is unmoved by the spirited display:

How they thundered the floorboards and rattled the rafters
While the whitecoats ogled in sore surprise
As that horde of the old moved athwart the morning
Of the risen Christ's rooster-red Easter Eyes.

(ll. 65–68)

The image in the last line reminds one of the roosting Holy Ghost in "First Confession" and the brooding bird in "Requiem in Hoboken." These poems and a number of later ones help us see that, for Kennedy, heaven—whether represented by God, the bird, or a portrait of Christ—may bear witness, but it does not intervene in human affairs to save, ease, or lead. Aunt Rectita's response to an unresponsive heaven is to jam a thorny crown into her surrogate Savior, who is, by the color of his eyes in Mabel's poem, associated with a rooster. The comparison craftily expresses the idea that if God remains indifferent, Mabel and her like have ways of registering their outrage and sense of injustice.

These negative images notwithstanding, Kennedy is not always intensely grim when he considers the relation of God to humans. Throughout the years of his religious reformation, he often lightened the mood without losing the serious import of his subject, if only to explore his subject from a different perspective—and to give expression to a part of his spirit that cannot resist a humorous pun or a wry smile even in the face of awful mysteries. One of his most widely known poems of this sort is "Nothing in Heaven Functions as It Ought," in which Heaven is peopled by clumsy, almost clownish souls, and the monotony of machinery dominates Hell. *Bulsh* has much satiric fun with a corrupt, depraved prelate. "Ultimate Motel," subtitled "A Hymn in Common Meter," uses an elaborate conceit and ballad measure to develop the ironic relation of a truck stop to God's "Holy Inn." Addressing Jesus throughout the poem's four stanzas, the poem's "common man" is a trucker hoping to find a motel and to write his "license-number" on "Thy line / And stay for endless night" (ll. 3–4). He envisions a chlorinated swimming pool, a roof "more high than reach of voice," and a "room than mind more large," exhorting the Savior to "Make fresh my bottom sheet" (ll. 9–10, 14). The humor is in the trucker's describing Heaven in terms of his own experience, which measures the comic limits of his imagination. The portrait is heightened by the trucker's inability to see the absurd discrepancy of his conceit, which reduces Heaven to a gaudy, trashy haven given the title, "Thy Holy Inn." Making ironic fun of the popular tendency of people to view

Heaven in human terms, Kennedy ends with the idea that the Heavenly seat is a toilet, wrapped thoughtfully with Christ's "seamless tissue band . . ."(l. 15).

Not having spent all of his animus against religious corruption in *Bulsh*, Kennedy turns again to this subject in "A Penitent Giuseppe Belli Enters Heaven," this time with as much low humor as he displays in *Bulsh* but with less bitterness. The sonnet's octave recounts the last words of Belli as he begs God to forgive him for writing "those infernal sonnets." In his retraction Belli recounts some of the raunchiness for which he is guilty, telling "how monsignori dine / On whores' hair-pies and lust for bishops' bonnets" (ll. 3–4). His sonnets describe "Luke dead drunk with wine . . . blest Bellini / Wiping that hole . . ." and "The Holy Father himself with stiff, sticking-out weenie" (ll. 5–8). The sestet presents God's answer to Belli, explaining that he, not Belli, is responsible for "the grape that could knock out Luke . . ." (l. 10) and for making "Poppa" so that "he has to get on a bone / Like anybody else. . . ." Kennedy's language both celebrates and reproduces the earthy quality of Belli's poetry, but, even so, the principal targets of the poem are the monsignori and other church officials. Perhaps Kennedy felt the poem goes too far in his coarse humor, or perhaps his animus against the church had waned, for he did not include this rollicking satire in *Dark Horses*, his next major collection. What is more likely, however, is that the irreverent humor of this poem would unsettle the staid ambiance and uniform seriousness of *Dark Horses*, from which, except for nine somber couplets in "City Churchyard," Kennedy excludes even his favorite form, the epigram.

Although critic David Harsent referred to one of Kennedy's epigrams as "little more than a five-finger exercise," good ones require extraordinary skill, and Kennedy has won considerable respect for his epigrams. The epigram especially seems to trigger Kennedy's irreverent spirit, or this spirit often seeks expression in brief, biting bits, as when he takes a moment to mock the founder of Christian Science, Mary Baker Eddy, who believed that illness and death could be willed away. If so, the poem challenges Eddy: "rise up—change your mind!" Elsewhere in *The Epigrammatist*, Kennedy gracefully combines the secular and the Catholic to compliment a favorite poet: "Leaden, my thoughts. For saving grace they grope, / Lightness their God the Father, Pope their pope." Though the epigram offers quick insight and trenchant satire, Kennedy's emotional attachment to his subjects, including not only Catholicism, but religion in general, seeks a broader range of effects and a greater length with which to convey his message. In the process of expressing his feelings, he seems to have achieved a measure of enlightenment, if one considers a recent poem from *Dark Horses*, "Song: Enlightenment."

In this poem, Kennedy's playful commentary on Buddhist ritual turns into serious thought on religious belief and the nature of holiness in general. A news dispatch announces that a tooth of Buddha has been transported by elephant to "Sri Lanka's holiest shrine." From the report arises a vision of a "two-ton elephant with a bobbing teak / telephone booth" (ll. 1–2) transporting a tooth to a new shrine. The poem's language, sound, and bobbing rhythm—all reminiscent of Kennedy's verse for children—create a comical context for the serious event: "Hear the bong of the gong and the sigh as the throng / of worshipers whooshes aside . . ." (ll. 5–6). When we ordinary mortals lose a tooth, the poet notes, "nobody prays on our holy days to a scrap of our / castoff bone. . . ." In the final stanza, Kennedy comes back to the title and grows more serious: enlightenment arises from the realization that "any old tooth [is] as immense in truth as that elephant-borne incisor" (ll. 23–24). It is significant that this poem is among the many in *Dark Horses* that reflect Kennedy's continued interest in religious themes, for it expresses a breadth of vision and a lightness of tone that previous religious poems do not, and it hints at a resolution of the personal conflict that has inspired many poems over many years, including several in *Dark Horses*, whose overall somber intensity nevertheless suggests that any enlightenment Kennedy may have come to may be more intellectual than emotional.

Although Kennedy most often blames heaven for abandoning humans, he occasionally lays the blame on humans for breaching the connection between heaven and earth. In one of his earlier poems, "Space," which he has not reprinted since *Growing into Love*, he suggests that something in human nature drives humans from their earthly roots and, in the process, causes technology in general and space flight in particular to supplant religious faith. The first stanza develops the notion that space travel frees humans from having to contend with weight and bulk to achieve their goals, and Kennedy wonders how it will be "when all the strength it takes / To rip moons loose from planet boughs (ll. 8–9) . . . will require nothing more than a twist that opens a door a crack . . ." (l. 12). By the end of the poem, his speculation arrives at a vision:

> We clerks-without-church look on while slide-rules
> Render our lusts and madnesses concrete.
> It may well be that when I rev my car
> And let it overtake and pass my thinking,
> It's space I crave. . . .
>
> (ll. 27–31)

Space flight is evidence of mankind's lack of religious faith and its desire to be disembodied, to "shrug the world's dull weight." Science, like liquor, offers humans the chance to be free, but something thereby would be lost. Ironically, space flight would free the body but "our lusts and madness," our wild desires, would be reduced to "concrete."

Human Nature and the Modern Condition

Many of Kennedy's poems capture the spirit of the times and characterize modern conditions.[29] As he matured as a poet, he turned again and again to portraits of modern characters who are victims of their environment. Often, modern technology is the bane of the individual as he argues in "Space." Nature also threatens, as though it expresses the judgment of a higher power intent on punishing humans for their waywardness. If nature is not rising against them, many modern individuals are trapped in an urban setting that is congested, squalid, bureaucratically run, decaying, impersonal, hostile, spiritless, merciless, and unfulfilling. Kennedy is also fond of characterizing Americans in social groups that are either isolated or characteristic of a debilitating mentality or both. Whether it be tourists at a national shrine, a gathering of academics, a rowdy bunch in a saloon, or oldsters barely alive in a nursing home, Americans in social groups seldom offer an attractive picture as Kennedy portrays them.

At times Kennedy makes fun of characters who hazard to speak of lofty subjects, as he does in "Ool about to Proclaim a Parable." The humor of the poem derives in part from the contrast between the seriousness of the subject—the nature of humankind—and its comical, sometimes bawdy treatment. In Ool's world, which is the inside of a tavern, human nature is discussed in low terms; as one character declares, " 'The human race, the head on draft beer is!' " (l. 7). Someone asks, " 'But what's below the suds line . . . ?' " (l. 9). Before Ool can reply, another shouts, "*Gas with your ass, man, give your mouth a rest.*" Unperturbed,

"Ool poured / A second glass, blew off the human race, / And drank deep of the fullness of the Lord" (ll. 14–16). By placing the drama in a saloon, Kennedy can have fun with Ool's high-mindedness by suggesting that any attempt to consider such weighty matters is ridiculous in a world where ordinary humans gather and become boisterous, drunken, and vulgar.

Though among "Light Verse" in *Cross Ties,* "Gold Bought Here" does not present a light view of the human condition. The poem's speaker is standing in line with "fellow sellers-out" to sell "old gauds and baubles." A woman is selling her wedding band; for her, "love's worth had done its nose- / Dive . . ." (ll. 7–8). Another wants to sell a school ring "whose vined brass / Looks overgrown with weeds—just how I feel— / Missing both stones. Fit emblem for its class" (ll. 10–12). The speaker himself sells a ring inscribed, "SECOND OUTSTAND- / ING STUDENT 1950 DEP'T OF ED." Whatever its value to him, "its heart proves lead." Outside the shop, the world is grim and mildly threatening: "Cold neon-lighted sleet / Nibbles with costly fillings at my neck." Human nature and the human condition are symbolized here as stained brass, broken rings, and a wedding band. These people have lost, like their baubles, their former brightness and their lives have become, again like their baubles, all but worthless. The blank resignation of the buyers and the anonymity, yet universality, of the sellers are succinctly expressed in the phrase that opens the second quatrain, "*Who's next?*" Life itself, like the "bright medallion" here being sold, comes to this: "its heart proves bad." In his characteristic quatrains—five in all—Kennedy reduces the human spirit to a commodity bartered for.

When he considers the male-female relationship, Kennedy often sees it fraught with antagonism and disillusion. In an early poem, "Barking Dog Blues," he finds humor in the antagonism. The poem is the form of a song sung by a man whose woman has thrown him out of the house. He is in the street asking to come back in and bemoaning her "messing round my little dog / Cause my big dog got a bone" (ll. 15–16). The song plays on the sexual meaning of "bone" as the young man characterizes himself as a dog that would rather bark "in the driving rain" than wear a woman's chain. Another poem, "Her Thinking Man," also portrays a man and woman in conflict. The woman chides her man for worrying about his job and what the preacher next door will say, and whether he is "any good" in bed. Thinking interferes with his natural impulses, she believes. In addition to their own conflict, they both are victimized by other people. Life, she implies, will go better for both of them if they do not question why events happen and how one performs. She asks rhetorically, "*Does a red leaf crossing the street wait / for the light to change?*" Like the leaf, the individual is controlled by outside forces. Her man is so beat upon by unnamed forces in his environment that he has lost touch with nature, and they both are, like leaves, blown about by the wind. Significantly, the female plays a dominant role in the relationship, and the man has somehow failed her.

Kennedy has frequently shown an interest in, even a fascination for, dominant women and those who cast a spell over men. "Ladies Looking for Lice," for example, depicts a scene in which "Two enchantress big sisters steal close" to the bed of a boy whose "forehead is afire with red / Tortures and he longs for vague white dreams to come" (ll. 1-3). As they examine his head for lice, "He traces the song of their hesitant breath" and "hears their black lashes beat through the perfume" as "in him a wine mounts." He is intoxicated by their "sorceress hands." His relationship with these "queens of his indolent gloom" is sexual, and the languor the women induce is like that which follows a sexual experience. The women are introducing the boy to the dilemma of male adulthood, which is to suffer either the "Tortures" of sexual desire or enervating indolence, once one has submitted to them. They control the ebb and flow of sexual desire in the male, who is in a state of perpetually wanting, never fully realizing, always feeling "the desire to cry" at their hands.

Kennedy also shows great sympathy for women who have suffered at the hands of men. Bulsh's sins are represented in large part by his concupiscence and by his inordinate penchant for using woman for his pleasure. "Solitary Confinement" portrays a woman trapped in a loveless relationship with a man—Kennedy is especially sensitive to this aspect of the male-female relationship, returning to it in many poems throughout his career. More often than not, as he shows in "Solitary Confinement," his sympathy lies with the woman. The first stanza introduces the idea that the woman could have "stolen from his arms," and through the rest of the poem's sixteen lines, Kennedy weaves together the idea of her leaving him and thieving. She could have left him, but she finds "nothing left / To steal"; there is "the crucifix / Of silver," but it would not bring her enough to "steal away with and lay down / By someone new in a new town . . ." (ll. 1–3, 7–8). In the second stanza, she notices the clock, as fixed as she is, as much a thief (of time) as she would be; it measures the years she has been with this man, who has "nailed her fast / Between two thieves, him and herself" (ll. 15–16). The woman is a sacrificial being, Christlike in being "nailed," not to a cross, however, but to the man's bed. The sexual implication of the image (and the clause, "breath / By breath . . . he'd nailed her fast . . .") further separates her condition from that of Christ, and the irony of the final line is that she has stolen from herself for not leaving him, and in order to leave him, she would have to steal something of value to hock. Kennedy's imagery captures the paradox of fixed motion, of being free to move but only in a confined and confining way:

> the clock,
> Green ghost, swept round its tethered hand
> That had made off with many nights
> But no more could break from its shelf
> Than she could quit this bed. . . .
>
> (ll. 10–14)

Her life is as fixed, her motions as prescribed, and her future as bleak and blank as the clock's. The religious element of the poem suggests that the woman is being punished for giving herself to a loveless relationship. Her fate is to be in "solitary confinement," solitary because she cannot share her thoughts or her love with the man, and confined because he has "nailed" her so fast that she cannot free herself.

Women generally have attracted Kennedy's attention from the beginning of his career. The title poem in *Nude Descending a Staircase* typifies one aspect of his interest, the female's visual appeal, her capacity to give motion a special quality and for motion to define her in an unforgettable way. In other poems he has portrayed the abused, frustrated, neglected, fallen, seductive, hung over, schizophrenic, and irreverent woman. His respect for women is based in no small degree on their ability to give birth, as he demonstrates in "Pottery Class," a poem from *Growing into Love*. Woman's capacity to give birth not only differentiates her from man but gives her a natural superiority over him. A contrast is also drawn between the universal woman and a group of modern wives who attend pottery class. In this poem, the modern woman is shown to perform a routine, making little distinction between doing the dishes and taking care of her children. On Wednesday nights the wives go to pottery class, leaving their children "rinsed and stacked" and their husbands "closeted with *Time*." This latter phrase suggests that the husbands are bound by time, whereas their wives are not. The family house becomes a symbol of the present, finite time that the wives escape temporarily to make pottery, but, in universal terms, always by virtue of their ability to give birth to generations. The universal, timeless element these wives share is reflected in what they do in pottery class: they "travail in the elemental slime," and the result is human history:

> Thwack! and a hunk of muck hung by the heels
> Has its back slapped, its breathing made to come.
> Great casseroles take shape on groaning wheels,
> A vase commences, vast as Christendom.
>
> (ll. 5–8)

The poet asks the wives why they busy themselves with making pottery. Is it "The drag of being wives? / The deep grave that a birth leaves after it?" (ll. 11–12). The final stanza assures the "dears," that however much they busy themselves with pottery, "Yours is that furious core man stands outside / Gazing, stone-helpless. . . ." Women are the "core" out of which generations are shaped; they have the power, the central place in creating humans; men are excluded, are in fact passive creatures, both the product of woman's power and the material women mold. Women are a universal force outside time, working on "elemental slime" to create man, and the implication is that a man is as fragile and replaceable as pottery, blasted "till he's dried," and if broken, easily replaced by another.

Kennedy explores the complex female mind from the perspective of a mother in "Pacifier," a later poem reprinted in *The Lords of Misrule.* Its subject is the sexual element in a mother's relationship to her nursing child, who is a male. This element gives the poem considerable tension as we follow the "night-thoughts" of a mother as she lies next to her baby, who is still in the nursing stage. At the opening, the mother announces that her baby "wails," and so she gives him a pacifier instead of her breast and he is quieted. In the second tercet, she confesses that she has tricked her child, but she has done no harm, has raised "no Berlin Wall / Between the two of us at all . . ." (ll. 7–8). Later that night she will "open to him like a door / And give him all he wants and more" (ll. 11–12). The sexual suggestiveness of these two lines is developed in the rest of the poem as the woman draws a parallel between her relationship with the child and her relationship with a man. She advises her child that at times a lover's "tide may rise in flood," when one is not in the mood; at such times, then the child should "let that raging bull chew cud / . . . And fall to sleep" (ll. 18–19). In the final two stanzas, the woman blurs the distinction between the grown man and herself and herself with her child:

> Let him return
> When in coincidence you burn.
> Fire lingers near a kindled urn,
>
> And lives to burn again, and spreads
> On real as on imagined beds
> Held fast by things that stand in steads.
>
> (ll. 19–24)

The final line of the poem makes clear that she sees the child as a replacement of the man, and the man as a replacement of the child. They both "stand in steads," and the pun on "stands" reinforces the sexual meaning of her thoughts and feelings.

Sometimes the relationship between the man and woman encounters difficulty not because of any defect in the nature of either person or by inherent differences; sometimes forces outside the relationship undermine or destroy it, as is shown in "Barking Dog Blues." A much longer and more complex poem, "The Man in the Manmade Moon," plays on the idea that modern technology is the evil force that destroys true love.[30] The poem humorously tells a story of true love in four parts. Part I introduces the reader to the major's plan of sending Bill Beale into space, although the airman is reluctant to risk his life since he plans to marry Lizabeth Bligh. In part II, Beale is on the launching pad, strapped into "a ball of steel," wondering whether he is "doing his Lizabet dirty." His doubts notwithstanding, he is blasted into space, circles the earth, and, reminded of "his woman behind," suddenly wants to return to earth. Unfortunately, his space capsule collides with a meteor and "Bill Beale and his soul met the perfect hole" (l. 59). Part III shifts to Liz, who sees her lover blazing away in the night sky. Having vowed to "keep him my soul like a glowing coal," she is sent his remains, "a little black pill." Before Congress she protests her loss and tells of seeing her lover in a dream as "a featureless face . . . on a neck like a jet exhaust" (ll. 35–36). In part IV, Bill's corpse is buried, and Liz throws herself on his grave, screeching. It begins to snow, but she remains at her lover's grave, where she eventually dies. From the site grow

"A sweet pea vine and a blackeyed pea vine / And a rose in a vacuum bottle" (ll. 11–12). The vines, in true ballad fashion, entwine, and the lovers' spirits, symbolized by, or transposed into, the gas created by the decomposing rose and Thermos bottle, waft away together.

Part of the fun of this mock romance comes from the puns—"Bill accepted a butt and bit it." Part of the comedy comes from the mocking logic: Airman Beale's test scores are so normal that he is "abnormal." The ridiculous storyline also adds considerably to the array of comic effects, and much fun is had from seeing Kennedy wrench rhythm and rhyme into his nonsensical story and use the ballad form to tell a modern tale of space travel that blends traditional love with space flight and modern militarism. The moon-June storytellers are mocked—"On a moonlit night while the hills lay white / On a night of a crescent Bill" (III. ll. 1–2)—and courtly love is caricatured: the rose, traditional symbol of romantic love, is placed on Beale's grave in a Thermos bottle. At the fade-out, Kennedy spins a final meaning from the premise that *Amor vincit omnia* by having the lovers' spirits transcend technology. Technology, symbolically, encloses the rose, which is "rust-red," but as "pea" with "pea" entwine, nature reduces metal and rose to gas, and love triumphs in the air. The wrenched rhythms and playful rhymes mock the tragic events of this modern romance. Kennedy implies that the kind of devotion and sacrifice shared by this pair of lovers is found only in make-believe, and even then, they are not to be taken seriously. The space program may represent an advancement in human evolution, but this sort of progress renders obsolete a certain kind of human experience that may be worth cultivating.

The role played by technology in modern life is treated with humor again in "The Medium Is the Message," though the humor masks a serious point: the individual has become attached both physically and spiritually to electronic devices. Today, people are "Plugged in, stone deaf, sleepwalking into trains." In time, each child shall have an antenna implanted in the brain to receive radio and television waves, making "words in lines" obsolete. One of the lines voices the principle of a free-verse poet: "Fresh beats the age insists on—not the heart's. . . ."[31] Would the narrator drop out of these times? "You bet!" he answers, and he would devote himself to art—but he would retain his "hi-fi set / Electric light . . . canned beer / To help keep medieval ardor clear." The final message is that the prevailing medium is electronic and, as one of the line says, "The rude beast slouches."

Elsewhere Kennedy suggests that space exploration threatens to supplant—or is evidence of a loss of—religious faith. In "To Mercury" he again looks upon space exploration with some doubt as to its effect on other aspects of human values.[32] He laments the loss of what Mercury, both as a heavenly body and as a concept, has represented throughout the centuries, for space exploration threatens to destroy something worth preserving by turning the planet into a mere scientific specimen. To Kennedy the planet's name itself evokes various associations: in Greek mythology it was the "Quicksilver lord" and "swayholder over thieves" (l. 4); later, Mercury the god became the guide and protector of travelers, but science has replaced these images with photographs of a surface that "Now fries, now freezes . . ." (l. 5). The poet urges the planet to "Stay for a while inviolable," for, untouched by man's presence, the planet would remain "ghostly pure," would not be demeaned as the moon has been,

> now that men
> Steeped in a hate for beauty left obscure
> Patrol her ashpits in a golfer's cart
> And grave her face with Nixon's signature.
>
> (ll. 13–16)

Kennedy sees such scientific achievements as a despoliation of the "obscure" beauty of extraterrestrial bodies. Violating Mercury, reducing it to a junkyard of space probes and to computerized data pored over by scientists, would diminish its power to receive "The homage of our Mariners" and to "lend heart / Back to our daydreams . . ." (ll. 10–11).

Early in his career Kennedy created a vision of modern conditions in a poem, "Inscriptions After Fact," that is one of his most complex, ambitious, and imaginative poems.[33] It sweeps through human history from the time of the Greek gods, through biblical Eden, to modern times. The poem's five parts total a hundred thirty-two lines. Quatrains are used in each section, and each section has its own title. As the poem advances from section to section, the use of rhyme and line length displays increasing freedom and less regularity. Within this structural framework, Kennedy, inspired by his visit to Athens in 1953 while in the navy, ponders Greek and Hebrew myths and envisions a journey that begins, in "Declare War against Heaven," with gods running rampant on earth:

Truant from home stars and from right spouse,
A god by self conceived and of self born
Sets out for manhood, halts in the halfway house
Of beast. But it is man he caps with horn.

(ll. 5–8)

From the gods' acts come distrust and perpetual strife between Heaven and earth. Kennedy captures the distrust in an image that is as striking as it is frightening: "What child under a rooftree can sleep safe / While skies uncoil and phalloi slither down?" (ll. 17–18). He lightens the dark mood that this image generates somewhat by turning to playful language in the same quatrain: "Will woman, the onslaught of a swan once known, / Think man a goose and give him up for life?" (ll. 19–20). The basis of the strife between Heaven and humans, Kennedy posits, is jealousy, and the section ends with a call for war against the gods, all done in the language of a salty seaman that borders on the comical: "Drive! Drive them back! . . . Let not a man-jack among them batter through!" (ll. 21, 23).

In the second section, "Lilith," Kennedy addresses the biblical story of Adam, Adam's first wife, Lilith, and his second wife, Eve. Again, Kennedy is not entirely serious as he describes Adam's bumbling attempts to "complete what God had left half-wrought" in a series of images that are both strange and humorous: "He looked her in the eye, back looked a hole. . . ."; when Adam tried assembling the woman,

He practiced in a looking lake, he taught
Stray rudiments of wriggle, where to stand
Her liltless feet. She handed him her hand.

Her breasts stood up but in them seemed to rise
No need for man.

(ll. 6–10)

Having failed to assemble a whole woman, Adam is reduced to praying for help: "*Sweet Lord . . . with what shade do I lie?*" Only then does Eve arrive.

Shifting to shorter lines and looser rhymes in the third section, "The Sirens," Kennedy depicts the moment when Odysseus encounters the Sirens. This episode introduces the image of the voyage and suggests that the entire five sections comprise a history of mankind, which grew from classical rebellion and biblical conjugation and passed through moments such as this one, which brings Odysseus to a revelation:

> And when those soft sounds stole, there grew
> The notion as he champed his bit
> That love was all there was, and death
> Had something to be said for it.
>
> (ll. 13–16)

Heretofore, he was "Imprisoned in propriety / And pagan ethic. Also ropes." Now love supersedes pagan ethic and propriety, and death becomes attractive. The romantic spirit is born, and Kennedy signals this turn in stunning images: "round each oar / Broke like the grapes of Ilium / Ripening clusters of blue air" (ll. 10–12) and "The keel drove tapestries / Of distance on the sea's silk-loom" and "Woven undone rewoven foam" (ll. 21–22, 24). Kennedy, however, continues his playfulness. The phrase "Also ropes" at the end of a previous stanza, positioned like an afterthought, deflates the image of Odysseus's roaring "as the music sweetened" and railing "Against his oarsmen's bent wet slopes." Kennedy repeats this maneuver in the last stanza: "Impelled him to his dying dog, Pantoufles, and Penelope," she, by position, almost an afterthought as well, but certainly second to the dog. In this section Kennedy suggests that man passes through a stage in which man's passion for woman is awakened along with the realization that love is everything. If the Sirens' song lures man to his destruction, man's lust drives him into mistaken perceptions of the female.

The fourth section, "Narcissus Suitor," combines the myth of Leda and the swan with that of Narcissus, who represents the eternally lustful, eternally frustrated, self-absorbed male. He is also a type of Adam, whom we see in a previous section trying to assemble Lilith by using an image of himself that he sees "in a looking lake." This image resurfaces in "Narcissus Suitor" in the line: "He loved her as it were / Not for her look though it was deep / But what he saw in her" (ll. 2–4). Narcissus seeks sexual union with an image of himself: He "would have joined the two of him / In one cohesive Greek." Both Odysseus and Narcissus are bound, Odysseus by ropes, Narcissus by a curse. Both experience powerful lures. The man who seeks love and love alone is doomed forever to lust and to remain incomplete. Kennedy again keeps the mood from remaining serious for long by shifting abruptly from Narcissus attempting to mate with the swan to the cry of a female outraged when she finds a swan on top of her: "'Oh keep your big feet to yourself / Good sir, goddammit stop! . . . I'll scream! I'll call a cop!'" (ll. 13–14, 16). The woman's language also signals a shift from the mythical Leda to the modern woman threatening to call a cop.

The unity of the poem's theme is sustained partly by the water that Odysseus sails and in which Narcissus is immersed. Connections are made, too, between the Narcissus episode and that of Ulysses when the woman tells the man to put her back in her "'right bed / Or you shall edge your skiff / Through ice as limber as your eyes, / As blue, as frozen stiff.'" (ll. 17–20).

The final section, "Theater of Dionysus," takes place in March 1953, when a sailor from the U.S. Sixth Fleet is visiting Athens. Odysseus's journey has led to this: a sailor drawing pictures of Mickey Mouse for Greek children in a place "where queen-betrayed / Agamemnon had to don / Wine-purple robes, boys in torn drabs / try my whitehat on . . ." (ll. 13–16) and where "Girls hawking flyspecked postcards" pursue tourists. The tawdry commercial aspect of modern Greece—the home of Aristophanes, the Parthenon (now "sacked"), Agamemnon, and others of a great tradition—symbolizes the decline of this heroic tradition as the garish glow of neon obscures the sunset. In addition to the decline from the heroic past to a squalid present, current conditions also threaten, and in this respect, the young sailor is not Odysseus returned in modern uniform but an outsider confronted by Andromache, who challenges: "'Young man, / Aren't you from Schenectady?'" (ll. 23–24).

Through a series of episodes, Kennedy has envisioned human history to be the result of bestial coupling, misdirection, and thwarted dreams. The purposeful merging of one myth, Leda and the swan, with another, that of Narcissus, suggests that all of history is interwoven into the same line, which ends, for the moment, with a young sailor in a tourist trap retreating into the darkness. Kennedy positions his lines to show how certain ancient figures have taken modern forms:

> Over stones where Orestes fled
> The sonorous Furies
> Girls hawking flyspecked postcards
> Pursue the tourist.
>
> Here in her anguish-mask
> Andromache

Mourned her slain son—"Young man,
Aren't you from Schenectady?"

(ll. 17–24)

Again Kennedy deflates the heroic figure by juxtaposing images that contrast the past with the present. If the past, as Kennedy envisions it, is rife with monstrous behavior and lustful coupling of humans and animals, at least the action took place on an epic scale and the figures were central to a high drama. Kennedy's final vision is that of a cosmic stage reduced to a theater peopled by hawkers, "boys in torn drabs," and a sailor intimidated by the night, which "unsheathes / Her chill blade," and driven offstage by "inaudible laughter." Odysseus, braving soul-embracing hazards, has dwindled into a young sailor who realizes that his "radared bark" has "No thresh of oars, sails with gods' crests," and his heroic spirit has fled; this modern voyager trembles in fear, wondering, "Does the wind stir through the dark / Or does a throng of ghosts? / / I run" (ll. 39–41).

Kennedy addresses this theme in another poem, "Where Are the Snows of Yesteryear?" which borrows a refrain from a poem by François Villon, "Ballade des dames du temps jadis" ("Ballad of the women of former times"),[34] to contrast the heroic past with the less-than-heroic present. The site where Alexander the Great is buried, for instance, is to be found by means of a Baedeker tourist guide; Helen now is "Indistinguishable loam"; heroes, heroines, epic grandeur, and historic sites have been reduced by the tourist trade to modern radio tunes, paperweight souvenirs, and the guided tour. The august spirit of the past has been transformed by commercialism into a clutter of tourists, for whom answers must be fast, superficial, and easy.

"All-Knowing Rabbit" paints a grim picture of modern times from the curious perspective of a rabbit. The poem's imagery suggests dissolution, madness, destruction: "Hart Crane's bridge is falling down, / The hangman's knot, the stock quotations slip . . . while promenading madboys leap through June" (ll. 5–6, 12). The logic of the poem's events also is sprung: "The stoic chops his beet-patch with a hoe." Nevertheless, running through the poem is a bizarre celebration of spring. Images of and references to fecundity and procreation abound. The rabbit, for example, "Would swallow earth, envelope all of spring. / Her middle waxes big around with womb / Where fetuses like peas in peapod swing" (ll. 2–4). The poem's central figure, the "wise rabbit," symbolizes a power that serves as a stable center amid chaos, a force with abundant procreative powers that can ponder "on her tail / All secrets of tomorrow, of the Nile," linking past, present, and future. To the extent that this figure represents nature, or a force that is in harmony with nature and its generative power, the poem offers a vision of a world in which the animal and vegetable kingdoms are united, while the human world is disintegrating.[35]

More than two decades later, Kennedy returns to this theme. Taking a cue from William Shakespeare's idea that "Not marble, nor the gilded monuments / Of princes, shall outlive this pow'rful rhyme," Kennedy responds with "Not Marble," a sonnet placed near the end of *Cross Ties*. The two sonnets also share the same theme, that the woman's beauty will survive after she is gone, thanks to the poet's powerful rhyme. Both poets develop the notion that the woman's beauty is entwined with the fate of his own poem, and on that conceit the sonnets proceed in very different directions. In Kennedy's sonnet, the fate of the woman's beauty is ironically reduced in importance to environmental issues, and the sonnet's focus shifts to the survival of the race. What happens to the woman's "peerless eyes" pales beside the prospects that await the human race. Kennedy contrasts Shakespeare's "gilded monuments / Of princes" with his own stark vision: "When one twin tower of the Board of Trade / Works like a domino its mate's collapse . . ." (ll. 1–2). In just two opening lines, Kennedy transposes Shakespeare's Elizabethan setting to the corporate offices of the princes of industry in modern skyscrapers, even hinting at the domino theory, which was used to justify the Vietnam War (and unintentionally featuring future terrorism). In doing so, Kennedy's focus shifts from the contrast between gilded monuments and powerful poetry to the collapse of the Western world, if not the entire world. He also has shifted from Shakespeare's grand style to something less noble: "These potent lines might stick around, perhaps. . . ." Thus he demonstrates, as well, the collapse of poetry, which precedes his dire vision of a collapsed civilization in the rest of the octave:

> Or come to mind in some dim Everglade
> Should one survivor still have tongue to move,
> Stealing a moment from his fishing-hook
> To mutter what he read once in some book
> To another half-starved victim whom he love.
>
> (ll. 4–8)

The ostensible subject of the poem, the poet's beloved and her beauty, has become lost in the vision of the collapse of civilization, a lone "victim" fishing for food. The sestet, in good traditional fashion, appears to shift focus to counter the contents of the octave, but in fact Kennedy's vision does not improve very much:

> But what if doom's no circus of MacLeish?
> Suppose no black pall drops, and none but flies
> Settle upon my words—then PhDish
> Plodders alone may engineer your rise
> And once more, through a frame of microfiche,
> From footnotes' knotholes stare your peerless eyes.
> (ll. 9–14)

The playful rhyme of "MacLeish" with "PhDish" further illustrates the collapse of poetry—Kennedy making the point at his own expense—and the collapse of civilization is contained in the poem's grand final vision, a world reduced to plodding engineers laboring in shadowy archives on footnotes and microfiche. A reference to the woman's beauty, all but forgotten by now, gives the poem its final image, which sums up in a pun on *peerless* the poem's principal theme, the collapse of civilization, for in that tragic time the lady will indeed be without peers, and all that shall remain of her will be eyes.

In some poems Kennedy suggests that modern conditions are somehow the cause of the individual's misery and loneliness. The modern world has become so rigidly defined and insensitive that individuals who do not fit into the mainstream of society exist in a kind of limbo, facing a future of continued lonely alienation. One of the problems, Kennedy suggests again and again, is that the modern world has lost its sense of community. Several poems that show people enjoying one another's company are set in pubs and taverns, where conviviality and sociability are encouraged by music and drink. "In a Prominent Bar in Secaucus One Day" rocks with high spirits; Ool reflects on the human condition in another tavern ("Ool about to Proclaim a Parable") and complains of the writer's life in yet another ("Uncle Ool's Complaint against the Ill-Paid Life of Verse"). As late as *Dark Horses*, Kennedy returns to the tavern for some reflection and potation ("Dancing with the Poets at Piggy's"). In this environment, music, dance, and drink offer humans an attractive, if temporary, respite. Outside the tavern, in the suburbs and in the streets of the city—and in many a home—humans become isolated, insensitive, indifferent, and at times hostile. Many of them live lonely, unhealthy lives whose future is dark and depressing. Besides, as Kennedy says in one of his early, four-line poems ("Cities"), the city looks better from the inside of a bar, and may even be safer:

> Old as a rind of moon, half cracked they are,
> Bleary-eyed, better looking in a bar,
> Pale as if sick, each smelling like a nurse,
> A sawed-off shotgun in her beaded purse.

"B Negative" is one of the darker poems, also an early one, in which Kennedy describes depraved conditions in a modern urban setting that degrade, isolate, and ultimately destroy the individual and threaten human relationships in general. The speaker of the poem is introduced in the jargon of a medical or police report: "M / 60 / 5 FT 4 / W PROT." This old, short, white Protestant male ponders his condition, and, as the title indicates in a pun on "B," the emphasis is on being negative. Now he is on the street among the homeless, in the snow and on the subway, where he feeds pigeons and sleeps under a newspaper. This life takes him down streets, "Till in a cubic room in some hotel / You wake one day to find yourself abstract" (ll. 55–56), perhaps committing suicide. Two images blur together: the derelict picks up debris and the policeman picks up the body of a murder victim. Nature records one's passing: "The snow, at least, keeps track of people's feet." Ironically, the record will soon melt away. Calling this one of Kennedy's "most ambitious and moving poems," critic Forrest Read focuses on the poem's speaker, who has become "spectator, mechanism, artifact, and cleaner-up after perverts." The rhythm of the lines, Read observes, "suddenly evokes a deeper insight:

> It used to be that when I laid my head
> And body with it down by you in bed
> You did not turn from me nor fall to sleep
> But turn to fall between my arms instead. . . .[36]
>
> (ll. 17–20)

Kennedy often portrays individuals who have somehow come to grief. Another of these portraits was published in *Three Tenors, One Vehicle* and not reprinted, but the seventeen lines of "The Moths Have Eaten My Butterfly Collection" capture vividly the condition of someone who suffers an advanced state of deterioration:

In my televisioned room I sit and listen to
Distant plops like heavy letters that you mail,
And those several blurry channels that have served me well,
My seeing hearing tasting and my sense of smell
And the whole damned picture tube begin to fail.

(ll. 1–4)

The poem's imagery continues to entwine the speaker's decay with broken pieces of modern society, as in the line, "the plastic seal's / Slithering loose from my Texaco card" (ll. 12–13). His body has been transformed into failing artifacts from a broken society, and the implication is that the rot is caused by his having lost connection with vital forces outside modern society. Too much television and too much plastic not only rot the body and mind but erode one's humanity.

"Rat" contrasts a woman's freedom to the condition of inmates of the Suffolk County Jail, which the woman passes on her way to "Mass. General Hospital / For her radiation treatment . . ." (ll. 1–2). The poem questions whether the woman, free to stroll down the street, is better off than the prisoners. These two locations, a jail and a sidewalk, are opposed yet shown to be very similar. Ironically, what connects the two worlds is symbolized by the dead rat the woman sees on the sidewalk, and she wonders, "Had a prisoner / Arrested it by the fur, / Knocked out its brain against a wall / And flung it through the bars?" (ll. 5–8). Like the rat, both the woman and the prisoners have been battered by misfortune and discarded. In their anger and entrapment—she by her disease, they by their incarceration—they share a similar condition, outlook, and anger. This is a world in which one's anger and destructive outburst are liberating: Thinking of the jailed individual, she is thrust, "strangely, into cheer: / That someone trapped had to be / Locked up inside with a scampering brood / While she in the sun walked free . . ." (ll. 9–12). The final image blurs the distinction between the woman and the imagined prisoner:

And though a beast with pinpoint teeth
Scurried in her own shadow,
She felt at one with that urge to kill
And throw out and clean house.

(ll. 13–16)

Both individuals are, like the rest, beaten, bashed, discarded; both are imprisoned by authority, the prisoner of one or another kind of institution. Ironically, the living are bonded by their desire to bash and to kill, and they are bonded to the dead by their feeling of being bashed and discarded.

Earlier in his career Kennedy was able to see comedy in a female character fallen on hard times, and he regards this type of woman with affection. "In a Prominent Bar in Secaucus One Day" is a song[37] delivered by "a lady in skunk with a topheavy sway."[38] In her glory days, she would drive to the track in a car so long that "'it took you ten minutes to see me go past. . . . Now I'm saddled each night for my butter and eggs'" (ll. 24, 27). Her self-satire is shot through with lively but coarse details: "Two toadstools for tits and a face full of weeds." At the fade-out she is carted off to jail blowing a kiss. Of course Kennedy is interested in the poignant balance between tragedy and jollity in this comic portrait, and at least one early critic saw much more beneath the poem's humor. Theodore Holmes thought the poem would last "as long as men and women do" because of the skill with which Kennedy combines humor, pathos, and allusive power. "In what conducts itself with the good-hearted cheer of a robust drinking song," Holmes argues, "the whole pattern of the psyche's involvement with sex looks out from apparently accidental allusions taken for the sake of their rhyme," as in these two lines especially: "'All the gents used to swear that the white of my calf / Beat the down of the swan by a length and a half'" (ll. 9–10).

In the first line, Holmes sees allusions to "The fatted calf, the innocence and the corruption of society"; in the second line, "the Leda and Helen myths."[39] Not a little of the festive spirit in this poem derives from the setting. Kennedy has a fondness for taverns and places many of his poetic efforts in them.

Not a little of the poem's energy comes from Kennedy's appreciation of women who have passed their prime and are regarded with humor by others, most of whom cannot see their endearing human qualities. In a later poem, "Snug," Kennedy portrays a woman who has died, first showing how she was viewed by her family when she was alive:

> What, dead? Aunt Edith, whom the children dubbed
> The Bug behind her back? Have limp hands dropped
> That sheaf of metered mail
> She'd leaf through for live letters? Have her frail
> Clock-stockinged legs, now done with running, stopped?
>
> (ll. 1–5)

During her "seasonal" visits, she was like a migratory bird fluttering through, wearing "insect spectacles." Her "Giving each pillowcase a keener crease" made the household "nervous," but her caring was given to "gently folding things, / To children, creatures." The poem's thesis is that a somewhat derisive characterization of the woman by the children and the resentment of the household were not only unkind but short-sighted. Her unselfconscious individuality and particular habits made her a nuisance, but she had a graceful ability that ordinary mortals lack, to "skim away" on wings.

By the time he published *Dark Horses*, however, Kennedy had lost much of his festive spirit when considering lost souls. "Rotten Reveille" describes in vivid detail the morning of a besotted woman, who lies in bed watching "her dreams / Drizzle to daydreams . . ." (ll. 1–2). As her dentures "marinate" in a glass, her mind cannot untangle, and her dreams "dissolve to thought, / But thought that had what thought ought not have: knots." By contrast, the day is "precise and green," and "a possessive cat" judges her, "Preparing for a hurtle through her head." Humans do not manage as well as nature and its creatures in the modern world. For Kennedy, the portrait of human depravity seems all the more shocking and telling when it is that of a female. A festered lily is far more unsettling to Kennedy than weeds.

Kennedy's interest in the condition of the modern church is seldom strong or passionate, although his feelings about his own Catholic faith find expression in a number of poems throughout his career. His most extensive treatment of this subject is found in *Bulsh*, his only major statement about religion in modern America, perhaps because he believes the church is peripheral to the conditions in which the modern individual is confined. Kennedy further distances Bulsh's Catholic world from his own by giving the poem the character of a medieval attack on the church. Insofar as religion plays an important role in an individual's life, "First Confession," "West Somerville, Mass.," and "Cross Ties" may represent Kennedy's views on the matter. The context of "First Confession" is a church, but Kennedy focuses on the young man's struggle to break free of authority, which happens to be Catholic. Religious faith is something the young man wishes to escape, as it is a restrictive force in the guise of religious authority. In "Cross Ties" religious overtones give generational ties additional significance and force, but the religious faith implicit in this poem remains distant throughout the poem, suggesting that it is correspondingly distant from the speaker's concerns.[40] The subject of "West Somerville, Mass." is the mental state of an individual whose sense of inadequacy and alienation is cast in religious imagery. The man's malaise is associated with the failure of his religious faith, but by the end of the poem, the focus has shifted to the man's environment, in which nature itself has become hostile. Kennedy's Catholicism threads through a number of poems, from "First Confession" to "Cross Ties," never wholly dismissed yet never fully embraced.

In the secular realm, Kennedy explores the psyche of a wide variety of individuals who appear to be trapped and victimized by a despoiled and fallen world. "For Jed" portrays another doomed individual, this one a patient in a cancer ward, who is playing a game of chess. In a mock-epic contrast between heroic knighthood and Jed's current state, the poem's speaker instructs Jed to "Stand guard" on his "state of quilted covers." The poem associates Jed with all humans by speaking of the universal human condition that makes death inescapable—"It wastes us all" and "nobody human / Stays immune forever." The human condition is akin to confinement in a cancer ward in which patients face "A Great Ming Wall of boredom."

"Absentminded Bartender" continues Kennedy's interest in portraying the mental condition of the unusual, even perverted, individual, using structural devices to interweave the past and present and to characterize the character's confused state of mind. The poem opens with the bartender recalling an encounter with a woman, whom he has apparently killed. The past and present merge in the image, "Cut off head dribbling from the tap" (l. 5). The "head" is that of the woman and that of the beer he is drawing. Later, in his room, he goes "for ease / In fresh positions legs and arms / Severed, alive, in bed with his" (ll. 16–18). The woman in his past is now present in the form of "legs and arms / Severed"; her parts mingle with those of a new woman and with his own. The image suggests that the present woman will end up like the previous one, dismembered. The poem's gruesome subject ironically contrasts with the designation of the bartender as "absentminded." In reality, he is probably a serial killer, a lonely and confused nomad seeking refuge in drinking in sunless hotel rooms, trying to escape the past while imprisoned by his compulsive urge to kill and dismember.

"Schizophrenic Girl" portrays yet another mentally disordered individual, a young woman fixed in a state of suspended animation. Kennedy devotes eighteen of the poem's thirty lines to casting the girl's condition in a series of striking images. She is first seen as a kind of menacing animal in a cage:

> Having crept out this far,
> So close your breath casts moisture on the pane,
> Your eyes blank lenses opening part way
> To the dead moonmoth fixed with pins of rain,
> Why do you hover here,
> A swimmer not quite surfaced, inches down,
> Fluttering water, making up her mind
> To breathe, or drown?
>
> (ll. 1–8)

Kennedy skillfully controls the stanza's development, using rhyme to knit some of the lines together unobtrusively and creating a sense of ebb and flow by varying line length, balancing images of motion with those that slow it down, coming to the poem's best pair of images in the next stanza: "You'd sit, / Petrified fire, casting your frozen glare. . . ." It is not clear whether her condition symbolizes the isolation of the modern condition; Kennedy has made his poem as inscrutable as the young woman: we stand before it as the speaker in the poem stands before the young woman, stymied by her blank stare, helpless to understand her condition, unable to penetrate her mind. "If you'd just cry," the speaker says, helpless before her blank stare. She is not far removed from those other individuals whom Kennedy renders in vivid, unsettling detail—the onanist, the serial killer, the arsonist—all of whom withdraw into their own dark worlds.

Kennedy pays particular attention to the modern home environment, its appearance, the individuals in it, and how it reflects them and their values. Mothers are trapped in "Drivers of Diaper-Service Trucks Are Sad," which takes a dim view of childbearing from the perspective of the drivers, who are "sad" because they and women have been "had" and because they have to "dredge their pails for wet ones lying loose . . . From which they wring a temporary juice. . . ." Babies burden women, truck drivers, and the earth, which must bear the "brat's abuse." The poem asks, "What's the use?" and does not offer an answer.

"Evening Tide" depicts another suburban world, this one inhabited by a father who has retreated into hazy intoxication. As he lolls on a recliner with a container of beer, dark forces creep forward, but he is too disengaged and too full of beer to be aware of them or to be moved by the "cry of a child protesting bed. . . ."

Mentally and emotionally at sea, he remains suspended among impressions that pass him like "driftwood." In this suspended state, he is not very different from the schizophrenic girl, but the dark forces around him give ominous warning that some dire force is afoot: "Darkness invades the shallows of the street," and "Under the parked car in the driveway, shadows seep." This suburban island is surrounded by forces that threaten to engulf it.

Even his own child does not raise Kennedy's spirits. "Last Child," one of Kennedy's most popular, is, like "Cross Ties," concerned with the father-son relationship and is a companion piece to "The Shorter View," a poem in which Kennedy considers the "burden" of having children—in this poem Kathleen, his daughter—in a world whose future is "Littered with ashes, too dried-up to bear." The father in "Last Child" is in anguish as he regards his child, whom he addresses as "Small vampire, gorger at your mother's teat." The poem is replete with the language of disgust, loathing, and resentment: "I bear you to be slaked, / Your step-and-fetch-it pimp. / Fat lot you care, / If meadows fall before your trash-attack . . ." (ll. 4–7). This little monster might destroy the planet: "Will yours be that last straw that breaks earth's back?" The only positive feelings the father can muster are expressed in the negative: "I cannot wish you dead."

In many later poems, Kennedy broadens his vision of modern life. "City-Quitter," in *Dark Horses,* opens on a scene of commuters traveling Highway 93, converging on Boston. The dominant image of the stanza is of arrows converging on Boston, the center of the target:

> Down inbound Ninety-three, straight route that wings
> To bullseye Boston through concentric rings
> Of ringroads, faster than the sun can drive,
> Young brokers from New Hampshire farms arrive
> Like thudding arrows at the Charlesbank merge
> Painstakingly inch forward to converge
> In three contending lanes.
>
> (ll. 1–7)

The three lanes into the city become increasingly crowded, and the way is obstructed by a truck, which has "slimed the road with shells and scrambled eggs." The commuters' attitude, ironically, is to "savor to the dregs" a mishap that has happened to someone else. The city itself is "where it's at . . . / Craftshops, theaters, being stood to lunch, / Cop sirens and the subtly lurking fear /

Of slashers' blades . . ." (ll. 11–14). The speaker has "opted for the outer dark," the country, accepting his "doom." A note of despair pervades the final stanza, for conditions in the city and the isolation of the country offer the speaker little hope of a fulfilling life. The train commute only underscores how little control he has over his existence, his fate: "I / Am driven to a safer place to die / Where privacies are clung to like beliefs / And separate houses wall in separate griefs" (ll. 26–28). The irony is in the safety in the country, where one is walled in. In the final stanza the image of a bow and arrow returns: "But soon / The hills of Lexington accept a moon / Drawn like a bow. . . ." The crescent moon arches toward the hills of Lexington, beyond reach, a symbol perhaps of the romantic past that is too distant for him to be a part of, a faraway beauty disappearing from view. Kennedy has gathered these images of things being driven forward, of the individual being propelled to his doom, to characterize the predicament of a generation of commuters who have been driven from the city into the dark entrapment of country life.

The house in "Empty House Singing to Itself" offers another kind of doom: it is "instructed . . . to exude / Ninety minutes of Mozart on tape" to ward off potential burglars and to turn lights on and off at certain times while the owners are "gone to the Cape." The programmed routine of the lights and machines in the house is meant to suggest that the inhabitants are at home, and Kennedy, seeing fertile meaning in this arrangement, creates an amusing cast of ghostly figures "Who neither consume nor cast shade," but who go about as humans would, sliding into bed "impalpable." These ghostly figures mirror the humans they represent, and their lives are reflected in their mansion, which they have "computer-programmed / To make threatening noise: a machine / For confining the souls of those damned / To a heaven of perfect routine" (ll. 13–16). Kennedy sees in utopian perfection, founded on modern technology, a damnation of the soul.

In "Dump" discarded and broken objects in a city trash heap suggest lives in similar condition. The poem paints a dismal picture of impending disaster, of failure and hopelessness, opening with "The brink over which we pour" and closing with a resigned acceptance of death: "Our emptiness may rankle, / But soon it too will pass." Along the way the poem never lightens the dark picture of human waste: "Here lie discarded hopes," the speaker notes, his eye catching sight of rotted roof shingles and "Paintings eternally stale." The poem's neat appearance and orderly structure belie the chaotic heap of junk:

The brink over which we pour
Odd items we can't find
Enough cubic inches to store
In house, in mind,

Is come to by a clamber
Up steep unsteady heights
Of beds without a dreamer
And lamps that no hand lights.

(ll. 1–8)

The previous owners of these items are dismembered hands, and the empty beds reflect the fate of those who dream. The lines of the first stanza teeter at their ends and fall into the next lines, bringing with them jarring qualifications: "The brink over which we pour / Odd items"; "we can't find / Enough." The fourth line breaks from the regular, three-stressed previous lines by having only two stresses, those phrases themselves broken in two. Into this broken container, Kennedy pours disturbing images: "Pink dolls with skulls half-crushed, / Eyes petrified in sleep. . . ." He builds a world of putrid junk and broken lives and implies that it has left us empty: "Our emptiness may rankle, / But soon it too will pass" (ll. 59–60). Our civilization, symbolized by the junk heap, inevitably will come to this end.

Kennedy continues his gloomy discourse in *Dark Horses* with "Summer Children," which sees in a simple picture of children playing on a beach the decline of modern civilization. These children, "quickly made / In marriages that came undone . . . ," symbolize the uncertain treasures of the future. As products of broken homes, they represent the dissolution of the modern family unit, and their behavior does not bode well, either, for "Like creaking-pulley gulls, they quarrel / They've taken too much sun today." All around them nature seems to conspire against them and to promise troubled times ahead:

Now foam consumes their castle keep,
Draping their towels with sodden laurel.
Children, it's high time. Come away.

Concussions of the surf resound
As though in shells. Once sunken deep,
Like driftwood a September chill
Rises, returns.

(ll. 8–14)

In the sense that they embody the past and represent the future, the children's value is recognized and kept when all else is lost: "These children may be all we keep." They might even possess a knowledge we do not have, as the poem intimates with a question: "What currents do they understand?" Typically, Kennedy's skill with puns brings together in this line the natural currents of the sea and the trends in public life, suggesting that these children will not be able to understand the world in which they will travel as they will not understand the ways of the ocean. The question is rhetorical. The children are viewed as a group, one that is distant from the speaker and the "we" referenced in the final line, "These children may be all we keep." None is given a specific identity or much humanity. They are referred to as "they," "their," and "these children." Despite the lack of individuality, however, they are creatures of the summer, the apex of the year, the sunny season; they represent a life force that may withstand the rising tide and September chill or survive them.

Even among his light verse Kennedy places poems that voice frightening implications. After the quite playful "King Tut" in "Intermission for Children" in *Cross Ties,* Kennedy offers us "Where Will We Run To," a six-line poem of aphoristic force that asks a serious question about the future of the human race:

> Where will we run to
> When the moon's
> Polluted in her turn
> And the sun sits
> With its wheels blocked
> In the used star lot?
>
> (ll. 1–6)

The final image is especially witty in that it plays on the notion that in Roman mythology, the sun is a flaming chariot whose wheels could indeed be blocked.

Kennedy's doubts concerning the benefits of modern society, particularly American society, is reflected even in his diet. "Dirty English Potatoes" is a confession on the part of the speaker that his preference in potatoes stems from a defect in his New-World character. He has become so accustomed to the American potato that he cannot adequately appreciate the British variety. American potatoes from Idaho and Maine are "Steam-cleaned . . . tied in their plastic shroud" and "so groundless you'd believe / Them exhaled from some passing cloud . . ." (ll. 1–2). British potatoes, on the other hand, have the marks of the earth on them and have substance, personality. The speaker's preference for the American potato is evidence that he suffers from "the new world's impatient taint," which makes him curse the "mucked-up sink" where his British potatoes are cleaned. Americans destroy the vitality of Earth's fruit with their passion for cleaning and packaging.

The academic world fares no better, in Kennedy's opinion. Whether in a group, as in "Reading Trip," or in individual portraits, this aspect of American life does not present an attractive picture. "Leave of Absence" portrays a college teacher growing old while trying to write a book and teach at the same time. He is frustrated by his failure to complete his book and is doomed to mark student essays. "Scholar's Wife" deals with another kind of academic failure. Reminiscent of the woman in "Her Thinking Man" who thinks her mate thinks too much, this academic wife resents her husband's work on his scholarly project. Her husband works on a book entitled "*The Doric Mood,*" which befits the poem's imagery that contrasts this modern woman's sexual thoughts with her husband's preoccupation with Grecian architecture: "the skin / Of suburbs pierced, your column spurted in" (ll. 5–6). In her journal she imagines "The new-mown snow soft toppling down in stacks"; licks her ballpoint; "To relax / The pelvic girdle" takes "endless baths"; and goes to confession, where she is told to "*See five Days of Wraths / And ten Potemkins . . . avoid your husband's friend.*" Sexually frustrated and resentful, she imagines herself talking to her husband—the only way she can have a conversation with him—and tells him:

> Don't come back
> Unless for who I am, not for some pack
> You rip the tab from, give a flick, unzip,
> Puff and crush out. Your sexual Reddi-dip.
>
> (ll. 20–23)

The woman is widowed by scholarship, sexually unsatisfied and emotionally mistreated by the husband, whose scant attention is rife with insensitivity.

"Among Stool Pigeons" depicts a very different picture of a teacher in the classroom from the one we find in William Butler Yeats's "Among School Children," which Kennedy wants us to remember as we read his poem. Yeats's solemn and philosophical reflections on the past as it is reflected in the faces of his pupils contrast sharply with Kennedy's picture, in which a teacher's drunken collapse turns a schoolroom into a surreal vision of present education. Kennedy's teacher is beset by the strict, sober, orderly world of the school, represented by "Miss Runcible's smart peck of heels" and the school board members, who disapprove of his "yawp." Creativity is altogether squelched in this jejune environment, and to combat these demonic forces, the teacher rebels and, ultimately, withdraws into an inebriated world and is destroyed.

Another retreat from the world is depicted in "For a Flung Cyclist," which speculates in somber tones on a cyclist killed accidentally by hitting a pole. The poem hints that the cyclist was a social rebel who did not take advice well and grew "Tired of a speed that grew like mad." The final quatrain eulogizes him by declaring that he remained true to his star, now a "paving stone"; in that way, he was unlike "those of us who have lied / And not so soon are overthrown." "Flung" aside by "those of us who have lied," the cyclist chose "To drop out of the human race."

In all these poems Kennedy suggests that human failure results from the inability to achieve and sustain an emotional and intellectual connection with others and with the part of oneself that, if it has not been eradicated by too much civilization, would allow for fulfillment and free, creative expression. Even in "West Somerville, Mass.," which traces the collapse of another academic, the teacher's loss of religious faith represents a disconnection from something vital and emotionally sustaining. Too much worldly ambition, too little freedom to express oneself, or too little faith in oneself stifles the individual spirit and cuts one off from the past and present and from nature and the community. Kennedy generalizes these portraits and the circumstances that surround these people who are troubled and in trouble, generalizes them enough to suggest that they represent people and conditions in contemporary America. Yeats's world of classical greatness is the backdrop to the events in "Among Stool Pigeons," and the teacher's collapse suggests the fall of the human spirit in America in general, and his vision of the future includes us all: "Here comes that star-splashed dark" (l. 19).

Throughout his career Kennedy has shown great interest in the American landscape outside urban centers and in the individuals who inhabit those conditions. "A Water Glass of Whisky" is one of Kennedy's earlier poems that creates a vivid and memorable picture of a place that defines what Kennedy means when he says conditions are "God forsaken." The irregular stresses in a few of the lines reflect the theme of disorder that runs through the poem. Some of the lines seem to emphasize their irregular beat: "Through the hill by the Rite Nite Motel," "There is no good book but the Good Book," and "You don't die for want of TV." As these lines show, the poem repeats sounds and double stresses, creating rhythmic emphasis along with discordant sound: "Rite Nite," "falls halt," and "TV" (these two letters of course pronounced "Tee Vee"). The unpleasantness of the scene—a tawdry motel in the empty stretches of the American midwest—is underscored also by the assonant sounds that end the second, third, and fourth lines:

> Through the hill by the Rite Nite Motel
> Not a picture unbroken can reach:
> An old famous head in the screen
> Facelifted, falls halt in its speech. . . .
>
> (ll. 1–4)

This part of the American landscape has become a cultural wasteland, whose inhabits are connected to the outside world only by television. Though the inhabitants have the Good Book, Heaven is out of reach: "Only outer space answers your stare" (l. 12). The title of the poem suggests that those who pass through this dismal place, or those who remain here, are compelled to anesthetize themselves with whisky, which is more effective than the Good Book in helping one through. The speaker senses that an ominous force has isolated this area, a force that is "more than night or a hill." This far out, this cut off from communication with the rest of the world, the inhabitants are lost:

> You don't die for want of TV
> But even so, here lies a lack
> As though more than night or a hill
> Had walled you in, back of its back.
>
> (ll. 13–16)

In this final stanza the speaker uses "you" both to generalize about the place and to enlist the reader's assent, distancing the town even further from contact with the rest of the world and suggesting that when communication with others is lost, Heaven loses interest too.

Ten poems gathered in *Cross Ties* under a single title, "Traveler's Warnings," demonstrate the importance Kennedy gives the modern American landscape. "Main Road West" begins the series by describing a tawdry, desolate spot on the highway. It gives a snapshot of a little town where light from a sign in a used car lot "keeps hard stars from piercing through to town."[41] "Edgar's Story" records the grievances of a traveler who discovers on a trip with his wife that tourist stops and national shrines have been desecrated by tourism. Edgar and Nell strike out to do some traveling, bored with "stoking up the coffeepot at dawn . . . sitting working on some beers, / Watching the sprinkler going on the lawn . . ." (ll. 2–4). Edgar, preferring to admire trees, is impatient with his wife's wanting to "Gawk at some china plates and hand-carved looms," dislikes "plastic squirrels" with inscriptions "on their butts." Edgar's affections for trees causes his mind to "hurt, / Thinking . . . Of redwood forests melted down for pulp," and he even is anguished using toilet tissue and paper towels. At Mount Rushmore, Edgar asks: "*Abe, Abe, how does it feel to be up there?*" To his amazement, "that great rock he has for a pupil budged," and the figure replied, "*Alone*" (ll. 26–28). The poem suggests that the attractions Edgar and his wife have been missing out on "all those years" was not worth going to see; in fact, Edgar's reward for his pains is to find razed forests and plastic souvenirs. Although the figure of Lincoln reflects Edgar's feelings, the poem makes an ironic point: a talking stone monument is worth traveling to see, but its message is that mankind and nature have become separated. By imposing his vision on the land, mankind has disfigured both.

"National Shrine" elaborates this idea, focusing on the court house at Appomattox, where Lee surrendered to Grant, ending the American Civil War. The first quatrain introduces Lee and Grant as they arrive, take off their swordbelts, smoke, and pose for a photograph. The second quatrain shifts to the present site, where glass showcases display "Kentucky rifle . . . Parrot gun," and automobiles from Connecticut and Alabama "waxed sleek in the sun, / Reflect like sisters in the parking lot." The final quatrain juxtaposes images of the past and present: Lee's defeated troops "led home to gutted field and farm / Mules barely stumbling" and departing cars carrying "The wounded sun and instant Kodachrome . . ." (ll. 9–11). The double meaning of "wounded sun" adds a solemn tone to the final image, for it suggests that the Civil War "wounded" the sons (and daughters) of subsequent generations. Tourism distorts the past, rendering "our truces brighter than they are," the final lines says. The events of the past are not diminished; in fact, the poem ennobles them by making them human—the image of the troops being led like mules home to gutted fields conveys considerable sympathy for the defeated army. Tourists receive less sympathy, however. Their character is only implied by their cars and Kodachrome pictures. The "sisters in the parking lot" reflect, but do so in the way the cars in the parking lot reflect, on the surface only, no depth, no understanding. The poem offers a view of what happens at national shrines: the past is encased, mummified, diminished in the present because its human element is gone; the present is diminished, too, for it lacks a vital human element.

In "Peace and Plenty" the natural landscape is so desecrated by human traffic that it actually commits suicide. The poem opens on a picture of a landscape blighted by the waste produced by a modern industrial society. Natural features are personified victims of humans and their machines. Hills of pine, "Bound to the road by chains / Of motels . . . lie stunned" (ll. 1–3); the mountain, like a mother, missing her young, gropes "for her firs" as "Engines are gunned." The river, like a dying animal, "Choked with refuse / Upturns a blithering stare / To the exhausted air" (ll. 9–11). The poem closes on a note of despair, rendered in a series of images that concentrate beauty and meaning in a grand finale:

> Let the new fallen snow
> Before she change her mind
> Lay bare her body to the Presto-Blo,
> The drooped rose her
> Quietus find
> Head down inside the in-sink waste disposer.
>
> (ll. 13–18)

Kennedy subtly contrasts the heroic past with the very unheroic present scene by calling on the landscape to choose an honorable suicide rather than to continue living a dishonorable life, subtly alluding to Hamlet's contemplation of suicide in the use of "Quietus," and, in the symbol of the rose, echoing the Romantic tradition of delicate female beauty dying for love.

"Ant Trap" sees "the rank-and-file of working stiffs" as ants lured into a life of benumbing repetition, failure, and unfulfilling relationships. Throughout this long poem (seven stanzas of eight lines each), Kennedy underscores the very unheroic quality of his modern figures with references to warriors of classical antiquity, particularly those returning from the Trojan War. The modern soldier has been lured by a "Siren in a tin can," and the heroic march to and from battle has become a flow of commuters shuttling back and forth in trains. The overriding image is that of an army of doomed worker ants. The poem illustrates the way Kennedy often uses references to the past as a context for, and as a commentary on, present conditions. The father in the poem is a relic from World War II, one of a generation of men who have come home to a life in which the typical man is a "kempt creature treading in straight files . . . / Hopping the shuttle daily . . ." (ll. 25, 27). As the father and others like him sip their scotch and waters "in a state of shock," their sons mock them and their beliefs, turn to drugs, and "die from speed." A British reviewer senses "fear and trembling" in Kennedy's picture of "the alienation of the new young from the new old,"[42] and certainly the poem paints a grim picture of current conditions in suburbia, building to a final scarifying image of the death throes of a generation:

> their pulsebeats falter and stall
> When, clutching sides, they double up in pain
> And footholds loosening, they begin to fall,
> Cast forth fast feelers, grope, catch fast again:
> Stiffening columns in behind a wall.

The puns in the last line heighten the effect of the poem's themes: "stiffening columns" reduces epic heroism to the death throes of the ants, and "in behind a wall" reduces the father's plight to that of hemmed-in and destroyed ants, showing the extent to which, in modern times, classical grandeur has fallen.

The subject of "Best Seller" is the reaction of people in a small town to finding themselves portrayed in a best-selling novel. They react in anger, burn the author in effigy, and call him names. But when "the guided tours hit town," they begin to capitalize on their notoriety, concocting tall tales to dazzle the tourists and profiting on the increased sale of gasoline. In time they discover that they must remain like the characters in the guidebooks to sustain their prosperity. In the end, they have become victims of their own greed and lust for fame.

In "What She Told the Sheriff" Kennedy returns to the subject of social misfits and twisted minds. This poem is one of Kennedy's longest—one hundred and twenty lines—and demonstrates his great skill in sustaining a long narrative. He was to repeat this level of performance in an even longer poem—one hundred and thirty-four lines—collected in *The Lords of Misrule*, "The Ballad of Fenimore Woolson and Henry James," which is a somewhat fictionalized account of a relationship James had with Constance Fenimore Woolson. In "What She Told the Sheriff," the lines alternate in three-stress and two-stress rhythms and the rhymes also alternate, most of them slanted. The imagery and other formal elements are so well blended together that they compete with the poem's subject for attention, as in these lines, in which the narrator is a crazed woman:

> Next noon, out choosing ears
> For the lunch pot,
> I'd come on sin's arrears
> Still body-hot:
> There in the scrambled dirt
> The telltale pressings
> Of buttocks, a torn-off shirt,
> Love's smelly passings.
> Father, how could your Hand
> Deign to forgive?
>
> (ll. 41–50)

The woman's choice of detail reveals her fascination for the sexuality she herself misses, the body-hot evidence of love making, the revealing indentations, the smells that both disgust and arouse her. All the while the woman is revealing herself, Kennedy's hand is at work heightening the tension between her disconnections from logic, from human contact, from sexual pleasure. By breaking the first line at *ears* and, in the next line, saying that they are for the lunch pot, Kennedy hints at physical dismemberments. The use of *arrears* hints at the human "rears" that have stirred her emotions, and the Lord's hand suggests another ambivalent meaning in this context.

The poem opens with the woman recalling sexual escapades in which she cannot or does not wish to take part, visualizing "Hot nights out in the cornshocks, / Snakelike they'd go / Bashing about in pickup trucks . . ." (ll. 1–3). Surely these sinners do not deserve forgiveness. "Smite them!" she prays. Claiming God is her lover, she kills her parents with a cleaver and sets the house, henhouse, and silo ablaze. When caught, she justifies her actions by quoting the Bible: Paul said, *Our days in earth / Are as a shadow . . .*" (ll. 33–34). Irony develops from the incongruity between her Biblical quotations and the description of the bloodbath "*Render unto Your Father on high / Your father's silo*! (ll.

103–4). Oddly, her narrative skills and clarity of recollection mask the dark turmoil that drives her destructive passion.

In "Driving Cross-Country" Kennedy returns to the Iowa landscape where he placed the deranged woman of "What She Told the Sheriff." The degraded condition in one of the towns is contrasted to an ideal past, and the poem's speaker asks, "Where is the prince of yesteryear / Beneath whose lip princesses roused?" Here Ella Ashhauler, the resident barfly with the self-revealing name, searches for a meal. To get it, she "has to scrounge, / Her slipper tilted, for some heel." Like drugged victims of "Some hag's black broth," the travelers continue, doomed to pass through blighted town after blighted town. The fairy-tale past seems all the more attractive and impossible in these conditions. The end is ironically ambiguous. "We had a home. It was somewhere. / We were there once upon a time" (ll. 27–28). The final phrase, "once upon a time," recalls the signature beginning of a fairy tale and suggests that the poet's home, the ideal place that contrasts sharply with the Iowa landscape, seems like a fairy-tale world when set against these surroundings.

This series of travel poems culminates with "Reading Trip," which gives another look at an academic community, this one sterile and benighted. Too much attention to drinking and eating has rotted the poetic sensibility and appreciation of literature. The speaker has also lost his way: "I grope for balance, break off and discard / . . . the lies / I stick out with all over, fumbling for / A means to shrivel back to some sort of core . . ." (ll. 87–90). Like the academics about him, he has lost touch with a spiritual or cultural center. Diminishment ends the poem along with a sense of imminent doom as the speaker edges "out into the dusk to claim my slot / . . . less and less / The bard on fire, more one now with the blot / That hoods the stars above Los Angeles . . ." (ll. 91–94).

Though not part of the series in *Cross Ties*,[43] "Loose Woman" nevertheless reflects Kennedy's negative view of people in small-town America and is among the many poems in which a woman figures prominently. The poem portrays a woman considered "loose" by the townspeople. She is found murdered and no one knows who killed her. The townspeople never will find out who the murderer is, for they are more interested in the victim's sexual conduct than in the identity of her murderer. The poem's central point is revealed in the speaker's comment: "It still occurs / To wonder had she been our fault or hers . . ." (ll. 10–11). The true perpetrators of the crime are the town gossips. As Kennedy shows in "Best Seller," the townspeople collectively share some of the blame for what happens, though they remain ignorant of their own responsibility.

As if to balance the picture, Kennedy has considerable sympathy toward those who remain close to soil, and he expresses his feelings in a poem that was grouped with songs in *Cross Ties.* "Talking Dust Bowl" describes the life of a poor farmer who, in a long list of grievances, describes the severity of his circumstances:

> Old cow's almost dry now, her hooves scrape hard dirt.
> Where's the man going to pay me what I'm worth?
> Forty acres played out, soil like the corn meal low in the can,
> Reminds me of a woman holding back on a man.
> Nights, hot nights I walk by the warped board fence
> Hoping to find a fresh water break-through or some sense.
>
> (ll. 1–6)

His "kids run round in washed-out flour bags," and so on. Out of work and angry, he decides he has had his "fill of hanging around this town," a sentiment he repeats a dozen lines later, adding that he is "Going due west" to escape the "Dust clouds bearing down now, dust stretching from pole to pole" (l. 31). The poem focuses on the plight and character of the people who migrated from the Dust Bowl to the Sunshine State in the 1930s. Into this elemental mixture of humanity and soil, Kennedy injects the idea that the farmer's relation with the earth is partly sexual. The man feels betrayed by the land, expressing himself in sexual terms more than once in the poem. The grim picture the poem paints comes partly from the crowded, heavy look, rhythm, and feel of the lines, many of which are loaded with vivid, specific details that accumulate as one reads; they reinforce the sense of being overwhelmed by the same frustration and despair the speaker feels. By staying close to things, "nine stew beans," "Stalk of corn, " "an old Ford," and "patched tires," and so on, the poem reveals a mind that cannot escape elemental life, partly because of circumstances, partly because of character.

The closeness of humans and the earth is explored again in "Mining Town,"[44] where those who work the mine lead precarious, dangerous lives. Kennedy focuses sympathetically on the buildings that bear the hardships of this life, the sheds that "Hug dirt for dear life," the houses that "lose / Gray clapboards the way a dying oak sheds bark" (ll. 2–3), the gas stations that "inch up near," and so on. Man, building, and nature are linked as they endure in a world dominated by hard labor, danger, and fear. The landscape and people are fixed yet intermingle. The buildings become like "dying oak" and "Like boys in sneakers testing limber ice"; the townsmen become "like their trees / Locked to the wind's steep angle." No malevolent force dooms them; no curse has placed them here. The poem makes no moral judgment, and its tone is matter-of-fact. It is as though Kennedy has discovered a world in which animate and inanimate objects have become a single being that is gradually dying as it struggles under the weight of its own purpose.

Although he is profoundly interested in and concerned for the American landscape and its relation to the humans who inhabit it, Kennedy devotes many poems to an exploration of human nature as it is reflected in sexual behavior that is wholly self-centered and reduced to physical gratification only. "Hearthside Story" is about a young man's visit to a prostitute, and the experience is cast in the image of a hearth and its attendant features. This approach to a situation that lacks beauty, dignity, and spiritual elevation Kennedy characterizes with wit, humor, and indirection. In place of the coarse expression "piece of ass," for instance, the young man buys "a piece of ash. . . ." (echoing Kennedy's play on the name of the prostitute Ella Ashhauler in "Driving Cross-Country"). Instead of a bedraggled whore, the image is of "Two legs attached like logs of oak / Stacked for a burning." Despite the artful playfulness, however, the young man sees its wretched side, though the experience is not altogether unpleasant for him. The woman's skill with cigarette smoke, not to mention her other skills, elicits his admiration: "What perfect ovals she could blow!"[45] At the time he "had no heart to fan a fire / That chilled" and "gave it up for good," but as he looks back on the experience, he lapses into a romantic ardor that, for all his new knowledge and firmness of heart, bespeaks an ironic callowness: "O Mistress mine, my kindling wood." At the same time, the young man understands that the woman will remain a part of him and that, while quenching one flame, she has lit another.

"For an Exotic Dancer" takes another look at sex degraded by commercial exploitation. The poem makes a metaphor of the exotic dancer's activity, which consists of "undoing feeling / Like a tied string" and letting "fall all beneath." The woman is tired of her occupation and is at the end of her career. "Drums bumped," suggesting a monotonous, spiritless accompaniment to her dance, and she performs before an "Old Boneyard" that whistles "through cracked teeth."

People whose sexuality stirs outside the procreative function or who have an abnormal interest in sexuality also receive Kennedy's witty portraiture. "The Self-Exposed" looks into the mind of an exhibitionist. The speaker's depiction of events and scenes alternates between his seeing harsh reality and his feeling of pleasure. After exposing himself in a Pullman car, he asks, "What gets into me?" and answers, "my bird-out-of-hand longs to take its stand / On the farther side from what's allowed"(ll. 11–12). Social restrictions create social rebels, he argues. "How I yearn / To scribble with the dibble on their neat-ruled norms. / They'll nail me yet" (ll. 14–16). He hints that those who witness his act share some of the responsibility, however, for the "world's warm look" arouses in him a hunger to be "dressed" in it. Exposing himself actually makes him feel clothed. The mind of the exhibitionist inverts the "norms" of others, and his inversion is but one manifestation of his mental derangement.

One of Kennedy's earliest poems, "Faces from a Bestiary," shows interest in the individual whose self-absorption is expressed in sexual terms. The poem borrows imagery from "the twelfth-century *Livre des Créatures* of Philip de Thaun" to condemn those who are self-absorbed and sterile. The poem offers contrasting figures: the noble lion is Christ, symbol of procreation and eternal life, and the despicable Hyena is "a beast to hate," for "No man hath seen him copulate." As the quintessential narcissist, "He is unto himself a mate." Unnatural and doomed is such a creature, and the poem ends with a warning:

> You who this creature emulate
> Who with your mirrors fornicate
> Do not repent. It is too late.
>
> (ll. 10–12)

"Onan's Soliloquy" also looks into the mind of the masturbator, whose experience during masturbation is rendered in religious overtones. The poem works like a pun, both a contradiction and a confirmation: given the nature of masturbation and of imagination, a single person can be two people. The first line of the poem illustrates this duality: "She'll none of me? Like Hell. She's mine alone." The woman is indeed his "alone" because only he possesses her in his fantasy, and he does so when he is alone. The poem's final line confirms the ambiguous nature of the onanist's experience: "Darkness all mine for lover. And I its." The darkness envelops him in a shroud of moral condemnation. The possessor has been possessed by his own dark passion.

"Flagellant's Song" presents yet another individual caught up in sexual pleasure, this one "A lecher by persuasion" who derives sexual gratification from being whipped. The poem's speaker argues that his advanced age and the decline in his sexual prowess have made him dependent on "the birchbark's thwacking!" He recommends it to others too: "If more wives flayed / They'd be well laid, / And rare would be divorces" (ll. 28–30). The Marquis de Sade appears to him in a dream, and he asks the Marquis, "*How did you die? / By little bits,* said he." This last phrase gathers together the ideas of being flayed (to bits) and dying gradually in successive flayings. The irony is capped by the suggestion that the speaker's passion for being flayed is so intense that nothing short of being cut to bits will suffice. The addiction, that is, is self-defeating and self-destructive.

In "On the Liquidation of the Mustang Ranch by the Internal Revenue Service," Kennedy looks again at how the landscape reflects the character of those responsible for it, connecting this theme with commercial sex, which degrades all involved, including the landscape. The poem's imagery suggests that the ranch's former clientele are the "paying herd"; the women, "waterholes turned dust." The discarded crates of condoms, lingerie, and mirrored orgy chamber offer a tawdry reminder of what has destroyed the place. The business has left the landscape in such a degraded condition that the "frustrated rain / Refuses to descend" (ll. 3–4), as though commerce in sex has made the landscape too unpalatable even for the rain.

Some humans receive Kennedy's sincere praise because they have not made the world worse than it was before they arrived and have not made fools of themselves. Some have even improved the world, often in a modest, uncelebrated way. "Consumer's Report" venerates John Dowd:

> who'd bring by rolling store
> Horse radish to our kitchen door
> He'd make from cream and home-ground roots.
>
> My God. The heat of it would burn
> Holes through your beef and knock your tongue out.
> (ll. 3–7)

Dowd's dedication to high-quality workmanship bespeaks his admirable character, and his unrelenting pursuit of high standards would be felt by his customers in the quality of his product. The old merchant had spunk, too, for he "ground right on with open eyes," knowing that the fumes would eventually kill him. Kennedy's language in the last stanza is particularly apt to his subject and meaning:

> But ground right on with open eyes
>   And, grinding, stared straight at his killer.
> I bet theirs takes them by surprise
> Though they can see, today-type guys,
> The guys who use white turnip filler.
>
> (ll. 16–20)

The various ways "ground" is used throughout the poem—"home-ground," "ground," and its variant, "grinding"—keep Dowd in mind, as his essential activity, nature, and product all are close to or from the "ground." Dowd had roots, like his horseradish, and his dedication to the daily grind is bound up also in the poem's key word, *ground*. Dowd was enduring, like the earth from which he took his materials, making his deliveries with a cane even when he could not drive. The entire first line of the last stanza, "But ground right on with open eyes," is a pun on the idea that the old man went right on with his rounds just as he ground right on with his horseradish, and he was so unblinking in his work that no part of it would surprise him. Sound in the poem's final lines reinforces the contrast between the sturdy, reliable Dowd and his rivals, who are "today-type guys . . . guys" with no names and whose designation, *guys*, is attuned, by virtue of Kennedy's skill with rhyme, with *surprise*, a word that conveys a great deal about them, their character, and how little they know their business. Kennedy defines Dowd's character in the evocative language of the old man's trade—a man like Dowd would of course have a *trade*, not a *job* or *profession*—but at the same time, by implication, Kennedy is defining the character of good workmanship and the enduring aspects of good people in general, those who endure and who do not compromise their standards even when they know the inevitable end.[46]

John Dowd is among those characters whose eccentricity, individuality, and, in most cases, integrity set them apart from the masses of silent toilers who dwindle away in suburbia or whose nightmarish existence is reflected in the violence and macabre settings of the city. Some may play along with fools and buffoons, like the visiting poet in "Reading Trip" who finds a measure of self-respect in standing apart, though in the end, he too disappears into the outer darkness. Still others lose control, like the teacher in "Among School Pigeons." Professor Backwards and Aunt Rectita are but two of many characters whom Kennedy portrays with admiration and affection.[47] Some of these likable souls protest loudly, like the woman from "In a Prominent Bar in Secaucus One Day" who has lost her beauty and youth; or contemptuously, like Ool in "Ool about to Proclaim a Parable," who blows off the human race like foam on his glass of beer. Others, like the old men pitching horseshoes, or like John Dowd, continue with quiet dignity through their singular lives.

Another praiseworthy individual is portrayed in one of Kennedy's best sonnets, "To Dorothy on Her Exclusion from *The Guinness Book of World Records.*" The tone is tongue-in-cheek, and Kennedy feigns regret because Dorothy[48] has failed to qualify for the famous record book. The octave characterizes those who win records in images of high drama and extreme, breathtaking action:

> Not being Breedlove, whose immortal skid
> Bore him for six charmed miles on screeching brakes;
> Not having whacked from Mieres to Madrid
> The longest-running hoop; at ducks and drakes
> The type whose stone drowns in a couple of skips
> Even if pittypats be counted plinkers;
> Smashing of face, but have launched no ships;
> Not of a kidney with beer's foremost drinkers. . . .
>
> (ll. 1–8)

Deftly, Kennedy shifts from death-defying feats to a ridiculous ploy to set a record—rolling a hoop. The language lowers the bar even further: "Even if pittypats be counted plinkers." The penultimate line demonstrates Kennedy's skill in weaving multiple strands of meaning into a single thought: "Smashing of face, but have launched no ships" turns on Christopher Marlowe's famous line about Helen of Troy in *The Tragical History of Doctor Faustus,* "Was this the face that launched a thousand ships, / And burnt the topless towers of Ilium?" In the sestet, Kennedy continues this sort of skillful play but focuses on the understated excellence with which Dorothy has won the poet's heart and admiration:

> Yet you win
> The world with just a peerless laugh. I stand
> Stricken amazed: you merely settle chin
> Into a casual fixture of your hand
> And a uniqueness is, that hasn't been.
>
> (ll. 10–14)

Whereas others must risk their lives or perform almost superhuman feats, Dorothy achieves her uniqueness by being herself—simply but magnificently—and Kennedy with impeccable courtesy injects a hint of sexual attraction at the end of a line, to give it added emphasis, in the simple statement, "I stand." The sexual reference is disguised somewhat in the other meaning of the phrase, to rise in a show of respect. Kennedy is frequently accused of being "academic," and one might argue that one needs some "bookish" education to see the allusion to Marlowe's line and to appreciate the sexual allusion in "I stand," but the poem works well without the connections being made. Anyone who reads poetry would probably know enough literature to appreciate the wit.

In such a playful, teasing guise, Kennedy develops the poem into a serious statement about the nature of human excellence, about human nature and the way it can be excellent and appreciated in a world in which some people receive public admiration for deeds of far less importance than being an excellent human. The poem celebrates a kind of excellence that public notice and record books miss. The poem's unstated moral is that the world needs more of them. To Kennedy, the best humans are those who do not try to be more than simply human—the ordinary, in some cases, is positively extraordinary, like Dorothy. This is what R. S. Gwynn is saying as he concludes his review of *Cross Ties*: "If we count ourselves human and remain ruefully proud of being so, then one measure of the praise we extend to the poet is the degree to which we recognize in his work a fellow member of the species."[49] And this is what Kennedy himself is saying in "To Dorothy on Her Exclusion from *The Guinness Book of World Records*."

Later in his career, Kennedy became increasingly interested in the elderly and in the aging process in general, entwining his own aging with his feelings about modern Americans. In "Ambition," which concludes *Dark Horses*, the aging process is cast in the imagery of the seasons, the coming winter seen by the speaker as the coming of old age. The oak leaves falling from the trees remind the speaker of his own lack of freedom. The leaves detach from their branches easily, whereas he is "hanging on, gathering gold."[50] He cannot give himself to "whatever a wind bestows," as the leaves can, for his ambition provides "roots," as the tree has roots. As it is the nature of the leaves to be free, it is his nature both to be rooted by ambition and to grasp "for light and air." Ironically, his ambition has not brought him freedom and security; rather, it has brought dread. The final stanza expresses the speaker's shaky courage:

> I'd be glad to go out on a limb with those
> Who can live with whatever the wind bestows
> Were it not for these roots, dug in deep to bear
> Never being done grasping for light and air.
>
> (ll. 9–12)

Part of Kennedy's poetic acumen is to see when a pun is ideally suited to enhance a thought over and above its unexpected cleverness, as the first line quoted above demonstrates: the original freshness of the phrase "to go out on a limb" is recaptured because the image is ideally suited to this context. The last two lines continue the idea of a tree blown by strong wind and suggest that his ambition gives him "roots," whereas the leaves have none. As it is the nature of the leaves to be free, it is his human nature both to be bound by ambition, to be rooted, and to grasp "for light and air." The implied permanence of the human's rootedness is ironically not a beneficial exchange for the rootlessness of the leaf, for the human's condition is one of envy, dread, and confinement. Grasping for gold results in the "gathering of gold," but one loses what has greater value, light and air, which the leaf enjoys without labor, simply by casting off. In the vivid imagery of seasonal change, Kennedy opposes heaven and earth, spirit and flesh, and earthly commitment and the freedom that death promises.

"Old Men Pitching Horseshoes," on the other hand, gives an affectionate picture of a group of old men "in shirtsleeves" who are pitching "Dirt-burnished iron." The horseshoe in flight reflects the course of their own lives, landing around the peg "Like one come home at last to greet a brother" (l. 11). They "stand ground, fling, kick dust with all the force / Of shoes still hammered to a living horse" (ll. 17–18). Though slowed by age and playing a seemingly trivial game, they are capable of graceful moves and still bear the dignity of a fine animal.[51] Their portraits are cast in language that associates them with elemental Nature, animals, the soil, and simple actions.

Not all humans age thus gracefully, however. In "Reunion" the class of 1934 arrives "In wheelchairs, coned with paper hats" (l. 4). President Till works the crowd, pumping the guests for donations to "his new stadium." The class tycoon is a crass materialist with "Four hog-hairs bristling from his chin . . ." (l. 10) who has a habit of grabbing waitresses by the buttock. They are all comical and pathetic figures whose behavior mocks the solemn occasion and the dignity of human nature.

Whereas "Invitations to the Dance" gives a rousing call for old people dying in a nursing home to dance in defiance of decrepitude and death, "The Old," from *Growing into Love,* characterizes the gloomy conditions of old people in rest homes. The old folks are compared to "Mushrooms, their deafnesses / Feed on their heads and sprout / In circles round them" (ll. 1–3). Their activities include "snatching obituaries" and living "for death's evening race results." The heirs of these dying souls are asked to "Let them lack / Nothing they'll need to have a ball," including "instant splints in case shins crack" (ll. 14–16). Unfortunately, these sad seniors are housed behind rubber shrubs and locked behind an electric gate. They are isolated from their relatives by their age and from those who care for them without caring for them. No one goads them to dance, and nothing here celebrates life.

Other individuals are isolated by an apparent diminished capacity to love other people. "Family Reunion," a poem from *Dark Horses,* portrays humans gathered on a festive day as ghostlike figures without identities, formless creatures who bear "glazed looks of cheer," benumbed by drink and the repetitive, mechanical, spiritless ritual of Thanksgiving. The members of this family are barely more human than the turkey that has been cut up and roasted. In the first stanza, the good cheer is a glaze of inebriation; in the second, final, stanza,

> Each spine erected in its seat,
> Each head bowed low for grace,
> All wait the word to fork white meat
> In through the family face.
>
> (ll. 5–8)

The imagery of both stanzas reduces the family members to a state resembling that of the turkey itself: dead, stuffed, basted, and roasted. The first two lines show the family members in respectful silence as grace is said; the third line tells us that they, like any typical family, are hungry and impatient to eat. Not until the final line do we understand their intense dislike of each other and the fierceness with which they would express it. Kennedy's way with imagery is especially effective here, for he plays on a somewhat comical, harmless expression, "to feed one's face," and mingles it with an expression of pathological hatred toward another human being, in this case a family member, making that final line all the more disturbing and shocking.

Kennedy's epigrams aim stinging criticism at a wide variety of modern characters and social situations. Social refinement, sexual peccadilloes, and snobbery make inviting targets, and if those afflicted by these ills do not represent his final judgment of human nature, at least they demonstrate an abiding disappointment. Kennedy aims his epigrammatic wit at the deceived husband, the masturbator, and the one who sends off for a "penis-extender." Sexual behavior may cause certain kinds of social problems. "*Stud* has a way with women . . . ," but his indiscriminate sexual activity makes him unfit for a long-term relationship with a woman, and "Old *Self-esteem* can manage an erection . . ." but his self-absorption is such that he can achieve an erection "Only by long and loving introspection." Although he is being witty at the expense of these types, Kennedy sees sexual dysfunction as darkness and derangement, and its worst manifestation is the destruction of the individual's life.

For Kennedy, human nature prompts ridicule as well as admiration. Those with integrity, selflessness, and unflagging spirit and joy in living are portrayed with not only admiration but affection. He is interested in the abnormal individual who retreats into a dark isolation, as in "Schizophrenic Girl," or becomes murderous, as in "Absentminded Bartender." But he reserves his contempt for the fatuous, the pretender, the self-deceiving, the crass, and the cruel. His vision sweeps large landscapes—a rural or desolate area, for example, a freeway or modern street scene—and large groups, tourists, old people, and academics, but often his focus narrows, settling on the family, couples, and, finally, the individual. Kennedy has been called the poet of the middle class, but he is more truly a poet of human nature and the human condition, especially in modern America.

Death and the Modern Experience

Death—the inevitable experience—is a subject Kennedy considers with a frequency and variety that suggest a desire somehow to come to terms with it, even to understand it. How he viewed death changed with advancing years, and he came increasingly to rely on epigrammatic brevity and wit to address the subject. The prospect of death casts a gloom over some poems, reflecting an almost bitter protest. In other poems he focuses on the effect death has on individuals and on the human condition. These poems seem to increase in gloominess and in number as Kennedy aged. *Cross Ties* contains many of this kind of poem, but they are especially prevalent in *Dark Horses.*[52] In his epitaphs he comes to see that in some instances death is a state in which individuals receive well-deserved—and humorous—justice.

In several early poems—those printed in *Nude Descending a Staircase* and *Growing into Love,* for instance—death is viewed as an unjust event, especially in the case of a child's death. In "On a Child Who Lived One Minute," which opens *Cross Ties,* Kennedy expresses impatience with a universe in which a new being "so fragile" is not allowed to live, is overwhelmed by "the waiting shape of evil." The child's death symbolizes the failure of not only the healing arts but art itself, and death interrupts the flow of generations.

The premise of "At the Stoplight by the Pauper's Graves," from *Nude Descending a Staircase,* is that the poem's speaker is more helpless than those in their graves, who paradoxically remain alive and protesting, in their way:

> Skull against skull, they won't stretch out at ease
> Their jammed arms, won't set grass to root for good.
> Perennials that came up only once
> Struggle and dry down from their stones of wood.
>
> (ll. 5–8)

Death for the paupers is not a passive condition. They are less helpless than the driver, for they have become part of the grass and the earth, and in that condition remain "active," recalcitrant though decomposing. The driver, on the other hand, is stopped by a mechanical light, directed by a remote power:

> My engine shudders as if about to stall
> But I've no heart to wait with them all night.
> That would be long to tense here for a leap,
> Thrall to the remote decisions of the light.

His inability to run the light, having "no heart" to do so, stands in stark, ironic contrast to the protest and the struggle of the dead. The extent of the driver's submission is measured by the difference between his authority, a mere red light, and theirs, the leveling power of death.

"Conspirator My Rose," also from *Nude Descending a Staircase*, views death as little more than a literary device in the tradition of Andrew Marvell's "To His Coy Mistress." The poem's speaker addresses the rose as a fellow conspirator in a "plot" to demonstrate to the speaker's beloved that, like the rose, she will change with the seasons and die—so she should not waste time resisting his advances.

Still in his first collection, Kennedy returns to the death of a child in "Little Elegy," in which death is a universal force that again disturbs his sense of cosmic justice, and he is challenged not to see death as the end of spiritual and physical existence.[53] The poem implies that although earth's motions eventually slay humans, earth itself can both shelter and protect:

> Earth whose circles round us skim
> Till they catch the lightest limb,
> Shelter now Elizabeth
> And for her sake trip up Death.
>
> (ll. 5–8)

In the previous stanza Kennedy entwines the world of astronomy with a child's game of jump rope to reflect the cycle of life and death in an image that is visually stunning and manages to portray night as Time's scythe: her "quicksilver toes not quite / Cleared the whirring edge of night." In the second stanza the use of *circles* and *catch* suggests that the child's death is as unexpected, and as meaningless, as a slip of the hand in rope jumping. Such a trivial event leads to such awesome consequences: Kennedy both underscores the chasm that separates the two and, at the same time, makes us feel their closeness. In the end he sees that the child's death, like her rope jumping, mirrors great circles of meaning, the swiftness with which death can occur, and the fleeting moment in which the greatest events can take place.[54]

Death, too, can cause a family to fall apart. In "O'Riley's Late-Bloomed Little Son" the child is compared to a flower that sprouted, became frostbitten, then "shrank back in again." The child's death sets the parents adrift. The mother plants a white birch tree in the backyard while the father pitches ball with the girls, standing "on a mound / No higher than that where their hope lies . . ." (ll. 10–11). Death not only shatters family order but breaks generational ties, those Kennedy ponders in his very personal poem "Cross Ties." The injustice he feels when children die he also feels when he envisions the fate of other good and innocent mortals, such as the central character in "Aunt Rectita's Good Friday." This solitary woman, feeling the misery that too many humans suffer, asks, "How can He die and birth and death go on?" One can almost hear Kennedy's own voice in that plaintive question.

In a lighter frame of mind, Kennedy brings his playful wit to bear on the subject of death. In "On the Proposed Seizure of Twelve Graves in a Colonial Cemetery," ghosts debate whether the graves should be moved to make way for traffic. One of the debaters voices the poem's theme, that the living do not respect the past and its relics, including the dead: "''Tis plain / They'd amputate Christ's outstretched arms / To make a right-turn lane'" (ll. 42–44). Kennedy's view that the grave should be safe from disturbance or intrusion underlies the poem's debate.

Despite his ability to treat the subject of death with humor, Kennedy demonstrates in *Dark Horses* that the gloom has not lifted. In "The Woodpile Skull" the discovery of "a black ant's severed head" in a log causes the poet to "think less of whatever Fate / parts heads from shoulders with indifference, / Decrees the moment of our going hence" (ll. 21–23). He thinks now that "Their Enmities" would "thin us out . . . / With sudden unpremeditated blows / And bask in comfort from our overthrows" (ll. 23–26). Feeling a chill wind blow through the woodpile, he realizes that he can blindly kill and, like the ant, be killed. Kennedy's earlier sense that death is unjust and threatens a wrenching separation gradually turns into a resigned acceptance.

By the time he wrote "Coming Close to Drowning," Kennedy could look upon death with a detached intellectual interest. This poem portrays an individual suspended between life and death, eyeing with dispassionate interest what appears to be the face of death beneath the water's surface. The poem begins as the speaker is on his third descent in a lake or river, and Kennedy is distant enough from the individual's predicament to play with words:

> The third time I submerged,
> I couldn't see to drown.
> Salt bit my eyes. There broke
> A breaker in my mind.
>
> (ll. 1–4)

Line three, breaking at the word *broke* and running into the image of a "breaker" in the next line, emphasizes the idea of separation and suggests that the speaker crosses some line of demarcation, perhaps the threshold between life and death. The second stanza focuses on the visual aspect of the experience and asks, "What did I see down there . . . ?" The third stanza answers: "Nothing but weeds that made / A clear stair dwindling down. . . ." The first word of this stanza, "Nothing," suggests an answer to the question about death: what does one see as one is dying? Nothing. The final stanza carries this answer further by presenting an image that characterizes death, or what lies beyond dying, as an impenetrable barrier, something that can be seen but cannot be understood or, unless one dies, entered: "The deep stood full as stone" (l. 16).

A similar interest in death is evident in "Finis," whose matter-of-fact tone is reflected in the title itself. The poem draws a series of parallels between the end of a child's party and death. "It's late," the poem announces, and the ice swan is melting. The cake splatters "in bullets"; puddles of grape Kool-Aid suggest pools of blood; and fudge sauce "eats through each sodden paper plate" like a disease. A child's "little star-decked paper bag" broadens the scope at the end, giving a vision of the night sky's dark expanse. What the poet sees as he stares into the universe is not comforting, and he sums up his feelings in a final chilling line: "It's cold, it's growing dark. You go off screaming" (l. 10).

Kennedy seems fascinated by the strange moments in an individual's mental life that in some respects simulate death or a suspension of consciousness, for he includes a poem similar to "Finis" in *Dark Horses.* The poem, "Staring into a River till Moved by It," translates a moment in the lives of two people into a metaphor of a river passing under the bridge on which they are standing:

> Down bedrock rails the river shot,
>   Scattering pebbles. As it went,
> The bridge we stood on lost in thought
>   Broke from its shoulders of cement
>
> And backwards made off with our looks
>   Resistless as a ship departs.
> As if some knife had twained our necks,
>   No heads stood lookout for our hearts.
>
> (ll. 1–8)

The metaphorical translation continues: They are sinking ships, and their thoughts are the keel that "ballasted" their minds. Finally, the couple returns to land by stepping on the rocks in the stream. The trees by the stream are "drydocked" and they raise "hulls of wood." Staring at the river from the bridge, the couple has taken a mental voyage, but metaphors depict the experience as violent dismemberment and then transform the couple into a vessel that "roared / At breakneck speed though still moored fast. . . ." The mental experience is the focus of this poem; the couple is "lost in thought," and the meaning of "lost" controls the poem. For a moment the two people lose their sense of reality, of place and of themselves. The experience makes the speaker feel detached, separated from his head; then he feels as though he has lost his mooring and is sinking; finally he regains consciousness of time and place. The total effect of these images and of focusing on only parts of the couple is to suggest that the experience of staring at the river has been disorienting, has detached the speaker from himself, and has given the couple a fragmented view of themselves and the world around them. A larger meaning is difficult to fathom in this poem; in its portraying humans in images of dismemberment, it is reminiscent of the ant's severed head in "The Woodpile Skull," the doll's crushed skull in "Dump," and "One claw like a doll's hand" in "Coming Close to Drowning." Kennedy is clearly interested in experiences in which the individual becomes fragmented by experience and is detached somehow from ordinary controls and thereby sees life from a perspective that teaches a lesson or an awareness, which must be learned before one is made whole again. One of the lines in "Staring into a River," for example, seems to sum up Kennedy's point: "No heads stood lookout for our hearts." The poem's elaborate metaphor dramatizes the truth of this statement. "In Faith of Rising," from *Nude Descending a Staircase,* shows Kennedy's faith is being "reconstructed" in the afterlife, but two decades later he believes only fragmentation and dissolution follow earthly existence.

As early as *Nude Descending a Staircase,* Kennedy showed a liking for writing epitaphs. Six of these early epitaphs were reprinted in *Cross Ties* as "Last Lines," followed by four others in "Last Lines for Athletes." *The Epigrammatist* contains ten new epitaphs among its forty-six epigrams. It is probably no coincidence that the number of these poems grew as his mood became more gloomy and satiric following the death of important people in his life. In his epigrams Kennedy finds that humans carry to the grave and beyond the same qualities they held in life. The dishwasher's bones "rattle about in the suds of the grave," for example, and the financier's ashes are locked "in his safe-deposit box." The wordplay diverts, of course, but the individuals themselves and their flaws give ample proof that human nature and the human condition remain unimproved and deserve Kennedy's sharp satire.

One of Kennedy's first epitaphs, aptly named "Epitaph," summarizes a whole life of marital misery in a mock wedding vow spoken by the husband who has drowned himself: "I take this wave to be my mound." The postal clerk, on the other hand, lies in his grave, "wrapped up tight in sod" like a package that God might open for inspection on Judgment Day. Several epitaphs characterize life as a sports contest in which the athlete contends with death. When the boxer is knocked down in the boxing ring, he will not "get up again for any amount," and Crusher the wrestler is "pinned for keeps." The football quarterback is "brought down on the two-yard-under line," and the tennis star "who battered frisky balls" finds that "At breaking balls, Death's service has no peer."

The epitaphs in *Dark Horses* form a series of poems titled "City Churchyard." These epitaphs focus on the ironic futility of human endeavor. The Lecher, Watchmaker, and Writer all devote themselves to activities that lead finally to a state that mocks their earthly occupations and preoccupations. Kennedy may have had Dante's circles of hell in mind when he penned these satiric pieces. The "Bitter Man," who was "screwed tight" from birth and "writhed" inside his soul, now fills "like a screw . . . a twisted hole." The Preacher is now a "wordless worm" and lies with the wordless worm, who "best knows how to convert you." The headstone of "Anyman" contains a message that mocks modern conveniences—the man beneath the marker is not in, and his tombstone is "A mere answering machine." The Misanthrope's epitaph expresses the man's continued antipathy to others, summed up in his final command: "Keep away." The Attorney's pragmatic logic and self-interest surface in another epitaph, which has the attorney scribbling "briefs for Jesus, just in case." The Lecher's tombstone is a phallic symbol with which he salutes the passerby. The "throbbing bone" he "could once erect" has been replaced by a lifeless stone. The Writer's epitaph ironically sums up his life in "a word or two. . . ." The final epitaph returns to Anyman with a grim reminder that the passerby is "only one" against the hordes who have died. One should not "try to fight" death, since "The odds are on our side."

In the epitaphs that conclude the series in *The Epigrammatist,* the satire is muted, and the tone, like that of "Anyman," is often resigned. "Further Retort from an Army of Mercenaries (in debt to A. E. Housman)" also shows Kennedy at his punning best. The dead mercenaries have received only the grave as payment, which they consider "rotten pay." Now they want "overtime," of which they already have too much. In "A Rail Traveler" poor Jonah Jordan was killed by a speeding train, and now his "uncoupled remains" lie buried; the poet hopes that "at the Trumpet" he will rise "to make connections." The untitled "I who in life stood upright as a tree" suggests, as many other poems do, that one has a fundamental relationship to nature, which is even stronger and closer in death. Now the poem's speaker is "more basic" since he is in the earth. "Earth was I made from, back to earth I went," which ends the collection, repeats this idea, calling for the reader of this epitaph to envy the speaker for having returned "back to earth": he is in his "element." The poem's final pun combines earth, heaven, death, and poetry making. Appropriately, Kennedy has come to the end of his journey and his labors are done, yet in death he shall find the union of the principal elements of his life: poetry and nature.

Lest he be caught being too serious too long, Kennedy is as pointed as ever in *The Minimus Poems,* a recent collection of epigrams. In an imaginary card game, the Devil "calls the action," saying that humans think God and the Devil "mere orders of abstraction." Still, the Almighty remains preeminent: Edison may have brought light to humans, but the Lord eventually "Fingers the switch. And Edison goes out." Kennedy reserves his most sardonic statements for himself, however. On his poetic career, he says: "I promised epics, spawned an epigram: / A pig's ass shrunken to a can of Spam." His "Last Request," which he signs, removing all doubt as to whose request it is, expresses what one hopes is a temporary lapse into despair: "Upon my cold clay let no teardrop splash. / Stand me out curbside with your other trash." Whatever view he has of himself, the maker of all this poetry shall remain worthy of better treatment. On this point, Kennedy must leave the final assessment to others.

Thoughts of death often prompt in Kennedy thoughts of the relationship of the past, present, and future expressed in one of his later poems, collected in *Dark Horses.* "War Newscast in St. Thomas," finds the poet on a cruise in the Caribbean, where the tropical sea "has more blue shades than Eskimo / Has names," and the "Undulant palm fronds emulate each wave." This setting is invaded by the news of Desert Storm in "far-off sandclouds," its missiles and airstrikes envisioned by the passengers on the cruise ship. The contrast in settings continues: "Here, rain clouds congeal, / Drain for a minute, stop." It is as if the distant war coagulates the atmosphere of the cruise ship, turning the land "surreal." The war reminds the poet that even this Caribbean locale is violent, its history marked by human slaughter; just recently, the locals tossed coins at a "blind Jew, blood seeping from his head," betting on when he would "fall down dead." In both worlds, the violence arises from greed, and humanity is degraded by the lust for money. The world and its inhabitants do not improve, and the past, in this case, is partly responsible:

> Today the sun dives in a copper blaze
> To vanish as if flushed beyond lush cays
> Where old resentments gather to a boil
> Fueled by "white gold"—that's us. The Persian Gulf
> Lies slicked in oil.
>
> (ll. 33–37)

Kennedy's poetry has shown from his early years that death posed a great question and confronted him with an unsettling fact: children die suddenly and without apparent reason. Why? Kennedy has never accepted the mystery of God's ways as answer for anything. The creative process is itself a mystery—"Don't watch!"—but death is another matter. It does not round off anything, and though it stops an individual's life from continuing here on earth, it leaves much unanswered. The number of poems in which the "dead" speak and act is enough to show that Kennedy does not wholly believe in death, only in Death.

Chapter 4

X. J. Kennedy as Critic

X. J. KENNEDY'S CAREER AS A LITERARY CRITIC GREW WITH HIS DEVELOPMENT as a poet. Although he has so far not collected his critical pieces into a single volume, his published essays, reviews, and interviews, together with his public speaking, represent a large and important part of his literary career. In addition, three of his textbooks have become mainstays in academic institutions, each reflecting his critical ideas in his choice of literary works and in his comments on them and on prose and poetry generally.[1] His first review appeared in 1960 and it gave a perceptive analysis of the popular appeal of his favorite movie, *King Kong*. The review reveals early on Kennedy's keen insight into the American spirit, contemporary social conditions, and popular taste as well as his skill in analyzing artistic productions, in this case film.

It was not long, however, before Kennedy found himself deeply involved in issues directly related to his interests as a poet. Perhaps the overriding issue was the revolution that took place in poetry that resulted in an "explosion" of free verse. Kennedy traces the shift from Walt Whitman, who thought "rhyming metre" useless "except in 'persiflage and the comic,'" to Stephen Crane in the 1890s.[2] Rhymelessness in poetry surged in the 1920s in the work of Ezra Pound, William Carlos Williams, and Gertrude Stein. "Charles Olson and William Carlos Williams led the stampede that took poetry away from traditional forms, strict form, closed forms," Kennedy observed. When major poets "junked" meter and rhyme, hordes of lesser poets followed suit; there followed "a colossal explosion of informality down at the recent end."[3] Between 1940 and 1960, many poets defected from the free-verse ranks, creating a "'Conservative Counterrevolution,'"[4] and although a few contemporaries still wrote formal verse, such as J. V. Cunningham, Howard Nemerov, Anthony Hecht, among others,[5] the revolution, begun by Whitman, had arrived.

Kennedy's response to the onslaught of open form was to write in traditional forms, becoming what he calls an "endangered species," an outsider, born too late.[6] He also preached the gospel of traditional forms in his critical prose and began with his wife, Dorothy, *Counter/Measures* in 1972, a journal devoted exclusively to poetry in traditional forms in order to demonstrate that good formal poetry was still viable and that poets could still produce true, enduring poetry.[7]

In the inaugural issue of *Counter/Measures* Kennedy opened with a defense of rhyme and meter, one that he had been conducting for years and would repeat for decades to come. He could not accept Charles Olson's "theory of breathing as form," nor the idea that "white space and indentations counted with the spacebar of a typewriter can possibly denote with any accuracy the subtleties of the human breath-process."[8] Olson himself in conversation admitted that his theory "was all a song-and-dance he had made up to justify the kind of poetry he and his friends liked to write."[9] Nevertheless, Olson's revolution had succeeded in overcoming the supremacy of traditional forms. Even skilled, literate poets began to "preach the destruction of the entire metrical tradition," although Robert Lowell said he could not see how any poet who has written both metered and unmetered poems could abandon either.[10] According to the new orthodoxy, the old measures did not correspond to the "nervous, staccato rhythms of our civilization." To Kennedy, this claim was nonsense, and he argued that rhythm is too often misunderstood: it means "a pattern established through a recurrence . . . of metrical stress and non-stress. In this sense, free verse does not have any 'rhythms' to it—not for more than a line or so."[11] Randomly placed stresses cannot produce rhythm and be "true to the pace of contemporary life. . . . No rhythm can be reproduced except by repeating something."[12] As he continued to point out, the English language itself tends to be metrical, a fact many open-form poets seem to discount. Passionate language "tends to fall into meter,"[13] and rhythms are fundamental to enduring experiences, such as the seasons, the human heartbeat, and copulation, as the poetry of even Walt Whitman demonstrates. In the early 1950s Kennedy dismissed Whitman as a "wild blatherer," but Kennedy said he was disabused of this opinion in a college course by Lionel Trilling, who explained Whitman's "subtle sound-effects and mastery of metrical rhythms."[14] Kennedy also found support in comments on form by John Frederick Nims, who believed that form "as paced by line length and rhyme escapement, is the choreography of the poet's spirit."[15]

If poetry is to mimic the rhythms of human experience, as proponents of open forms seem to think it should, free verse is therefore inadequate, Kennedy argued, adding that, according to the new theory, a "true poem" had to have "organic form, discovering its individual nature as it goes along,"[16] but closed forms do an even better job in this way, too. Kennedy saw meter as a way to be physical, to "recall that heartbeat it abstracts from, that physical pulse,"[17] and the assumption that formal structure is a container into which the poet pours words is false. A sonnet, for example, when well composed, is just as "organic" as a poem in open form. The fundamental issue, according to Kennedy, is whether a poet takes pains to remove "language from that great, fluid stream of organic reality."[18] Organic-unity poets seem to think that poetry should not be labored or contrived and that their first thoughts are their best thoughts, but memorable poetry tends to come from the effort to produce poetry with a metrical pattern, with or without rhyme. Such labor "is likely to produce valuable poems"; a poem thus created "is a thing more or less achieved, a thing made."[19] "The less art, the more poetry" was the current faith, but Kennedy believed as did W. B. Yeats that revision itself can be "an act of spontaneous inspiration."[20]

In a written debate with G. T. Wright as late as 1990, Kennedy was still driving these fundamental points home. In his essay "Pulse and Breath," Wright maintained that "free or open verse is like the breath—variable, issuing in a stream—while metrical verse is like the pulse, domineering and inexorable."[21] Kennedy believed the physiological analogy is shaky, as anyone can see who reads a few free-verse poems, "pacing his breath to the apparent pauses and alterations in the poet's diction and emphases."[22] A better question to ask of poetry might be " 'Is there any energy in it?' "[23] Wright's view that metrical verse is "artificial and unnatural" denies that "any good poem entails artifice," making artifice part of its pleasure. Kennedy cited Jorge Luis Borges's belief that "No poem can be actual, unretouched life, and if it pretends to be, then it abdicates art's power over us."[24] It is wrong to assert that structured poetry cannot capture "immediate and urgent life." On the contrary, "to write in meter and rime you must blindly submit to a wild and surprising force. You allow a rhythm to take you over, let a rime-scheme suggest what you will say." The free-verse writer "has no such barbaric force to cope with, and be nurtured by." Meter requires that one plunge deep into the mind. Doing so, as W. D. Snodgrass asserts, "You may discover what you truly believe, as perhaps you didn't consciously know."[25] Wright conceded that " 'Traditional meter owes something of its power to the alternating pulse of sexual excitement" and that "Traditional verse after all is a verse of conflict and tension."[26]

Not content with simply stating his beliefs, Kennedy demonstrates time and again how rhyme and meter, traditional forms in general, empower the poet and are discovered in the best contemporary poetry. Reviewing the poetry of L. E. Sissman, Kennedy sees a poet concerned with the "moral and ideological confusions" of contemporary life, writing of these matters "in traditional patterns," showing that "by taking the nervous language of the moment and laying it against an iambic pentameter line, a curious tension will result."[27] A careful reading of Sissman's poetry reveals a superlative poet "striving to feel his way through his own experience into an understanding of the world at large." The search for understanding is revealed through traditional forms, and, Kennedy implies, the revelations and the forms are one, as though the forms give birth to the revelations. Another poet much admired by Kennedy for her transformation of traditional forms into powerful poetry is Marianne Moore. She has, as Hart Crane dreamed poets would do, acclimatized "the machine in modern poetry, using the vocabulary of science as naturally as Donne employed limbecks and compasses." Her poetry "seems a form of silent conversation. Often the pattern of sounds in a stanza seems decided not by the ear but by an architect's eye," and "her geometrical designs arise out of some passionate necessity . . .[;] she is faithful to life." As for her rhythms, Kennedy finds them quite different from the loose, formless motions of free verse: "Where at times the new free-verse falls apart and becomes simply boring, there are usually few heavy syllables, many lines with many weak ones. And there isn't any powerful metric drive—as Miss Moore has, almost always. She can maintain a steady wham, wham, wham of short stubby monosyllables; she throws stresses on an *a* or a *the* or an *of* by putting them in tight patterns and making rimes of them."[28]

Not that every poem that is written in rhyme and meter is a good poem. Kennedy is no doctrinaire in his convictions, and he is as quick as any free-verser to detect weaknesses in certain formal poems.[29] A stern critic of his own work, Kennedy naturally would exercise the same acumen when looking at the work of others. Reviewing the efforts of one poet, for example, Kennedy sees experiments with slant-rime that are not always successful, adding that the poet's talents are not in rhyme and scansion: "He emulates the pauses, line-breaks, and manner of William Carlos Williams so well that too often he sounds like Williams's very self and voice."[30] Another poet "can write in stanzas that rhyme," but "Internal rhymes go false, alliterations become interior decoration," producing "horrible" examples of them.[31] A poet writing in Great Britain, where traditional forms still flourish, yearns "to cast fresh life into a few traditional forms," but his tetrameter couplet fails.[32] Though Kennedy admires Thomas Hardy's poetry,[33] he thinks Hardy never did completely master rhyme, and his poetry suffers occasionally from a "laborious awkwardness."[34] Some poems of another poet writing in rhyme and meter "decline to fulfill their schemes, instead falling into hollow letdowns, meaningfully."[35] Assessing the poems of another contemporary poet, Kennedy sees rhymes "tossed off spontaneously, in a kind of ironic doggerel, and so appear contrived."[36]

Fundamental to Kennedy's view of form is a deep conviction that meter and rhyme inhere in the poem's very nature. He would agree with Emerson's comment that "what makes a poem is 'not metres, but a metre-making argument,'"[37] but he would add that rhyme, too, arises with the concept of the poem. "The meaning of a poem is not only the connotations of the words . . . but all the emotional effects . . . the sound of it, the rhythms of it." A poem is more than just beautiful sounds, which by themselves are "forgettable."[38] At his best, Miller Williams is an example of a poet who thinks in rhyme, who does not bend rhyme to his thought.[39] Williams also "knows that forms convey unexpected power when a poet chooses to shatter their rules." Without rhyme and meter, Williams's flawless epigram would be simply a one-liner. Successful rhyming "stamps its poem with a certain inevitable resonance." Williams believes that "The human mind has a rage for order. The sane mind seeks the order inherent in every event." For Williams, "meter and rhyme are instruments of feeling." Kennedy notes Nims's view of rhyme: we tend to think today of rhyme as a mnemonic device or mere decoration, but "Its worldwide popularity with primitive types—savages, children, folk singers, advertising men—should indicate that something about it goes very deep in the psyche, and not the psyche alone—what is the human body but a system of rhyming parts?"[40]

Perhaps Kennedy's most elaborate defense of rhyme appeared in an essay for an editor who asked for Kennedy's view "on the uses of rime, its origins and development, and its contemporary application."[41] To Kennedy, rhyme is a "device of songs, and of unsung poems that aspire to be songlike." End rhymes are "damned conclusive," and the mind needs "some silence afterward" to linger in, as after an orgasm. It is "Impossible to isolate rime from other elements of a poem." James Hayford, a master of the "made poem," finds that "'Rhymes keep our corners firm,'" and where the "beat falls on the word is crucial."[42] Rhyme illuminates the reader's mind, as well, and fulfills expectations. When it succeeds, it is as satisfying as a sexual act. Rhyme "deeply involves a poet with how the living world really works . . . with something like an organic process, in which a life-force fooling around just naturally hits upon good animals. . . . It is stupid and monstrous to deny poetry any of its possibilities. One of those possibilities is rime." Rhyme—and meter along with it—is order-making and order-revealing. Currently, Kennedy believes, rhyme is not respected, except in popular poetry (such as rock songs). Some believe with Robert Bly that rhyme in English is exhausted and that, along with meter, rhyme befits the English, not the American, mind: "As Whitman saw, the rhymed metered poem is, in our consciousness, so tied to the feudal stratified society of England that such a metered poem refuses to merge well with the content of American experience."[43]

Though certain word combinations may be exhausted, the "supply of available rimes in English, if you include off-rimes too, is nearly infinite," Kennedy argued. Children who rhyme while rope jumping reveal "the nature of riming poetry . . . a stringing-together of words for the sheer hijinks of so doing, the words broken loose from their strictly logical base. Indeed, if the meanings of rimed words clash, all the more fun." The most favorite poems of young listeners all along have been rhymed and metrical.[44]

Rhyme itself can help the writer hear that "voice of feeling" muffled by other ideas that "keep muddling into its way." For the reader, a well-placed rhyme illuminates the mind: "an expectation is fulfilled, and a great gong tolls in the mind." It can of course be the very essence of wit and humor, if used with the effectiveness displayed in one of Kennedy's latest poems, "To His Lover, That She Be Not Overdressed":[45]

> The lilies of the field
> That neither toil nor spin
> Stand dazzlingly revealed
> In not a thing but skin

And in that radiant state,
  Sheer essences they wear.
Take heed, my fashion plate.
  Be so arrayed. Go bare.

Despite the free-verse revolution, as early as the 1970s Kennedy saw evidence of a renewed interest in rhyme and meter among poets who had discovered that if you "toss away rime and meter, you junk some of your powers, some of your subtlest strategies for affecting a reader's unconscious."[46] Some American poets who abandoned meter in the 1960s had good reason to, and after, wrote better poetry—James Wright, Denise Levertov, Donald Hall, and others. But others "have stuck to their lonely posts with great integrity" and, Kennedy would add, success.[47] A resurgence in meter and rhyme may also be seen in the poetry of Theodore Roethke, John Berryman, and many other contemporary poets.[48] Such indicators suggest to Kennedy that many poets, along with having discovered new forms outside traditional structures, have also realized that traditional forms have not only not been exhausted but offer advantages missing in open form. A poet who writes fixed forms, such as the sestina, the sonnet, the ballad, and so on, has "something working" in his favor.[49] Form helps poets know when they are going wrong and leads them to what they really want to say.[50] Kennedy agrees with Richard Wilbur that "'the strength of the genie comes of his being confined in a bottle.'" Traditional form, Kennedy believes, has "the power to stir us to the core."[51] Writing sonnets, for example, can cause a poet to "discover a deeper individuality." As W. H. Auden pointed out, "metrical verse . . . requires its practitioners not merely to adopt its conventions, but to adapt those conventions to their own needs. In so doing, each practitioner tends to discover an individual voice."[52]

Discussing a poem by Miller Williams, Kennedy explains how Williams, for whom "traditional forms have long held a powerful fascination," illustrates in one of his poems "the power that strict form can give to language deliberately simple and (for the most part) ordinary":

Whatever else you come to be
you will always be a year,
with numbers starting out from here
and going past where I can see,
if you are clever and cock an ear
for beast of old and boast of new,

if you are careful and keep an eye
peeled for the trolls of derring-do.[53]

Pointing out the predominance of one-syllable words and the play on words (*beast* and *boast*), Kennedy sees the poem enter "the universe of fairy tales" with the introduction of trolls, adding, "Had it been cast in free verse, this winning poem could have seemed banal, despite its playfulness," and he illustrates (and proves) his point by reducing the poem to a rhymeless heap:

Whatever else you may be
You will always be a year,
With numbers starting out
And going past my line of sight. . . .

Anyone can ruin a good poem, one might argue, even a good poet, Kennedy demonstrates, to make his point, so we might look at the issue in a more even way. In an issue of *Counter/Measures,* Kennedy squared off with Robert Bly, the guru of free verse, each poet rendering in English a poem in German by Rainer Maria Rilke and one by Hugo von Hofmannsthal. Bly led off with an unrhymed version of the Rilke poem:

Just as the watchman in the winefields
has a shed for himself and keeps watch,
I am the shed in your arms, Lord,
my night is drawn from your night.

Vineyard, meadow, weathered apple orchard,
field that never lets a spring go by,
fig tree rooted in ground hard
as marble, yet carrying a hundred figs:

odor pours out from your heavy boughs
and you never ask if I am keeping watch or not;
confident, dissolved by the juices, your depths
keep climbing past me silently.

Kennedy's rhymed version of the same poem goes:

Like the vineyard watchman sheltered
In his arbors out of sight,
In your hands, Lord, I am sheltered
And my night, O Lord, is your night.

Soil never caught napping in April,
Orchard, meadow, and vineyard old,
Tree that from ground hard as marble
Bursts with figs a hundredfold:

From your globed boughs flows aroma.
And you trust that I watch. Past my eyes
Boldly, by loosed sap swollen,
Your deeps in silence rise.[54]

Kennedy's rhymes draw attention to themselves, of course, and their effect is pleasing to the ear; they combine with other sounds in the poem to create harmony. Repetition in both poems creates a different effect, to the disadvantage of Bly's poem, one might say. Bly's opening stanza reads thus: "watchman," "shed," "watch," "shed," "night," "night." Kennedy's first stanza emphasizes very different sounds: "vineyard," "sheltered," "arbors," "Lord," "sheltered," "night, O Lord," "night." The reader may prefer the harsher sounds in Bly's version over Kennedy's mellifluous choices, but it is reasonable to say that in a prayerful address to the Almighty, the more sonorous sounds of Kennedy's poems suit the poem's subject better and create a more appropriate atmosphere or mood than Bly's do. Kennedy continues this emphasis in the rhyming of *old* and *mold* in the next stanza and the use of *aroma* and *swollen* in the last stanza. Even when Bly uses the more sonorous sounds, as in *orchard, boughs,* and other words, their effect is undercut by the imagery, which emphasizes ideas of hardness and heaviness: "fig tree rooted in ground hard / as marble" and "odor pours out from your heavy bough.—" This second image, when placed beside Kennedy's equivalent, "From your globed boughs flows aroma," indicates how each poet's word choice creates very different effects, too, and meaning. Bly's odor pours; Kennedy's aroma flows. Bly elects to echo the vowel sound of *out* with *boughs* in the same line and he repeats the *r* and *o* sounds in *odor, pours,* and *your.* Kennedy, on the other hand, balances the heavier *b* sound in *globed* and *boughs* with the softer sound of four *o* sounds in *your, globed, flows,* and *aroma.* He further softens the line by repeating the consonant sounds in *From* and *aroma.* Bly's speaker views the Almighty with some fear, even resentment that the "field that never lets a spring go by" and that the ground in which the fig tree must grow is "hard / as marble." Kennedy's speaker sees the "ground hard as marble," too, but his tree

"Bursts with figs a hundredfold.—" Bly's tree carries "a hundred figs."

One would probably draw similar conclusions by comparing Bly's and Kennedy's translations of the von Hofmannsthal poem "Die Beiden."[55] Kennedy's version begins:

> Goblet in hand, she moved to him
> —Her chin and mouth poised as its rim—
> So light her stride, and she so skilled
> At fetching, not a drop she spilled.
>
> (ll. 1–4)

Bly's version of this same stanza reads:

> She carried the goblet in her hand—
> her chin and mouth looked somehow like its rim—
> and her walk was so light and firm
> not one drop rolled out.

By now it is clear that Bly prefers the more prosaic line—"She carried the goblet in her hand— / her chin and mouth looked somehow like its rim . . ."—at least in these two poems, perhaps associating it with a "freer, more open," and therefore more appealing, poetry. His diction, too, may have been chosen because it is "more modern"—compare his phrasing in the second and fourth lines to Kennedy's or his use of *walk* instead of Kennedy's *stride.* Although these choices create very different effects—and poems—the question at issue here is whether Bly's is poetry and Kennedy's is not, or whether Bly's is better than Kennedy's because Bly's is "more modern," and more suited to the American spirit and eschews "traditional" elements.

Only one who can read both German and English would know which version, Bly's or Kennedy's, is the more faithful translation, but if one considers the poems as original creations, other considerations are more appropriate in responding to it. Whether one prefers the harsher and more negative effects of Bly's poem to Kennedy's more deferential and sonorous version depends on taste, religious faith, and literary bias. Those who cannot abide "traditional" rhyme and meter in a poem will reject Kennedy's outright, but no reasonable person can deny that both poets use sound, rhythm, repetition, and other poetic devices to create their poems, and no objective person can deny that Kennedy's version is every bit as expressive, artful, and effective as Bly's. In this pairing of styles and traditions (leaving skill out of consideration), Kennedy's version does not stand out as old-fashioned, outmoded, unmodern, or otherwise anachronistic. Nor does Bly's version give one the impression that it is freer, looser, less restricted by the "chains" of tradition than Kennedy's. It would also be difficult to persuade an objective person that Kennedy's version is closer to the poetric tradition of England than Bly's or that Bly's is closer to the "American experience." Breath and pulse or the tap-tap of meter? Which measure is appropriate in judging the effects of either version? Kennedy's position regarding these issues is that both versions are acceptable and should be judged as poetry, irrespective of school or literary bias. To dismiss either because it is not of one's "school" is to lose access to some very good poetry.

When he looks at the mountain of poetry produced nowadays, Kennedy sees more than a loss of faith in traditional forms. He sees a generation of young poets who are ill prepared and misdirected. Kennedy addresses this important issue in several major essays. Currently, he says, poets lack readers, yet there is a superabundance of poets—3,536 listed in the 1980–81 *Directory of Poets and Writers, Inc.* The poet inflation "renders it impossible for us to know enough of the finest poetry alive." He thinks the glut is due to "dominance of immense, open and all-consuming form: that of the daily *Notebooks* or poem-diaries of Robert Lowell, the plotless *Gunslinger* of Ed Dorn, the *Cantos* that Ezra Pound didn't know how to terminate." Most poets today "prefer the poem that meanders and just peters out."[56] The poetry that "clutters our little magazines" seems "composed by a word processor smothered in mothballs . . . lacking in music and grace . . . passion and intelligence." This "superabundance" of poetry is perhaps the result of people turning off their TVs and declaring their individuality, made easy by "the cheapness and convenience of offset printing."[57] One cannot read, as one could in the 1940s, "all the poetry, both good and bad, published in English in the previous decade," and "Not knowing the finest work of our peers is to risk doing what isn't worth doing. When criticism gives up in despair, then the poet loses a sense of reality and of community." Delmore Schwartz's idea appeals to Kennedy: "write as much as possible and publish as little as you can."[58] Then, only the better poetry would be published.

Turning to some fundamentals of poetry writing, Kennedy believes a poet needs to begin by knowing how to use the English language, and then needs to acquire breadth of experience and quality of observation, keenly observing with even a narrow focus, like Emily Dickinson. College courses in poetry writing can benefit if the teacher has "innate ability, devotion to craft, and the strength to endure a professional training that never ends." Such poetry writing classes can help students to understand poetry and can enable them "to wield words with greater skill and keener sensitivity when they write term papers and job applications." These classes can also bring together "an inspired teaching poet and an inspired student poet" and can, "in a relatively small way," strengthen "the flickering light of civilization." The right textbook and teacher can also help. Although textbooks cannot teach one how to write poetry well, for it cannot be taught, they can offer good advice, such as reading good poetry, especially the great poems of the past, in order to know with whom one is competing. Good poets compete with the best of their age and of every age, Kennedy asserts. One should also write poetry with an eye "to the world at large" and its "varied knowledge" in order to shift focus beyond the self.[59]

In a half-serious essay, he counsels those who "fiercely crave" to be published to increase their chances by following the fashions. To do so, poets should follow these rules: they should center their poetry on their experiences, families, everyday concerns, or a popular affliction. They should write in the first person, present tense, for some editors think the present tense lends immediacy to poetry. They should yoke together disparate things and include "a dash of realism, preferably straight out of the current news." They should give their poems snappy titles to catch the editor's eye. They should never write in traditional forms, which will slow their production and reveal their lack of skill. And they should seek less-competitive markets, such as "a monthly for highway superintendents and directors of departments of public works."

Kennedy injects a sobering note, however, advising would-be poets that it is better to resist the urge to publish and to let their talent grow, and further stating that it is better to think about writing good poetry than to rush into publication. Literary history is full of great poets "who garnered no fame or praise or significance in their lifetimes." Those who want to grow in depth and skill should remain aloof to publication and should read poetry. As Keats avowed he would do, "write for the mere yearning and fondness for the beautiful." The only sure reward is "the joy of making a poem."[60]

Despite the surge in the production of poetry, the audience for poetry has diminished, Kennedy believes, addressing this subject in one of his most serious essays.[61] In the early part of this century, schoolchildren were made to memorize poetry, but since 1929 a "noticeable erosion of mass interest in poetry has surely taken place." Popular magazines that published some poetry have vanished, and radio and newspaper outlets have dried up: "Today, the habit of reading any serious works for pleasure has virtually disappeared even among the educated." For this "massive indifference and illiteracy," Kennedy blames television, movies, the VCR, less leisure, longer working hours, and a "national decline in reading ability. In an era of rapid communication (and even more rapid writing), a general decline in the importance of well-placed words" has occurred.

Kennedy also sees a possible correlation "between the rise of free verse in the 1920s and the erosion of a popular audience." The only popular off-campus poetry today, cowboy poetry, is dominated by rhyme. Pop songs continue to rhyme, and rhyme and meter are always popular with children. Optimists seem to believe that an audience might be created for poetry if poetry were mixed with popular entertainment venues, such as concerts and lecture halls. Radio, too, offers possibilities—Kennedy himself has had some of his work aired on public radio. Some find audiences on college campuses, too, and possibilities exist in "a revival of drama and narrative . . . in poetry of more broadly appealing content that takes in a wider experience."[62] Kennedy's experience in poetry reading for thirty years makes him pessimistic, however. Poems over the radio are listened to like commercials. Even academics not in English "are too busy to read current poetry. . . ."[63] Kennedy believes the only audience for poetry will be "an audience of the poet's own peers." In two-year colleges, the study of poetry has been replaced by film courses. We need more teachers committed to poetry of the past and "more challenging textbooks." Reading to children offers the hope of building an audience of future poetry readers—"In the elementary grades, poetry writing has taken off." Still, Kennedy does not "expect literary poetry to regain any vast popular following," as long as TV and VCRs remain: "Poetry in America will continue to be mainly a closet art, produced and consumed by a happy few." If nothing else, one might take heart in what W. H. Auden has said: the reading public consumes "even the greatest fiction as if it were a can of soup." Thank goodness, though, one cannot ingest poetry that way: "it still must either be 'read,' that is to say, entered into by a personal encounter, or it must be left alone." Even though the audience be small, at least the poet knows his readers "have a personal relation to his work. And this is more than any best-selling novelist dare claim."[64]

The principal aim of any poet, Kennedy asserts again and again in his critical prose and reviews, is not so much to get published, to get one's name in print, and to be known as a poet, but to write good poetry. If one does write such poetry, the market will likely come to the poet. But even if it does not, one must not forget that principal goal, and to begin, the poet must prepare himself. Those who reject traditional forms have not mastered them well enough to feel free within them. One must also have something to say, must be passionate about saying it, and must love words. To write in rhyme is "to buy certain old-fangled and currently spat-upon assumptions: that it isn't evil to revise, that poetic excellence cannot be instant and effortless."[65] Novice poets who try rhyme "get discouraged when they find they can't readily say what they want to, give it up in disgust and opt for the great untrammeled freedom of free verse . . . ," but rhyme is beneficial also because it prevents you from "uttering all those bright, significant ideas that clutter the top of your head."[66] Kennedy has no quarrel with a poet "who seriously practices the difficult craft of honest open verse." But a poet has to love words, "in a physical sense—has to love the weight and heft and motions of them."[67] He admires poets who handle words with the "intent joy of a little kid playing with blocks." So many poets today, he continues, tell us intimate details about themselves and think us boors if we do not listen respectfully, yet we have a right to stomp on the "unwanted gift" just as we have a right to discard junk mail.[68]

The future of poetry depends on the continuance of the poetic tradition. As Kennedy told John Ciardi in an interview in 1972, the "made" poem finds itself in an exercise of the poet's total ability. What, he asks rhetorically, "can be more socially useful than an example of man at his best exercise of himself?" The made poem implies permanence. The formal poets "are the only ones to affirm some hope of the future."[69] Gary Snyder sees continuity in Oriental patterns of thought and "a sort of primitivistic closeness to nature." Some believe that to write a sonnet is to be "reactionary and in favor of the war in Vietnam," but those who write in traditional forms are not fixated on some kind of golden age of poetry in the past. On the contrary, poets writing in traditional forms affirm a continuity, begun long ago and continuing into the future. Writing good poetry generally holds promise for us all, whether it be in traditional or open forms. Nearly twenty years later, Kennedy has not lost his faith in the value of continuing to write good poetry. Asked why he keeps writing, he replied, "Well, to sustain the rest of civilization."[70]

Chapter 5
X. J. Kennedy and Light Verse

BETWEEN X. J. KENNEDY'S POETRY FOR CHILDREN AND HIS ADULT POETRY stands a group of light verse poems that, along with his poems for children, show his deep and abiding commitment to playfulness, high and low humor, and, above all, wit. Despite the unavoidable classifications, Kennedy does not set neat or strict boundaries between the poems for children and adults. He is not completely convinced that they are necessarily separate. Speaking on this matter in 1986, he confessed: "I've never been able to tell the difference between so-called light verse and so-called poetry. . . . Some of the best of Yeats is both funny and moving. A lot of the verse I've written has been put down for being nothing but light verse, and dismissed for that reason. But I don't buy it; I don't see why a good poem can't be funny."[1] Speaking again on this subject in a 1976 interview, Kennedy explained even more clearly the relation of light to serious poetry: "The late Randall Jarrell once made some penetrating remarks about how difficult it is to distinguish between so-called light verse and so-called heavy or serious poetry. I believe Jarrell was talking about those Oscar Williams poetry anthologies which always had a section called 'light verse.' Jarrell pointed out how heart-breaking some of the poems in the light verse section were. I'm intrigued by poems like that, where it's impossible to draw the line between humor and seriousness."[2] As if to make his point (and to follow Oscar Williams's lead), Kennedy includes some light verse in most of his major collections. In *Nude Descending a Staircase* and *Cross Ties,* he gives these poems a separate section, calling them "Songs" (or "Ballads"), "Light Verse," and "Epigrams and Epitaphs." He also hazards a definition of this kind of poetry:

> [Light verse] can be written about any matters, whether "high" or "low," and there is no language that a poet cannot make a poem out of. . . . Nor is light verse to be distinguished from poetry by its tone. . . . No, what separates light verse from poetry is something

> else—a certain degree of emotional intensity. For while poetry generally speaks with the deep voice of feeling, light verse tends to twitter and chirp. [Light verse] is a game of little consequence, and if in its midst a strong emotion should intrude, then its game is spoiled, like a Maypole dance disrupted by an outbreak of concupiscence among the dancers. As in the elderly man's damnation of the entire human race, a piece of light verse may profess strong feelings. Yet all the while it is affirming them, its jingly form and its verbal playfulness set up an ironic betrayal of that affirmation.[3]

In his review a year later of William Harmon's collection of American light-verse poems, Kennedy repeats the idea that light verse must remain free of too much emotional intensity, "things too subtle and demanding." He goes on to distinguish American light verse from the British version: "American light verse is more vulgar, more obstreperous," and the American light versifier is "an irreverent scoffer." Dialect and language also distinguish American light verse, and all light verse can include "poems that are bad unintentionally."[4] Nothing about Kennedy's light verse is ever unintentional, but he does offer many examples throughout his career of poems that are not emotionally intense or too subtle or demanding, and are playful and irreverent. They are poems in which he takes pleasure in deflating, debunking, and destroying pomposity, and in which he delights in rollicking vulgarity, mingling high spirits and low characters. We are talking here mainly of those poems of sustained hilarity and obvious playful mockery, whose language and subjects disqualify them as fit verse for children, but in some poems Kennedy mingles the serious and the light to the heightening of each. Reviewer Henry Taylor noted this quality in Kennedy's poetry, saying that "Kennedy's prodigious technical gifts often lead him into light verse," and Taylor instanced "Reading Trip," in which "Kennedy can make successful shifts of tone by increasing or decreasing his dependence on light-verse techniques," the playfulness being "part of a serious vision."[5]

Kennedy's interest in witty playfulness leads in two directions, into poetry for an audience of children and further into the serious poems. The more one reads these latter poems, the more one sees that play is basic to both kinds. They are complementary expressions of a single vision. When the playful elements of Kennedy's poetry are brought together in one poem, for example in "Flagellant's Song," one experiences the child's delight in rhythmic nonsense—which somehow makes divine sense—behind, or inside, a subject too serious for the child: "When I was young / And jackass-hung. . . ." The overtones of the nursery rhyme that such lines suggest modifies the experience of the poem significantly, however, giving the portrait a quality that both mocks and delights. Kennedy yokes two very different worlds together, and the estrangement enhances the wit and underscores the meaning. By the end of "Flagellant's Song" the severity of the flagellant's efforts, and the gravity and intensity of his derangement, is shaped into an image that is so witty and so keenly felt that one almost shudders:

> I dreamed a sight
> Of Sade last night,
> Alive like you and me.
> *Your grace,* said I,
> *How did you die?*
> *By little bits,* said he.

The poem works all the better because the character's mental condition, reflected in the short, choppy lines, is responsible for the discordance between light verse and dark subject matter—and its surprising concordance. Kennedy has said that poems of identical form can achieve very different effects with very different subject matter.[6] Here, the form could contain a child's nursery rhyme or an adult poem that makes light of a serious subject. Attention is sharply focused on the character and how he reveals himself in dramatic monologue, talking almost like a child, exposing a condition that the poem suggests we all share ("Alive like you and me").

To make his point unmistakable, Kennedy included children's verse in two of his most important collections, *Nude Descending a Staircase* and *Cross Ties,* boldly labeling them "For Children If They'll Take Them" and "Intermission: For Children," respectively.

The two children's poems in *Nude Descending a Staircase* illustrate Kennedy's skill in writing verse for children that allows free reign to his playful spirit and taste for wordplay. Later, Kennedy will devote himself to writing books specifically for children, but the inclusion of these poems here demonstrates that he does not see much difference between the adult and children realm when it comes to writing poetry. When he is at his most serious, his playful spirit is always near, and when he is at his most playful, he is never far from the serious. The eighteen lines of "The Man" run down the page in lengths of one to three words, giving the appearance of open form, and play heavily on these sounds: "The man" "With the tan," "Hands," "Who stands. . . ."

The second poem, "King Tut," makes more of sound and rhyme than "The Man" and is more complexly structured. Three of the four stanzas begin with only the name "King Tut," and the first line of the third stanza ends with the name as well. The verse develops a nonsense situation in which King Tut is seen crossing the Nile "On steppingstones / of crocodile" and being reprimanded by his mother, "*You'll get wet feet.*" This mother-son conflict is resolved in the third stanza with a pun—"And now King Tut / Tight as a mit / Keeps his big fat Mummy shut"—and the whole poem closes on another pun: "King Tut, / Tut, tut." As these two poems illustrate, Kennedy's poetics include a considerable interest in the coincidence of sound and sense, in the fact that the sounds of words can, in certain combinations and contexts, surprise, please (especially children), and create both humor and meaning. Nonsense is not entirely or merely nonsensical, he seems to be saying, echoing the view expressed by Emily Dickinson: "Much Madness is divinest Sense— / To a discerning Eye."

The comic side of Kennedy's wit is certainly not of secondary importance to everything he says and does. It informs and, as Laurence Sterne and other writers of serious play have shown, serves as a basis of and catalyst to the serious elements it accompanies. Kennedy's playful wit asserts a serious perspective and, in doing so, arrests the attention and focuses it on the inextricable relation of the two. As in "Flagellant's Song," the interplay develops startling and disconcerting power, but in the more comic poems, the art is no less effective and no less important to the poem's dual intent: to say something serious and have fun doing so. "Uncle Ool's Complaint Against the Ill-Paid Life of Verse" demonstrates this point admirably. Kennedy uses nursery-rhyme rhythms to portray a sot bemoaning the ill-treatment of bards throughout the ages:

> When Mother Church
> Preened on her perch
> Above the Middle Ages,
> No hunch-backed serf
> That dredged his turf
> Dared strike for living wages.
>
> (ll. 13–18)

Some of the poem's rhymes, too, are playful—*panties/Bacchantes*—and the language befits the playful theme. All these structural features emphasize a jaunty regularity that highlights the poem's serious subject. When Bard Orpheus is "Torn limb from limb," Uncle Ool manages to blaspheme and to deliver a hilarious pun in the same line, "By Christ, it was disarming!"

The poem is too artful and complex to be simply an offhanded bit of playfulness. It demonstrates the nature of Kennedy's light verse, how he exploits the conventions of traditional structures to create a moment of high comedy and low humor. "Uncle Ool's Complaint" reads like a Rabelaisian satire, but the coarse language and subject matter are not merely Kennedy's way of having fun by debasing the art of poetry writing and the church. The barroom language and drunken outrage of Uncle Ool, whose very name befits his fallen condition, underscore the poem's point: rhymesters throughout history have been neglected, even persecuted: "Today some starve / Behind iron bars, / Rage ravening their hearts" (ll. 25–27). This is not merely making fun; this outcry is heartfelt, and as we smile at Ool drooling in his beer, we feel some of his anguish. Kennedy would argue that without the devices associated with light verse, such effects would not be possible. The poet needs rhyme to create off-rhymes and needs meter to create Ool's bouncy lines. Light verse in Kennedy's hands is often a vehicle for mockery, and one of Kennedy's favorite targets in both his serious poetry and light verse is the Catholic Church, its members and its authority. The first poem in *Nude Descending a Staircase* takes a serious look at church authority, but Kennedy seems to have grown easier in his relations with this subject so that by 1970, he could publish *Bulsh,* a comical portrait of a corrupt Catholic prelate.[7] The poem's emphasis falls on Bulsh's corrupt nature, on the ribald humor and lewd goings-on. Like "Ool," the poem treats its subject with Rabelaisian humor and uses the couplet's brevity to sharpen the wit, its balance to create ironic counterpoint, and its rhyme to drive the point home humorously. What would be more appropriate to such a subject as the concupiscent Bulsh than to rhyme *Peter* with *sweeter, ass* with *gas,* or *boys* with *ploys*? Or to subvert the sublime by describing one of Bulsh's women as a "Hooker, her festered lips sublime with ooze"? These conventional light-verse techniques enable Kennedy to heighten the discrepancy between the ideal and the reality of Bulsh's world.

Much of Kennedy's light verse may be found in poems written to be sung to a popular tune. "In a Prominent Bar in Secaucus

One Day," one of his most popular poems, may be sung "To the tune of 'The Old Orange Flute' / or the tune of 'Sweet Betsy from Pike,'" Kennedy says, and "Sentimentalist's Song, or, Answers for Everything" is set to the tune of "Deutschland über Alles" (he himself is fond of singing "Song to the Tune of 'Somebody Stole My Gal'").[8]

In most of his light verse, Kennedy remains true to his conviction that what separates light from serious poetry is its "jingly form and its verbal playfulness." A bouncing meter also sets much of his light verse apart—"We merged our fleshes, I and she, / In mutual indignity" may be typical. He sometimes treats a subject of some consequence, however, as we have seen in his gloomy view of the poet's life in "Dancing with the Poets at Piggy's" and in "Great Chain of Being," which traces the fall of humankind. Kennedy enjoys portraying humans dislodged and disillusioned, displaying them in raucous surroundings as fools or fallen angels, then putting them into a song. Light verse affords Kennedy a chance to mock the august forces that seem to rule the universe and to sympathize with those ill-treated by that universe. Kennedy means that his light verse should be fun to read, and in that respect he is ever true. The verbal playfulness and mocking tone affirm their lightness. If they do not completely reassure, as they do in the children's poetry, that the poet is just being silly and having fun, they do remind us that nothing, not the futility of human effort, not human folly, not even death itself, prevents us from having a rollicking good time.

Chapter 6

X. J. Kennedy's Literature for Children

WHEN X. J. KENNEDY BEGAN VISITING GRADE SCHOOLS TO READ HIS POETRY for children, he quickly discovered that "Kids are a wonderful audience—they don't care about trends. They don't care if you're an old curmudgeon who writes in old-fashioned meter and rime. They rather like it, in fact, if the poem's got a nice bouncy beat."[1] He also learned that he liked writing such poetry and was very good at it. His poetry for children is written with obvious pleasure, skill, sensitivity, and respect for and appreciation of the child's world, outlook, and sensibility. Although for the child such literature needs no further justification, some adults need to be convinced that writing such literature is a worthy task, even for a serious poet such as Kennedy, and some need to be convinced that, though worthwhile, it is essentially harmless; indeed it may even be beneficial. Kennedy's poem "Mother's Nerves" was deemed "subversive of adult authority" by one school board, and the book in which it was printed was banned from school libraries. The poem does seem harmless enough, but board members thought otherwise:

> My mother said, "If just once more
> I hear you slam that old screen door,
> I'll tear out my hair! I'll dive in the stove!"
> So I gave it a bang and in she dove.

As Kennedy once explained, nonsense verse does have its salutary effects. For one, it "challenges . . . old reality."[2] Elsewhere he says that "poetry makes kids more aware of language and wakes them up to the real world . . . reminds them that they have senses besides sight, and that the world is full of wonderful things."[3] By giving children another view of the world in an entertaining way, nonsense literature reassures them that their feelings and thoughts about the world are not forbidden and that it is all right to have such thoughts and feelings. Reviewing the verse of Myra

Cohn Livingston in 1974, Kennedy agreed with her that "Learning to write poems 'can help our children to stay human,' nothing less," and he still encourages teachers to prod "the kids into trusting the feelings that come to them, into beholding with unmediated eyes."[4] Such sentiments certainly apply to Kennedy's serious poetry as well. As one reviewer noted, speaking of the poems in *Dark Horses,* "Written in sing-song, nursery-rhyme iambics, his best poems prove that irony need not be frivolous."[5]

Bringing to his children's verse a belief that poetry should make the reader or listener better off for the exposure to poetry, Kennedy believes that it is a mistake to offer poetry to children "like a barber bestowing a lollipop for good behavior." It is the same conviction that he brings to his adult poetry. For all their inexperience, children are keen detectors of condescension and insincerity, more so even than most adults. It is reasonable, Kennedy asserts, "to ask a child of third-grade maturity (or more) to examine a poem closely, think about it, and even analyze it." Such activity enables them to enjoy poetry "more deeply and more perceptively."[6]

By 1964 he was already admiring the children's verse of other poets and had views on its form and function:

> What ought a good children's book to be? We are hardly likely to agree on an ideal, though I'd think *The Wind in the Willows* as close as we might come to any. What a children's book surely ought *not* be, is a sort of poetic lollipop handed down with a condescending this-is-for-you-my-little-man and a knowing wink toward the adult onlookers . . . we might do well to reconsider the possibilities of a poetry immediately comprehensible and engaging. . . . Basically, I guess, a poem for a child must be as good as a poem for anybody else. A poet should be able to put it into his collected opera without blushing. Though written in a narrower vocabulary, it shouldn't be restricted in its honesty, in its confrontation of life. A children's poem need not prettify the world, nor make it out to be more innocent than children know it is.[7]

Kennedy warns that writing for children is, for all its playfulness, a demanding and complex endeavor.[8] It is more than making jingles, portraying goofy creatures, or poking fun at what adults call logic. Children must not feel threatened or humiliated by the horrors and chaos depicted in nonsense verse. They need of course to be entertained, and what entertains them is turning the world topsy-turvy, taking ordinary logic to silly extremes, and injecting a large dose of exaggerated wordplay, hopping rhythms, funny rhymes, and, above all, surprising turns in logic or situations. Children like to see common situations thrown into chaos, but they must be made to feel unthreatened by it all. Kennedy believes that "the medium is the message," for it prevents the child from taking the world of nonsense seriously. Illustrations that accompany the verse can help the child's imagination not only by giving visual reality to the verse and entertaining with their own sort of exaggerations, but by reassuring children that they are in the world of the unreal and that the play is harmless. Maturity, experience, knowledge and understanding of the world and human nature—certainly these factors distinguish adult from children's poetry, and they allow a poet to explore areas and address issues and subjects beyond the scope of children, but the two kinds of poetry do share common ground. Adults enjoy playful seriousness, and children enjoy serious play. Kennedy has mastered ways to speak to children and adults by knowing when to be either playful or serious, how, and how much.[9] In his view, successful literature for children depends on a few important features: the laws of nature and ordinary logic should be broken or suspended and replaced by the writer's own laws; and there should be an abundance of playful rhythms and sounds and much wordplay, including made-up words and puns. All of these features may be found in serious poetry, in different degrees and for different purposes.

Kennedy explains that the form of the work can itself provide children with the reassurance they need as they witness the ordinary world, or ordinary logic, come apart at the seams. The limerick, for example, or any short form that plays with rhythms, sound, and sense provides constant reminders that everything is to be taken in jest. Of children's verse generally, he says that the "hippitty-hop rhythm and tinkly rhymes . . . may help tell the child, 'This is only kidding. . . .'"[10]

The skill with which Kennedy writes this kind of literature is evident in the popularity of his books for children and young adults, which include not only books of nonsense verse and two novels but collections of verse by other writers—which demonstrate that he is not the only "serious" poet to write for children. His first collection of children's verse, *One Winter Night in August and Other Nonsense Jingles* (1975), is marked by those features that appear in most of his nonsense verse and in much of his serious poetry. The poems are mostly short, under sixteen lines, and all are rhymed, but rhymed in a flamboyant way so as to draw attention to this aspect of the poem—rhyme becomes a highlighted part of the fun. When they are used skillfully, rhyme and rhythm can be inherently funny, creating the kind of effect children's verse requires. Inanimate everyday objects of the child's world come to life and act in humorous, nonsensical ways, turning order into chaos. Nonsense occurs for its own silly sake; in one poem, for example, the child's logic asks a perfectly reasonable question of the dinosaur: why does the mother dinosaur not scramble her eggs when she sits on them?

The world is viewed as if through the child's eyes; the child's imagination gives it shape, or seems to, as the poems focus on bizarre characters and strange happenings. A dinosaur ambles along, a yellow telephone comes alive, turkey bones go hobbling, a kangaroo throws a pie, and Caleb Snyder turns into a spider. Ordinary situations are scrambled: a teacher makes her pupils talk backward—one is reminded of Professor Backwards, the subject of one of Kennedy's "serious" poems; an engineer builds a robot rabbit, and a baby cleans the rugs by eating them. Some of the verse is the occasion simply of making words play: "Look out, here comes Lucky Sukey / Sucking on her mucky-looking cookie." The poems capture the logic of dreams and the mystery of the world as the child might see it. What the child does not understand in that world is given voice and a nonsense answer. Childish fears are given shape in a manner that makes the child laugh and feel unthreatened. The verse brings into the open the darker aspects of a child's mental world, purging the ghosts, taming them with the humorous words and rhythms, and chasing them away in the process. Though they differ in obvious ways, many of Kennedy's serious poems aim to accomplish similar effects.

In some of his poems, Kennedy puts aside pure nonsense to show how the child's perspective differs from the adult's. Though children can be wildly "illogical" or innocent about what is and is not important, Kennedy has great respect for the child's understanding, as he demonstrates in "The Animals You Eat," which develops the relation of animal slaughter to human consumption, opening and closing with poignant sympathy for the child who cannot understand why adults kill animals:

> The animals you eat
> Leave footprints in your eyes.
> You stare, four-year-old pools
> Troubled. "They don't have souls,"
> I tell you, in defeat.

. . . .
The animals you eat
Start turning to your eyes.

The "you" addressed here is a four-year-old child, although the pronoun includes the reader as well. The second stanza develops a rhetorical question that appeals to and involves those beyond the narrow locus of this parent's relationship to this child, seeing the "Cuddlable pigs" from the child's viewpoint and linking the real pig to Peter Rabbit, saying that the two are associated "In that land of pure mind," the child's and that universal mind, where the fictional rabbit is not "stewed." The contrast and conflict in the speaker's mind between the child's world and that of the adult are expressed in the comparison of adults to "Foxy Loxy," a character in children's literature that uses deception to kill his victims. The final stanza entwines the fate of slaughtered animals with that of the human who eats them. The speaker sees the child as "Gravely wise," having to face "night" on his own. The language here suggests the fate humans themselves face: death and the dark unknown. The adult realizes that his world and that of the child are separated by the slaughter of animals, and the child sees through his feeble attempt to justify the practice. The poem's grim message, hinted at by the final image, is that the adult slaughters the child's purity, feeds on childhood, and consumes the child's innocence.

Kennedy's first book of children's verse was so successful that he published a second one, *The Phantom Ice Cream Man: More Nonsense Verse* (1979), which offers what the book's blurb describes as "wonderful, rollicking fun—absurd and free-wheeling," all of it in "tuneful rhymes" and "galloping rhythms." Nearly all the poems are under twenty lines, and they evoke surprise and humor with a play on word meanings and sound, a clever twist on an old theme, or simply nonsense. The subjects include birds and beasts, nonsensical notions—such as brushing one's teeth with ocean sand and having a mouthful of fish and clams—magical menaces, and family members. The menaces include the giant of Jack the Giant fame, who has updated himself by putting aside his "fee-fi-fo-fumming" and trading Englishmen's ground bones for peanut butter. When a space capsule lands on one of Neptune's moons, the locals see the visitors as "funny bugs." Occasionally, too, the reader is rewarded by arresting imagery: when the moon fell and broke apart, "Stars scattered like spilled jellybeans." In some of the verse, the publisher says, Kennedy "leads children into the more haunting regions of poetry." These haunting regions are conjured up in the book's final section, "Cheerful Spirits," in which we find such figures as a haunted oven, attic ghosts, and the title's Phantom Ice Cream Man, who entices the child with frozen treats that will turn the child into a phantom, and he will be made captive in a castle in another world guarded by "hounds with fangs that freeze." The child can only hide under his warm covers.

Kennedy's third book for children, *Did Adam Name the Vinegarroon?* consists of alphabetically arranged portraits of beasts, one for each letter of the alphabet. Four of the creatures are fabulous, three are extinct, and the rest are actual. The vinegarroon itself is a scorpion that emits the smell of pickles. Kennedy retains the verse forms of his other nonsense verse: all the poems are under sixteen lines, and nearly all of them are written in rhymed quatrains. Black-and-white drawings emphasize the beasts' outsized features, just as the verse features a humorous and bizarre quality. The Kraken, for example, is "One big fat soggy sponge below, / Huge bulging eyes above," and the Quetzal has a delicate taste and would be offended if you asked, "'Polly, want a pretzel?'" The book demonstrates Kennedy's aptitude for elevating what otherwise would be simply playful observations and humorous insights. It also shows his willingness to experiment with themes and subjects adroitly, a quality that keeps him from simply repeating past successes and keeps his poetry skills fresh. A similar play of imagination pervades his adult poetry, as well, in those poems in which form varies with subject and subject varies with form.

Kennedy has published, with Dorothy M. Kennedy as coeditor, two anthologies of verse for children. The first one appeared in 1982: *Knock at a Star: A Child's Introduction to Poetry,* revised in 1999. Though it contains none of Kennedy's verse for children, this book is nevertheless important in understanding Kennedy's own verse, for it says something about children making verse and, therefore, about making verse for children. It is as much about children's (and indirectly adult) poetry as it is a collection of poems that illustrate the principles of writing verse. In these poems the emphasis is on the senses, concrete experience, the everyday world, personal feelings, and the free play of imagination.

The poems in *Knock at a Star* were selected in part to demonstrate that poetry is close to the child's own world and experience, whether it be putting on stockings, waking up, going to sleep, having dreams, or simply looking at the sky. Language is made to be a part of the fun, creating pleasing rhythms, funny pictures, and silly sounds. Some of the poems show surprising likenesses by bringing unlikely things together in figurative language: "daisy" and "day's eye," for example. Fun can be made out of just sounds, with little sense, and words can also make music—some of the songs are even accompanied by musical notations. Sight poems show that words can both draw shapes in the mind and be twisted into shapes on the page. The book has children make up their own verse, play with images and sounds, or simply express their thoughts and feelings in words. The book's message is that poetry is in the daily lives of children, of everyone, in surprising ways; to illustrate the point, the Kennedys include some found poems.

Kennedy's second anthology, *Talking Like the Rain*, subtitled *A Read-to-Me Book of Poems*, appeared ten years after the first one, in 1992.[11] The most striking visual feature of the volume, which contains nearly a hundred twenty-five poems in just over eighty pages, is the large number of watercolor drawings by Jane Dyer that illustrates the poetry. Though the poems are meant to be read aloud, the illustrations are meant to be seen and admired, for they are artful, realistic, and attractive. The pictures and text together create a very pleasing visual and auditory experience. The collection is noteworthy also for the array of known and unknown poets represented by many verses probably already familiar to children and adults alike. The adult reader will recognize Ogden Nash, Wallace Stevens, and Emily Dickinson, among others famous poets. The Kennedys show that even "serious" poets are sometimes not too serious for young adults and, more important, that an element of play can be found in many adult poems.

In 1984 Kennedy went solo again and published his first novel *The Owlstone Crown*. Meant for children, it contains many of the qualities of the poetry for children: concrete observation, vivid imagery, inventiveness, bizarre situations, talking animals, villains, and high adventure. The story is filled with magic, charm, and menace. A pair of twins, Timothy and Verity Tibb, work on a farm run by their cruel adoptive parents. Learning that their grandparents are held captive in Other Earth, the twins persuade Lewis O. Ladybug, a friendly insect, to help them rescue their grandparents. To get there, they step on the reflection of the full moon in a stream, which is a magical portal leading to Other Earth, a land once ruled by wise old men and women called the Elders. On the other side they learn that a rascal named Raoul

Owlstone has declared himself dictator, covered the life-giving Moonflower with a dome, imprisoned all the animals, and enslaved all the people. His factory, which makes muck bombs, is blotting out the sun and killing all vegetation. Raoul's consort, Baroness Ratisha von Bad Radisch, wears a monocle that emits a red, hypnotizing light that she uses to subdue her enemies.

On their mission to rescue their grandparents and release Other Earth from the evil spell, the twins meet a variety of sharply drawn creations. Cressida Pond is a water woman whose voice sounds like a faraway tinkling. A prophet, Shelley Snail, joins the twins, and mud-slinging owls add excitement as well. Though the twins sometimes face danger—they barely escape when a cave collapses, and at another point they are separated and Tim is sent to slave in a mine—Kennedy surrounds them with plenty of light humor, entertaining characters, and opportunities to save all creatures, both small and large. The twins are driven by good will and the desire to preserve nature and to give all creatures the opportunity to live free. The villains are those who seek their own interests at the expense of the environment, animals, and humans.

Kennedy's second novel, *The Eagle as Wide as the World* (1997), continues the exploits of Timothy and Verity Tibb in the land of the Moonflower. As in *Owlstone*, the plot is replete with lively action, surprising twists, colorful and inventive descriptions, and imaginative characters and situations. At the start, the evil queen wants exclusive rights to the Moonflower nectar only for her colony. Since all the insects in Moonflower live off this nectar, her demand is for them a virtual death sentence. At the end, the queen is overthrown and chastened. She is even invited to remain in the Land of the Moonflower and live in harmony with everyone. The accent in *The Owlstone Crown* is on murk and muck, dungeons and darkness, symbolized by the mechanical owls and Owlstone Hall. *The Eagle of Wide as the World*, on the other hand, spreads its wings in harmony, sunlight, and freedom. The moral of both novels is that harmony and prosperity are achieved when people get along with one another and respect nature.

With *The Forgetful Wishing Well: Poems for Young People* (1985), Kennedy returned to writing children's verse. Several of the poems deal with assorted creatures and humans, wonders, and the seasons of the year; other poems offer a view of the world and its experiences that a child of mature years would have, discussing growing pains, family matters, and the city. The tone is less playful than one finds in Kennedy's first book for children. The adult's viewpoint is evident, though in many poems the speaker is still a child, and the emphasis is on observation and reaction to the world as adults might see it. The wonders of the world are those of an older child pausing to observe what the adult normally overlooks, such as the ant, the wind, the mole, and so on. It is as if Kennedy is reminding readers, old and young alike, that the world is made up of small events, small things, passing sights, and flitting experience. To appreciate that world, one must see it, watch it, and try to understand it.

In *Brats*, published a year later, Kennedy shifts focus from the world of nature to the world of the imp, whose mischief sometimes is the brat's own undoing. Lars, for example, showing off on his motorbike, topples over the handlebars. Greedy Greg gets his comeuppance by gobbling all the Easter eggs, not realizing they are dyed hand-grenades—"BOOOOM!" The book's jacket says that these "42 brief verses celebrate or denigrate the actions of mischievous children." Though playfulness predominates, some of the poems make a serious point—one should not ride a motorcycle with no hands, for example. What keeps them from being moralistic or preachy, aside from the exaggerations, rhythms, and wordplay, is that the events themselves are exaggerated, and nonsensical; a little girl stows away in a spaceship; foolhardy Sam "leaps inside a mammoth clam"; and so on. The "message" is so absurd and the caveat so unnecessary that part of the book's humor is generated by the nonsensical warning itself.

Portraits of impish children and their mischief proved popular, and Kennedy included several of them in *Cross Ties* and returned to this theme in two other books, *Fresh Brats* in 1990 and *Drat These Brats* in 1993, in which he portrays children in a variety of predicaments and doing much mischief. Steffan puts a dead mouse in a loaf of baked bread. Cass sets the school on fire with a magnifying glass—"Looks as if she'll never learn." Brent substitutes cement for his mother's mudpack and now she finds it "hard to crack a smile." Kennedy puts into language the what-ifness of the child's imagination and reveals a world in which children can be antic and, at times, cruel and destructive. The punishment, according to child logic, should fit the crime: overly curious Glenda in an everglade is eaten by a crocodile; incautious Desmond, offering Yellowstone bears part of his ice cream cone, is "now their favorite flavor"; Abner reaches down a shark's throat for his beach ball and is swallowed. *Drat These Brats* continues the zaniness of the previous volumes, though Kennedy varies the forms somewhat, retaining the couplet form. The dozens of surprising and funny antics in these volumes speak well of Kennedy's inventiveness and his ability to see the world through the eyes of children—even to be a child in his imagination. No less impressive is Kennedy's skill with rhyme, rhythm, tone, wordplay, descriptive detail, humor, and wit.

In 1989 Kennedy published *Ghastlies, Goops and Pincushions: Nonsense Verse,* playing again with bizarre and humorous situations and characters but becoming more inventive with form. Many of the poems are longer than eight lines, and the volume demonstrates Kennedy's skill with limericks—in fact, he has published a separate volume of them, *Uncle Switch: Loony Limericks.* In *Ghastlies* Kennedy returns to his fascination with the animal kingdom, often letting the jingle and jangle of sound carry an entire poem:

> The gnomes of Nome
> Are not at home . . .
> They live in a dome
> Of frozen foam.
>
> ("The Gnomes of Nome")

Sometimes his point is the pointlessness of, for example, orthography, rhyming *ravioli* with *sloli* (slowly), *spaghetti* with *Alretti* (already). However nonsensical the poem's premise is, though, the logic is evident; indeed, much of the humor derives from his treating extraordinary things with ordinary logic: a robot, for example, will need to oil his nose and replace his head when it burns out, as electrical devices do. The tone lends its own bit of humor, as these absurdities are delivered in a deadpan, matter-of-fact style. Implicit in the rhymes and rhythms is the idea that adult order can contain nonsense. In making the absurdity seem natural and unthreatening with deft wordplay, absurd humor, and fun-filled forms, Kennedy tames the wild, mysterious, sometimes frightening world of the child's and adult's imagination.

The seven sections of *The Kite That Braved Old Orchard Beach: Year-Round Poems for Young People* (1991) contain sixty-two poems that address the experiences of older children. The more complex stanzaic patterns reflect more mature themes and subjects, including a recurring sense of the passage of time. Someone remembers his first Thanksgiving, and someone else notes the passing of the seasons. In another poem the speaker realizes that every day is the earth's birthday. Although playfulness and absurdity abound, the nonsense is closer to the sense, even the wisdom that, for some people, comes with age: "Keep a hand on your dream," begins one poem, followed by two poems expressing the wistfulness of a youth remembering the wild dreams of his childhood. One youthful speaker even realizes that his father is not all bad, that many fathers "have their good sides."

Urban problems, the discomforts of travel, racial concerns, the kindness of a blind neighbor, gender bias, a lonely old Japanese woman getting through a morning—these are some of the subjects that reveal the world from an adolescent's point of view, sophisticated enough to express complex emotions in complex structures and imagery. The Japanese woman, for example, is described as sinking into her chair "As a fan might fold." Indeed, many of these poems have the voice and view of adult poems, but they retain an adolescent quality by addressing subjects close to the child's experience, associating a foghorn with a "frog-horn," for example, because it "mournfully croaks . . . ," walking a Saint Bernard when one is not very big, imagining a cricket wearing socks, reflecting on why canned tuna is can-shaped, eating a chocolate rabbit, or wishing for a school holiday and summertime.

Kennedy's inventiveness is again both entertaining and fruitful in *The Beasts of Bethlehem* (1992), which combines portraiture and religious devotion with colored illustrations. This collection of nineteen poems develops the folk legend that Christ's birth gave speech temporarily to all beasts. Each poem is devoted to a different animal, who speaks the poem's thought, and each thought is appropriate to the speaker. Always a part of Kennedy's light and serious poetry is discovering how many fresh delights and new meanings he can wrest from a form. *Uncle Switch: Loony Limericks* (1997) shows lighter fare, working with a form that is popular among children and adults alike. The premise of the book is indicated by the central character's name, Uncle Switch, who is so "turned-around" that he:

> milks the pup
> Walks the Jersey cow, sloshes a cup
> Full of hot exercise,
> Reads two fresh eggs, and fries
> All the morning news sunny side up.

In subsequent episodes he suffers the indignities and injuries visited upon both animate and inanimate objects by adults. He is played by a big violin, pecks seed while the Thanksgiving turkey dines, is hooked by a fillet of sole, is caught in a mousetrap, and is even used as a football on the gridiron. The moral of *Uncle Switch* does not dull the lustrous colors or diminish the humor; indeed, as in most of Kennedy's playful verse, the moral gives a gentle reminder with a cutting edge: "See, how would you like to be treated this way!" It is a moral that lies at the heart of all of his adult poetry.

To catch Kennedy's drift, one might consider a poem in *Dark Horses,* "The Arm," which combines the elements of the child's runaway imagination with the adult's inability to dismiss such "nonsense" entirely. Kennedy shows how adult fear may have its genesis in childhood experience. "The Arm" opens with a grammatically incomplete sentence: "A day like any natural summer day / Of hide-and-seek along the river shore." We come to realize that the sentence symbolizes what we are about to discover: a severed arm, as detached from the human body as the opening sentence is detached from what would make it grammatically complete. While the poem's narrator and a friend, "Snaker," are playing along a river, Snaker finds a baby's arm, shakes it in his friend's face "like some grim charm," and chases him with it. That night, the speaker is bedeviled by the arm, not knowing whether the arm was real or "only rubber wrenched loose from some doll / Who died and bit the trash. . . ." (ll. 14–15). Night after night he has visions of the arm: it taps at his windowpane, and he hears "Its cries squeezed shrill from trying to break through . . ." (l. 22). As he would in telling a child's horror story, Kennedy concludes the poem by assuming the voice of the severed arm: "*Why do you leave me out here in the rain? / It's dark and cold. Let me come sleep with you.*" The poem's imagery inspires the kind of spookiness that even the adult cannot shake off: "In nightmare even now, / Dribbling dark bottom-ooze, / Those fingers green with algae, infantile, / Reach out as though to fasten hold on me. . . ." (ll. 7-10). Though we know the image is that of the youth's imagination, the voice gives the arm a frightening reality, and Kennedy's wry playfulness—evident in his borrowing a cliché, to bite the dust, to fit his context—only enhances the scariness with a gleeful grin. The poem begins as a recollection and is transformed into a felt experience for both the youth and, through his imagination, the reader. Kennedy has used a trick that works on children to bring to life an experience that reminds the adult how the imagination can play tricks on all of us all our lives.

In some degree, too, it may be said that Kennedy sees the child's experience in the adult's, and vice versa, and so it is not such a leap for him to write verse for children and poetry for adults. Sometimes the child and the adult merge, as in a four-line poem from *Dark Horses*:

> Kicking and shrieking off to bed,
> Hand tugged in the Lord God's hand,
> He fought as he always did
> When day had to end.
>
> ("For a Small Boy's Stone")

The lines appear to depict a child in a common domestic moment, but something, perhaps the second line, transforms this scene into a universal one of the individual being "tugged in the Lord God's hand," like the child. The poem is saying that the child's going to bed, reluctantly, mirrors the fate of everyone and that in us all is the small child resisting the end of day.

Chronology

1929

August 21: born Joseph Charles Kennedy[1] in Dover, New Jersey, son of Joseph F. and Agnes (Rauter) Kennedy. Father is a timekeeper in a boiler factory; mother, a former registered nurse.

1950

Begins practice teaching at Dover High School.

Graduates from Seton Hall with major in English and minors in history, education, philosophy.

Receives gold medals as outstanding student in departments of English and education.

Begins study at Columbia University, attending lectures by Lionel Trilling, William York Tindall, Marjorie Nicholson, and Mark Van Doren.

1951

Earns M.A. in English from Columbia, with concentration in American literature.

Publications earn total of one hundred dollars. Kennedy abandons hope of making a living as a writer of science fiction.

Enlists for four years in U.S. Navy. After boot camp he attends the Naval Journalist School, Great Lakes, Illinois, and is then assigned as clerk-typist in a chaplains' office.

1952

Becomes speech writer for commandant, Ninth Naval District, working in the Public Information Office with professional newspapermen.

During the next two years, Kennedy serves on a destroyer assigned to take pictures and prepare press releases; he goes on cruises to Puerto Rico and the Dominican Republic, Scotland, London, the Netherlands, and Mediterranean countries.

1954

Transfers to the battleship *Wisconsin*, which takes him to Guantanamo Bay, Cuba, and Brest, France; visits Paris.

1955

Becomes the editor of *AIR*, official magazine of the Atlantic Fleet Air Force.

Begins intensive work on poetry.

Is discharged from the navy and begins a year in France on the GI Bill.

Spends August studying French in Tours, then attends the University of Paris for a year.

Visits Frankfurt and Vienna.

1956

Completes the French course and receives a *certificat littéraire* from the Sorbonne and a *certificat* from the Institut de Phonétique.

Takes car trip through England, Scotland, Wales, and Ireland.

Enters University of Michigan, Ann Arbor, as teaching fellow in English; begins study for Ph.D. in comparative literature. Forms friendships with aspiring poets Keith Waldrop, James Camp, Dallas Wiebe, and Donald Hope.

1957

Works as graduate assistant in drama and survey of literature courses.

1959

Translates Alfred Jarry's absurdist play *Ubu Roi* with Keith Waldrop; play is staged for two nights as *Go-potty Rex*; Kennedy plays title role. Besides teaching, he serves as assistant to John Heath-Stubbs,[2] a visiting professor at University of Michigan, 1959–60.

1960

Wins first place awards in Hopwood writing contest: fourteen hundred dollars for poetry (the judges are Louise Bogan and Henry Rago) and one thousand dollars for an essay (the judges are Irving Howe and William Van O'Connor).

Is appointed a Bread Loaf Fellow at the Bread Loaf Writers Conference, where he meets Robert Frost, John Ciardi, John Frederick Nims, David McCord, and others.

Receives a predoctoral instructorship at University of Michigan and teaches first course in literature.

1961

Nude Descending a Staircase is published by Doubleday.

Receives Lamont Award from Academy of American Poets for *Nude Descending a Staircase.*

Attends summer program with W. D. Snodgrass at Yaddo, a writers' and artists' colony at Saratoga Springs, N.Y.

The Wolgamot Interstice is published by Burning Deck Press.

1962

Marries Dorothy Mintzlaff.

Succeeds Donald Hall as poetry editor of *The Paris Review.*

Gives readings at Cornell, University of Wisconsin, North Carolina Poetry Circuit, YM-YWHA Poetry Center in New York, Washington University in St. Louis, and elsewhere.

Leaves Michigan, abandoning doctorate, having finished all requirements but the dissertation.

Appointed lecturer in English, Woman's College of the University of North Carolina, Greensboro, where he meets Randall Jarrell, who is on the faculty, and visitors Adrienne Rich and Eudora Welty.

Receives a commission from *Glamour* magazine to write a Christmas poem, "The Watchers," which is extended into *The Beasts of Bethlehem.*[3]

1963

Birth of first child, Kathleen.

Joins the faculty of Tufts University, Medford, Massachusetts, as an assistant professor of English.

Becomes the first poet to tour the New England poetry circuit.

Mark Twain's Frontier is published by Holt.

1964

Birth of son David.

Is appointed visiting lecturer at Wellesley College during the fall semester.

Is named Phi Beta Kappa Poet at Tufts.

1965

Conducts a summer poetry workshop at the Writers Conference in the Rocky Mountains, sponsored by University of Colorado, Boulder.

1966

Birth of son Matthew.
Joins staff at Bread Loaf Writers Conference, John Ciardi, director.
Is appointed visiting lecturer in the graduate Writing Program, University of California, Irvine, 1966–67.
Gives readings at several California universities.
An Introduction to Poetry is published by Little, Brown.

1967

Is promoted to associate professor at Tufts.
Receives a grant from the National Endowment for the Arts; lives for a year in London and tours England, Holland, Rhine Valley, northern France, and Italy.

1969

Takes part in "An Evening of Good Bad Verse" at YM–YWHA Poetry Center, New York.
Leads poetry workshop at Eastern Kentucky University Writers Conference.
Gives readings on the Wisconsin-Minnesota poetry circuit, visiting ten campuses.
Growing into Love is published by Doubleday.

1970

Birth of son Daniel.
Receives Shelley Memorial Award from Poetry Society of America (co-recipient is Mary Oliver).
Bulsh is published by Burning Deck Press.

1971

Breaking and Entering is published by Oxford University Press.
Pegasus Descending is published by Macmillan.

1972

Birth of son Joshua.
Gives reading at the Library of Congress with Anne Sexton.
Publishes first issue of *Counter/Measures.*

1973

Awarded a Guggenheim Fellowship for creative writing in poetry, 1973–74.
Is promoted to full professor at Tufts.

Reads with Philip Levine in New York for the Academy of American Poets.
Second issue of *Counter/Measures* is published.
Messages: A Thematic Anthology of Poetry is published by Little, Brown.

1974
Celebrations after the Death of John Brennan is published by Penmaen Press.
Emily Dickinson in Southern California is published by the David. R. Godine Press.
Receives Golden Rose Award from the New England Poetry Club.
Publishes final issue of *Counter/Measures.*
Appointed Bruern Fellow in American Civilisation, University of Leeds, 1974–75.
Gives readings at several universities in England and visits Paris, Nice, and Monaco with family.

1975
Death of father, Joseph Francis Kennedy, age eighty-nine.
Participates in a public debate at Tufts with Denise Levertov on open-form versus closed-form poetry.
Three Tenors, One Vehicle is published by Open Places.
One Winter Night in August and Other Nonsense Jingles is published by Margaret K. McElderry Books.

1976
Death of mother, Agnes Rauter Kennedy, age eighty-seven.
An Introduction to Fiction and *Literature: An Introduction to Fiction, Poetry, and Drama* are published by Little, Brown.
Colloquy for Tape Recorder and Orchestra, music by Vladimir Ussachevsky, verse by Kennedy, performed by Salt Lake City Philharmonic.
Gives reading at the Folger Shakespeare Library.

1977
Resigns from teaching at Tufts to write full-time.
Is appointed Phi Beta Kappa Poet at Brown University.

1979
The Phantom Ice Cream Man: More Nonsense Verse is published by Atheneum/Margaret K. McElderry Books.

1980

Attends reception at the White House with Dorothy to mark the anniversary of *Poetry* magazine, hosted by Mrs. Jimmy Carter.

1981

Is a speaker with Arthur Miller, John Ciardi, and others at Hopwood Festival, marking the fiftieth anniversary of writing awards at University of Michigan.

Tygers of Wrath: Poems of Hatred, Anger, and Invective is published by University of Georgia Press.

1982

The Bedford Reader is published by Bedford Books of St. Martin's. Bedford Books hosts celebration of this first edition at the CCCC convention in San Francisco, which is attended by 1,100 college English teachers.

Gives reading with Richard Moore at Books and Company, New York City, sponsored by *Ontario Review*, and on the Ohio poetry circuit.

Did Adam Name the Vinegarroon? is published by David. R. Godine Press.

Knock at a Star: A Child's Introduction to Poetry is published by Little, Brown.

1983

Is the keynote speaker at the Georgetown University Writers Conference.

French Leave: Translations is published by Robert L. Barth Press.

Missing Link is published by Scheidt Head Press; this is a self-published booklet of poems to be given away at readings.

The Owlstone Crown is published by Atheneum/Margaret K. McElderry Books.

1984

Reads on the Texas poetry circuit and at public libraries in Maine.

Gives program on the subject of bad poetry with W. D. Snodgrass at University of Tennessee, Knoxville.

Receives an award from Ethical Culture School, New York City, for *The Owlstone Crown*.

Reads at the University of Nevada, Las Vegas, University of North Reno, and Clark County Public Library.

Receives book award for *The Owlstone Crown* from the Ethical Culture School.

Hangover Mass is published by Bits Press.

1985

Cross Ties: Selected Poems is published by University of Georgia Press.

The Forgetful Wishing Well: Poems for Young People is published by Atheneum/Margaret K. McElderry Books.

Is Seeing Believing? is recorded for Watershed Tapes in Washington, D.C. and delivered live at George Mason University.

Cross Ties wins the *Los Angeles Times* Book Award for poetry.

Short story "Love 'Em or Leave 'Em" is chosen by PEN Syndicated Fiction Project.

Is appointed keynote speaker at national conference in Chicago titled "The Future of Literature in the Community College."

Travels with family to England, Norway, Denmark, Austria, Germany, and France.

1986

Leads a poetry workshop at Florida Suncoast Writers Conference, St. Petersburg.

Is appointed Phi Beta Kappa Poet at Bates College.

Brats is published by Atheneum/Margaret K. McElderry Books.

1987

Undergoes surgery on arm, possibly necessitated by overwork on textbooks.

Gives three readings in Michigan.

Reads poems on broadcast of PBS folk music program "Mountain Stage."

The Bedford Guide for College Writers is published by Bedford Books of St. Martin's.

1988

Is awarded an honorary degree, doctor of humane letters, by Lawrence University.

Reads light verse with George Starbuck at the Library of Congress, invited and introduced by Richard Wilbur.

Reads with W. D. Snodgrass at YM-YWHA Poetry Center in New York.

Is appointed to read and work with student poets at University of Arkansas and University of Arizona.

1989

Named the first recipient of Michael Braude Award for light verse, an international prize given by the American Academy and Institute of Arts and Letters.

Ghastlies, Goops and Pincushions: Nonsense Verse is published by Margaret K. McElderry Books/Macmillan.
Fresh Brats is published by Margaret K. McElderry Books.

1990
Is appointed to speak at Wesleyan University Writers Conference.
Gives first of four readings in Longfellow House garden, sponsored by New England Poetry Club.
Delivers 1990 Moore lecture on children's literature at the New York Public Library.
Maryland Public Television films documentary on Kennedy in Bedford for PBS series *Literary Visions.*
Winter Thunder is published by Robert L. Barth Press.

1991
Travels with Dorothy and son Joshua to Austria, Germany, Italy, Switzerland. Breaks wrist in car accident, requiring three operations and physical therapy.
The Kite That Braved Old Orchard Beach: Year-Round Poems for Young People is published by Margaret K. McElderry Books.
Talking like the Rain: A First Book of Poems is published by Little, Brown.

1992
Begins writing column "Outbound to Alewife" for *Harvard Review.*
Travels for two months in France with Dorothy.
Dark Horses: New Poems is published by Johns Hopkins University Press.
The Beasts of Bethlehem is published by Margaret K. McElderry Books.

1993
Reads at the University of the South, Sewanee, Tennessee; at universities in Austin and San Antonio, Texas; and at colleges in the Finger Lakes district of New York.
Takes part in reading nineteenth-century American poetry in New York City and at Harvard.
Drat These Brats! is published by Margaret K. McElderry Books.

1994
Makes video to promote the textbook, *Literature.*
Reads the poetry of e. e. cummings with W. D. Snodgrass at the New York Public Library.

Serves as a panelist at National Council of Teachers of English Convention in Orlando.
The Epigrammatist, a chapbook devoted to the epigrams of X. J. Kennedy, is published.
Nude Descending a Staircase is reprinted by the Carnegie Mellon University Press as part of its Classic Contemporary Series.

1995
Tours Moscow and St. Petersburg with Dorothy and friends.
Reads and works with poets in graduate program at McNeese State University, Louisiana.
Gives talk on poetry for children at Shenandoah University, Virginia, and Murray State University, Kentucky.
Writes the introduction for *Poets House Directory of American Poetry.*
Attends "An Evening with X. J. Kennedy" at the Bookcellar Cafe, Cambridge, Massachusetts.

1996
Tours Egypt with Dorothy.
Gives lecture and reading at Nicholls State University, Louisiana.
Reads at Bates College; reads and judges poetry contest for Newburyport (Massachusetts) Art Association.
The Minimus Poems is published by Robert L. Barth Press.

1997
Speaks at Children's Book Conference in Vancouver, B.C.
Reads and serves as judge for Glascock Poetry Contest at Mount Holyoke College.
Is the keynote speaker at Southwest Two Year College Conference, Austin, Texas.
Reads in Grolier Poetry Festival, Cambridge, Massachusetts; at Wells and Keuka colleges, Northern Essex (Massachusetts) Community College; and the Longfellow House.
The Eagle as Wide as the World and *Uncle Switch: Loony Limericks* are published by Margaret K. McElderry Books.

1998
Serves as the first judge for the X. J. Kennedy Poetry Prize, sponsored by the Texas Review Press.
Judges the competition for the T. S. Eliot Poetry Prize for Thomas Jefferson University Press.

Reads from his translation of Aristophanes' *Lysistrata* at Greek Institute, Cambridge, Massachusetts.

Gives talk on parody on PBS radio program "What's the Word?"

Tours western isles of England, Ireland, and Scotland with Dorothy.

Is awarded an honorary degree of doctor of fine arts from Adelphi University.

An Introduction to Poetry, ninth edition, is published by Longman.

1999

Receives Aiken Taylor Award for Modern Poetry, given by University of the South and *The Sewanee Review.*

Keynote reader at West Chester Poetry Conference. Keynote speaker, Texas Community College Teachers Association Convention in Houston.

The spring issue of *Paintbrush* is devoted to Kennedy and his work.

Travels to Spain with Dorothy; breaks leg and returns home for surgery.

Elympics is published by Philomel Books.

Lysistrata, a translation, is published by the University of Pennsylvania Press.

An Introduction to Fiction, seventh edition, is published by Longman.

Literature: An Introduction to Fiction, Poetry, and Drama, seventh edition, is published by Longman.

The Bedford Guide for College Writers, fifth edition, is published by Bedford Books of St. Martin's.

Knock at a Star: A Child's Introduction to Poetry is published by Little, Brown.

2000

Speaks at Brown University, the fortieth anniversary tribute to Keith and Rosmarie Waldrop's Burning Deck Press.

Reads at Sewanee Writers' Conference.

Receives Award for Excellence in Children's Poetry from the National Council of Teachers of English.

Takes trip on the Danube River to Budapest with side trip to Prague.

The Bedford Reader, seventh edition, is published by Bedford Books of St. Martin's

2001

Is the keynote speaker at the first Teaching Poetry Conference in Santa Rosa, California.

Travels to Greece and Turkey.

Speaks at the inauguration of the Center for the Study of Literature for Young Readers at Youngstown (Ohio) University.

Elefantina's Dream, a picture book for children, is published.

Launches website, <XJandDorothyMKennedy.com>, where news, uncollected verse for children and adults, and other material relevant to the Kennedys is made available to the public.

2002

Literature, eighth edition, to be published by Longman.

The Lords of Misrule: Poems 1992–2001 to be published by Johns Hopkins University Press.

Awarded honorary doctorate from Westfield State College, Westfield, Massachusetts.

The Purpose of Time published by Arabia Press in a limited edition of 130 copies, contains six poems already published in *The Lords of Misrule.*

In July, X. J. Kennedy and Dorothy boat down the Rhine river.

Appendix A

Influences

WHEN ASKED TO LIST THE WRITERS AND THINKERS WHO HAVE HAD THE greatest influence on him, X. J. Kennedy provided a narrative of his literary development that includes his encounters with literary figures and their works. It may be read as a history of the development of a poet's mind from his own perspective and in his own words. Kennedy wrote:[1]

> The early effect of Whitman and the *Rubaiyat of Omar Khayyám*, those two opposite extremes of enthusiasm and pessimism, breathy psalm-measures and chiseled formality, mattered greatly to me; I have mentioned this in the Contemporary Authors autobiography. As a senior in high school, I declined to study trigonometry and instead took a library period—a momentous decision that went against the advice of my guidance counselor—during which I simply read. I devoured Steinbeck and Richard Wright's *Black Boy* and Karl Menninger's *Man Against Himself*, and skimmed Untermeyer's *Modern British and American Poetry* anthology, glimpsing with uncomprehending eyes the wonders of Cummings, Williams, H. D., Stevens, and Pound, forming superficial acquaintance with them. John Crowe Ransom's ballad of "Captain Carpenter" entranced me, and for a long time I went around chanting its outrageous last stanza:
>
> > The curse of hell upon that sleek upstart
> > That got the Captain finally on his back
> > And the red red vitals of his heart
> > And made the kites to whet their beaks clack clack.
>
> At Seton Hall, to which I went directly from high school (almost all my classmates were veterans back from the war), my English teachers, the one or two honest, hard-working ones, were Romantics who adored Shelley and the novels of Thomas Wolfe; when I took a course in eighteenth-century English literature, I found myself Alexander Pope's solitary defender. We did read Blake's *Songs of Innocence and Experience*, though, and in admiring those, the instructor and I were on the same team. In truth, Seton Hall was not of much help, except

to put *The Oxford Anthology of American Literature* between my hands. The instructor never did get to the second, more modern volume, but I read it anyway and found it eye-opening. Discovering on my own the work of Hart Crane, I wrote a senior thesis on *The Bridge*—rather an iconoclastic move, I now realize, for the good priest in charge of the English Department had no use for modern poets, and I suspect he never found out that Crane was gay. (Indeed, for any English major to write about poetry was such an unheard-of thing that they gave me and my senior thesis a gold medal when I graduated.) I can't claim that Crane, the best of whose stuff is marvelous, exerted any profound influence on me; but his work, particularly the earlier formal lyrics and "Voyages" and the successful parts of *The Bridge*, confirmed in me a sense that poetry has to have music, or it is a bore. I loved Crane's ability to resonate, to sling about fearlessly the richest and most striven-for vocabulary ("The seal's wide spindrift gaze toward paradise").

The most pervasive influence was surely W. B. Yeats, whose poems I had hardly met till I took William York Tindall's graduate course in Modern British Literature at Columbia. Tindall had us buy the then-latest British edition of Yeats's *Collected Poems*, and when I entered the Navy in the summer of 1951 I took that holy book with me and kept it close to hand for four years, packing it into my seabag when making cruises in Atlantic Fleet destroyers. I wrote a good deal of imitation Yeats in those days at sea, but it all came out pitifully inferior to the master, of course, so none of it ever got printed. I remember trying to imitate Yeats's songs, with their inimitable refrains, and learned nothing except how hard a task he sets for any copycat. To Tindall's excellent course (much more informative than Lionel Trilling's), I also owed a close reading of Eliot's poems—I have never cared for the *Four Quartets* as I cared for, and still care for, "Prufrock" and the Sweeney poems—and Dylan Thomas's.

It was in 1950–51 as a grad student that I bought and read every extant volume by Wallace Stevens, and delighted in especially *Harmonium*, and tried to imitate "Cortege for Rosenbloom" and "The Emperor of Ice Cream" and other gorgeous items, and failed.

Theodore Roethke was another influence I gravitated to early on—at Columbia, I was reading his new poems as they appeared in *Poetry*—and I tried to imitate his less experimental work, unsuccessfully. I met Roethke at Michigan once, and got to talk with him for a few minutes, but he seemed indrawn and perhaps ill, and there wasn't any real conversation between us. Later, I learned from Sandra McPherson that he had once brought a copy of *Nude Descending* into one of his classes and had declaimed from it with some enthusiasm, which delighted my heart. He is one of the purest verbal musicians our poetry has had; he seems hardly ever to have let an idea into his head for long, except, "Hooray for green and growing things."

When I was a graduate-student in the later 1950s, there were two predominant models for us young poets to follow: the wild, violent formality of Robert Lowell (e.g., "The Drunken Fisherman" and other poems in *Lord Weary's Castle*) and the polished, witty formality of Richard Wilbur.[2] I tried to be like both of them. It was the pre-Beat era of the Iowa City kind of formal poem well exemplified in the first *New Poets of England and America* anthology edited by Hall, Pack, and Simpson. I was familiar with William Carlos Williams (who, elsewhere than in the academe, was then making converts)—indeed, I had written a master's essay at Columbia that dealt in part with his work—and I was fond of him, but it was the tight-assed rimesters that wowed me the most.

At Michigan, I profited from an excellent course in Renaissance poetry from John Arthos (ah! what a treat to study Herrick, Jonson, Waller, and the epigram-writers!) and another Medieval literature course from John Revell Rinehard. My early "Little Elegy" does not refer to any actual child, but was quite bookish in origin: an attempt to write a verse epitaph for a child in the tradition of Herrick ("Here she lies, a pretty bud / Lately made of flesh and blood") and Jonson. The rendition of Charles d'Orléans' famous spring song ("Le temps a laissie son manteau / De neige, de froidure, et de pluie"), which I translated in *Nude* as a rondel beginning "The world is taking off her clothes" dates from this period. I've long loved the Child ballads, but if I remember right it was from teaching that I got to know the great stuff like "Edward," "Barbara Allen," "Sir Patrick Spens" and "Get Up and Bar the Door." For my last two years at Michigan I was a "pre-doctoral instructor," a glorified teaching-fellow, and they let me teach a section of a sophomore genre course that included poetry.

The work of Robert Frost took a while to land on me, but when he hit, he hit hard.[3] When I went to the Bread Loaf Writers Conference on a fellowship (in 1960), I had never taken much interest in Frost's poems; they seemed tame and prosaic to me in comparison with the poems of those wild-eyed dreamers I preferred—Yeats, Stevens, Hart Crane. But the spell of Frost in person, surrounding a reading of his poems with long rambling remarks, quite captured me. Frost would sign his collected poems for all comers (provided they bought a copy at Bread Loaf), so I had him sign one to me, and went out under a tree to read it. What should I come upon but "Tree at My Window"—

> Not all your light tongues talking aloud
> Could be profound.

I was hooked. Ever since, Frost has been one of the poets nearest and dearest to me—I don't care that he was a mean old selfish bastard, he's great. If imitation is any tribute, then a number of poems I have written seem indebted to his kind of tone and language and measure: most obviously "Robert Frost Discovers Another Road Not

Taken" (a loving parody), and in *Dark Horses* "The Woodpile Skull" and "Ambition."

My debt to Emily Dickinson will be apparent from *Emily Dickinson in Southern California* and from another attempt to write in her voice—the one about the answering machine in *Dark Horses.* Shortly after her poems finally appeared in more or less faithful texts in the three-volume edition of Thomas Johnson, Keith Waldrop got some letterheads printed up and pretended to be a bookstore so that he and all his friends in Ann Arbor could order books at a discount of 40%, and I was able to acquire the Johnson edition and read all those miraculous poems and ponder them.

Never fond of the long poems of Edwin Arlington Robinson, I nevertheless gravitated early to his sonnets and short poems about people. "The Mill" strikes me as a masterpiece, so does "Haunted House." John Frederick Nims has shrewdly detected this influence in my "Loose Woman."

You learn from whoever you love. Hardy is another favorite. I bought his *Collected Poems* in 1957, but they took a while to sink in—"Channel Firing," "During Wind and Rain," "Neutral Tones," "The Oxen," and the much-maligned "Satires of Circumstance" (which I am very fond of; so was [John Crowe] Ransom). Wonderful poems. I would be hard-pressed to see specific Hardy echoes in me. Maybe in "On the Proposed Seizure of Twelve Graves in a Colonial Cemetery" (a poem inspired by an actual public dispute in Bedford, Mass.).

One other influence deserves mention. In Ann Arbor, I served for a year as graduate assistant to the visiting English poet John Heath-Stubbs, whose eyesight was extremely poor (and who later went quite blind). Heath-Stubbs could make out words in a book by holding the thing two inches from his eyes, and was able to plan his own classes, but needed help to read the student papers. An extraordinarily learned man with a deep knowledge of poetry and myth, endowed with a marvelous voice, Heath-Stubbs made a great impression on me. During his year in residence Keith Waldrop produced and directed a performance of Heath-Stubbs's verse play *The Talking Ass,* based on the Biblical story of Balaam. Draped with a blanket and wearing a papier-mâché ass's head, I was proud to play the front half-ass, the half that talked. (William P. Kenney played the silent half, a role that called for considerable skill and agility, so as to stay united with the front of the animal and not step out of the blanket.) I read Heath-Stubbs's poems too. They are predominantly rimed and metrical. In one of his early books there's a Villon-like ballade about a woman in a bar, who contemplates her body's deterioration: "The Lady's Complaint," reprinted in Heath-Stubbs's *Collected Poems 1943–1987* (London and New York: Carcanet Press, 1988). No doubt this barfly went into the making of "In a Prominent Bar in Secaucus One Day." So did Hardy's "The Ruined Maid," probably.

The extent to which this education, private and public, found its way into Kennedy's poetry may be traced through the readings of various reviewers and critics. From the beginning of Kennedy's career, for example, the influence of W. H. Auden was mentioned in several reviews. One of the better, most perceptive readers, John Gordon, with keen understanding, summarized Kennedy's career in terms of the influences on it:

> Kennedy seems to have been at least spottily bookish as a boy. He read Ulysses at fifteen and developed a love of science fiction during the golden age of that alternately hyped and scanted genre. His first published works were a number of science fiction stories which he has not collected and does not particularly wish to have remembered. . . . Still, could they be resurrected, they might just possibly snap into a glowing, gloriously inclusive continuity that suggests itself to me, and which goes like this: Catholicism—Science fiction—Yeats—Poetry. All of which evoke a mooninness, an opulent fantasticality, a veneration for form and structure, a love for the brilliantined machinery of the imagination (mottled gilded chalices and gem-studded monstrances; Bradbury's jewels of spaceships and fine ivory Martian chess cities; Yeats's aviary of singing symbols), which, among other things, may be seen coalesced in some of the poetry of X. J. Kennedy.[4]

Considering Yeats to be the "most important in the sequence," Gordon sees his influence on Kennedy's poetry manifested in a number of ways:

> the idiomatic tone (*increasingly in Kennedy's later poetry*) worked through expertly crafted traditional stanzaic forms; the quantum leaps from memory to metaphor; the love of song; the high wit, most intense in the gravest subjects; the sequencing of recondite, far-flung images into something that turns out to dovetail after all; and the growing confidence we feel that things will indeed come around at the end of the journey.[5]

Once a reader has glimpsed the rich traditional heritage that infuses Kennedy's poetry, one begins to see traces of virtually every famous poet who ever rhymed or wrote in meter and haled from the Continent. Many critics have noted—and both attacked and praised—the influence on Kennedy's poetry of metaphysical poets and the Augustan satirists. Certainly Kennedy's penchant for writing epigrams throughout his career shows an affinity for Augustan satire, with its focus on the pretentious fool and posturing buffoon.

So we also have Raymond Oliver seeing Kennedy's "main literary antecedents" to be the writers of the English Renaissance and detecting "the mark of Herrick" in "Little Elegy" as well as Baudelaire and Rimbaud elsewhere in his poetry.[6] We even have the tide turning in Kennedy's favor in one respect at least, according to Oliver: "Kennedy's very sharp 'First Confession' . . . is his answer to the 'confessional' poetry done so messily by Lowell and others."[7]

Kennedy models certain poems after an author's style. He has imitated Emily Dickinson in two poems; has taken the stanzaic pattern of the *Rubaiyat,* and has made the ballad stanza his own in many of his poems, giving it both a boisterous and baleful mood. He has also taken the sonnet form from all who have succeeded in that form. More subtle has been the influence of W. H. Auden, the poet most often cited as the greatest influence on Kennedy, although Robert Frost is also a major influence. Lachlan Mackinnon says that "sometimes the ghost of Frost is too much in evidence as in the sad 'O'Riley's Late-Bloomed Little Son.' The first stanza describes the infant's death, the second the surviving parents: 'They say she's past her change of life. / You'll see them Saturdays / In the back yard.' "[8] Mackinnon hears a "Wordsworthian echo" in "The Death of Professor Backwards" and sees Frost's poem "The Most of It" lurking behind Kennedy's signature poem, "Cross Ties."

Loxley Nichols sees Kennedy's style "of wit and argument characteristic of seventeenth-century metaphysical verse. In 'One A.M. with Voices' we hear traces of John Donne with a New Jersey accent: 'Hers: What do you squander night for / In coupling on a page / Rhymes no man pronounces?— / Is it love or rage?' "[9] Nichols also is reminded of "T. S. Eliot's depictions of the modern wasteland" in the "jarring dissonance" of juxtapositions found in some of Kennedy's lines: "Over stones where Orestes fled / The sonorous Furies / Girls hawking flyspecked postcards / Pursue the tourist" ("Theater of Dionysus"). Like Eliot, too, Kennedy is "unafraid to face the Gorgon" in those poems that "deal with the commonplaces of alienation, desecration, perversion, and violence."[10] Moore Moran showed a keen sympathy for Kennedy's metrical skills while reading *Cross Ties*: "Spellbound by the novelty of metrics, I at times thought I was back sharing an evening with E. A. Robinson—at other moments, Thomas Hardy. At still others, William Blake."[11] Michael True had a similar reaction reading other poems, only he was reminded of another influence: "Kennedy's early poems, including ['First

Confession'] resemble the best work of Karl Shapiro—'Drug Store,' 'Auto Wreck,' or 'University'—and of others who give back the exact dimension and character of particular moments in history."[12]

Perhaps Bernard Keith Waldrop put the whole question of the influences on Kennedy's work into the right perspective when he wrote: "That X. J. Kennedy has been influenced more by Herrick and Emily Dickinson than by Whitman seems to me all to the good. That Yeats and John Heath-Stubbs seem to mean more to him than William Carlos Williams is surely his own affair. His style is as much his own as that of any poet I can think of."[13]

Appendix B

X. J. Kennedy's Book Publications

Poetry for Adults

Breaking and Entering. London: Oxford University Press, 1971.
Bulsh. Providence, R.I.: Burning Deck Press, 1970.
Celebrations after the Death of John Brennan. Lincoln, Mass.: Penmaen Press, 1974.
Cross Ties: Selected Poems. Athens, Ga.: University of Georgia Press, 1985.
Dark Horses: New Poems. Baltimore and London: Johns Hopkins University Press, 1992.
Emily Dickinson in Southern California. Boston: David. R. Godine Press, 1974.
Growing into Love. New York: Doubleday, 1969.
Hangover Mass. Cleveland: Bits Press, 1984.
The Epigrammatist 5, no. 2 (August 1994) (a chapbook series).
The Lords of Misrule: Poems 1992–2001. Johns Hopkins University Press, 2002.
The Minimus Poems. Edgewood, Ky.: Robert L. Barth, 1996.
Missing Link. Bedford, Mass.: Scheidt Head Press, 1983.
Nude Descending a Staircase. New York: Doubleday, 1961. Reprint edition in Classic Contemporary Series, Carnegie Mellon University Press, 1994.
Three Tenors, One Vehicle (with James E. Camp and Keith Waldrop). Columbia, Mo.: Open Places, 1975.
Winter Thunder. Florence, Ky.: Robert L. Barth, 1990 (a chapbook).

For Children and Young Adults

The Beasts of Bethlehem. New York: Margaret K. McElderry Books, 1992.

Brats. New York: Atheneum, Margaret K. McElderry Books, 1986.

Did Adam Name the Vinegarroon? Boston: David R. Godine, 1982.

Drat These Brats! New York: Margaret K. McElderry Books, 1993.

The Eagle as Wide as the World. New York: Margaret K. McElderry Books, 1997.

Elympics. New York: Philomel Books, 1999.

The Forgetful Wishing Well: Poems for Young People. New York: Atheneum, Margaret K. McElderry Books, 1985.

Fresh Brats. New York: Margaret K. McElderry Books, 1989.

Ghastlies, Goops and Pincushions: Nonsense Verse. New York: Margaret K. McElderry Books; Macmillan, 1989.

The Kite That Braved Old Orchard Beach: Year-Round Poems for Young People. New York: Margaret K. McElderry Books, 1991.

Knock at a Star: A Child's Introduction to Poetry. Rev. ed. With Dorothy M. Kennedy. Boston.: Little, Brown, 1999.

One Winter Night in August and Other Nonsense Jingles. New York: Atheneum, Margaret K. McElderry Books, 1975.

The Owlstone Crown. New York: Atheneum, Margaret K. McElderry Books, 1983.

The Phantom Ice Cream Man: More Nonsense Verse. New York: Atheneum, Margaret K. McElderry Books, 1979.

Talking like the Rain: a First Book of Poems. With Dorothy M. Kennedy. Boston: Little, Brown, 1991.

Uncle Switch: Loony Limericks. New York: Margaret K. McElderry Books, 1997.

Textbooks, Anthologies, and Journals

The Bedford Guide for College Writers. 5th ed. Edited by X. J. Kennedy, Dorothy M. Kennedy, and Sylvia A. Holladay. Boston: Bedford Books of St. Martin's, 1999.

The Bedford Reader. 7th ed. Edited by X. J. Kennedy, Dorothy M. Kennedy, and Jane E. Aaron. Boston: Bedford Books of St. Martin's, 2000.

Counter/Measures: A Magazine of Rime, Meter, and Song. Edited by X. J. Kennedy and Dorothy M. Kennedy, 1972. A second issue was published in 1973, and a final issue in 1974.

An Introduction to Fiction. 7th ed. Edited by X. J. Kennedy and Dana Gioia. New York: Longman, 1999.

An Introduction to Poetry. 9th ed. Edited by X. J. Kennedy and Dana Gioia. New York: Longman, 1998.

Literature: An Introduction to Fiction, Poetry, and Drama. 7th ed.

Edited by X. J. Kennedy and Dana Gioia. New York: Longman, 1999.

Mark Twain's Frontier: A Textbook of Primary Source Materials for Student Research and Writing. Edited by X. J. Kennedy and James E. Camp. New York: Holt, Rinehart and Winston, 1963.

Messages: A Thematic Anthology of Poetry. Edited by X. J. Kennedy. Boston: Little, Brown, 1973.

Pegasus Descending: A Book of the Best Bad Verse. Compiled by X. J. Kennedy, James E. Camp, and Bernard Waldrop. New York: Macmillan, 1971.

Tygers of Wrath: Poems of Hatred, Anger, and Invective. Collected and edited by X. J. Kennedy. Athens, Ga.: University of Georgia Press, 1981.

Translations

French Leave: Translations. Florence, Ky.: Robert L. Barth, 1983.

Lysistrata. In *Aristophanes: Wasps, Lysistrata, Frogs, The Sexual Congress.* Edited by David R. Slavitt and Palmer Bovie, 2: 85–174. Philadelphia: University of Pennsylvania Press, 1999.

Miscellaneous

Is Seeing Believing? Watershed Tapes: Signature Series, no. C-186, 1985. A sound recording of X. J. Kennedy reading thirty-nine of his poems from *Cross Ties*; recorded at George Mason University, Fairfax, Virginia, April 10, 1985, and at Soundscape, Inc., Alexandria, Virginia, April 12, 1985.

The Beasts of Bethlehem. Lake Charles, LA: Epona Records, 2001. A compact disc containing poems set to music by Carol Wood and others.

Appendix C

Titles of Poems for Adults

THE TITLES OF THE POETRY COLLECTIONS ARE ABBREVIATED AS FOLLOWS:

BE: *Breaking and Entering,* 1971
CP: *A Controversy of Poets,* 1965
CT: *Cross Ties,* 1985
DH: *Dark Horses,* 1992
ED: *Emily Dickinson in Southern California,* 1974
EP: *The Epigrammatist,* 1994
FL: *French Leave,* 1983
GL: *Growing into Love,* 1969
HM: *Hangover Mass,* 1984
JB: *Celebrations after the Death of John Brennan,* 1974
LM: *The Lords of Misrule,* 2002
ML: *Missing Link,* 1983
MP: *The Minimus Poems,* 1996
ND: *Nude Descending a Staircase,* 1961
TT: *Three Tenors, One Vehicle,* 1975
WI: *The Wolgamot Interstice,* 1961
WT: *Winter Thunder,* 1990

Kennedy often reprinted poems in different ways from their original version. For example, he would reprint only part of a poem or move parts of poems around within the original poem; sometimes he would place a poem, or a part of a poem, among other poems under a separate title, *Japanese Beetles,* for one. He also made minor changes in the text and formatting of some poems when he reprinted them.

"Absentminded Bartender." GL, BE, CT
"Abyss." FL
"Acumen." CT
"Additional Lines for the Tombstone of. . . ." EP

"Advice to an Anthologist." BE
"Afterward." LM
"An Aged Virgin." EP
"The Aged Wino's Counsel to a Young Man on the Brink of Marriage." ND, CT
"Airport in the Grass." ND, CT
"All-Knowing Rabbit." ND
"Ambition." WT, DH
"American Cities." BE (titled "Cities" in GL)
"Among Stool Pigeons." GL, CT
"An epic on the conquest of Peru. . . ." EP
"An epigram, if buffed . . . " BE, ED
"Ancient Lovers." WT
"The Animals You Eat." DH
"Ant Trap." GL, BE, CT
"Anyman." WT
"Anyman Again." WT
"Aphasia." CT
"Apocrypha." GL, CT
"The Arm." DH
"Ars Poetica." ND, BE, ML, CT
"Artificer." GL, BE, CT
"The Ascent." GL, BE, CT
"At a Sale of Manuscript." ED
"At Brown Crane Pavilion." CT
"At Colonus." ED, CT
"At the Ghostwriter's Deathbed." ND
"At the Last Rites for Two Hotrodders." HM, CT
"At the Stoplight by the Paupers' Graves." ND
"The Atheist's Stigmata." BE, CT
"Attorney." WT
"Aunt Rectita's Good Friday." HM, CT
"The Author Receives an Accounting of His Sales." EP
"An Autobiographer." CT
"The Autumn in Norfolk Shipyard." ND, CT
"B Negative." ND, BE, CT
"The Ballad of Fenimore Woolson and Henry James." LM
"Ballade of the Hanged" (formerly "Villon's Epitaph"). LM
"Barking Dog Blues." ND, CT
"A Beard of Bees." LM
"A Beardsley Moment." CT
"Bells." ED
"Best Intentions." LM

"Best Seller." GL, CT
"Birth Report." GL
"Bitter Man." WT
"Black Velvet Art." DH
"The Blessing of the Bikes." LM
"Brats." CT
Bulsh. BE, CT.
"By the cold glow that lit. . . ." BE
"Carol." TT
"Carp." FL
"Carrying on Without Him." ND, CT
"Categories." ED, CT
"Celebrations After the Death of John Brennan" (published separately and reprinted in CT)
"Central Heat." FL
"Charities: I and II." MP
"Christmas Abrupted." DH
"Christmas Show at the Planetarium." LM
"Churchbells." DH
"Cities." GL ("American Cities" in BE)
"City Churchyard." WT, DH
"City-Quitter." DH
"Close Call." LM
"Coming Close to Drowning." DH
"A Common Attitude." EP
"Commuter." LM
"Conformity." FL, CT
"Conspirator My Rose." ND
"Consumer's Report." BE, CT
"Covering the Massacre." LM
"Crawfish." ED, FL, CT
"Creation Morning." GL, BE, ML, CT
"A Critic." EP
"Crocodile." CT
"Cross Ties." CP, GL, BE, ML, CT
"A Curse on a Thief." LM
"Dancing with the Poets at Piggy's." DH
"Dandelion Man." MP
"Daughter in the House." GL, BE, CT
"Daughter Like a Pendant." LM
"Day 7." GL, CT
"Death of a First Child." LM
"The Death of Professor Backwards." HM, CT

"Declare War Against Heaven." ND
"Décor." LM
"Deer Ticks." LM
"The Devil's Advice to Poets." ML, CT
"Diplomacy." BE
"Dirty English Potatoes." HM, CT
"Disinclination." MP
"Down in Dallas." CP, GL
"Drivers of Diaper Service Trucks Are Sad." BE, CT
"Driving Cross-Country." GL, BE
"Dump." DH
"Dusk Decides to Settle in Short Hills." LM
"Each other for some other spouse. . . ." BE, ED
"Earth was I made from. . . ." EP
"Edgar's Story." GL, CT
"An Editor." CT
"Elephant." FL
"Emily Dickinson in Southern California." ED, CT
"Emily Dickinson Leaves a Message to the World, Now That Her Homestead in Amherst Has an Answering Machine." WT, DH
"Empty House Singing to Itself." DH
"Envoi." CT
"Epigrams." WT
"Epigraph for a Banned Book." FL
"Epiphany." CT
"Epitaph for a Postal Clerk." ND (in CT as "For a Postal Clerk")
"Epitaph Proposed for the Headstone of S.R. Quiett." LM
"Epitaph." ND
"Epitaphs." EP
"Evening Tide." ED, CT
"Faces from a Bestiary." ND, BE, CT
"Fall Song." FL, CT
"Family Reunion." DH
"Farmer." GL
"A Farting Babbler." EP
"Fat Cats in Egypt." LM
"Fiat Lux." MP
"Financier." EP
"Finis." DH
"First Confession." ND, BE, ML, CT
"Five-and-Dime, Late Thirties." LM
"Flagellant's Song." TT, CT
"Flesh Is Grass." CT

"Flitting Flies." CT
"A Footpath near Gethsemane." HM, CT
"For a Flung Cyclist." GL
"For a Friend He'd Sent His Book." MP
"For a Maiden Lady." GL, CT
"For a Man Overboard." CT (titled "Epitaph" in ND)
"For a Postal Clerk." CT
"For a Small Boy's Stone." DH
"For a Teutonic Scholar." CT ("Teutonic Scholar" in BE, ED)
"For Allen Ginsberg." LM
"For an Exotic Dancer." CT
"For Children, If They'll Take 'Em." ND, ML
"For Jed." WT, DH
"The Fountain and the Drain." WT
"From *The Bestiary*." FL
"From the Greek Anthology." BE, ED, CT
"Full-nelsoned in earth's arms. . . ." ED, CT
"Further Retort from an Army. . . ." EP
"Girl Sketching Me into Her Landscape." GL
"Giving In to You." GL, CT
"Goblet." HM, CT
"Gold Bought Here." CT
"Golgotha." GL, BE, CT
"Grasshopper." FL
"Great Chain of Being." TT, (in CT as "Song: Great Chain of Being")
"Hangover Mass." HM, CT
"Hare." FL
"Harriet." LM
"Having gone prizeless. . . ." EP
"He lured her home. . . ." EP
"He'd show them—he'd win fame by suicide!. . . ." EP
"Heard through the Walls of the Racetrack Glen Motel." LM
"Hearthside Story." CP, GL
"Heavy Generosity." EP
"Help!" ML
"Her Thinking Man." TT
"Here lies a girl. . . ." BE, ED, CT
"Here lies *Top Seed*. . . ." CT
"Hired Pilot." GL
"Homeless Beggars in Cairo Cemetery." LM
"Horny Man's Song." LM
"I mean my work for none. . . ." EP

"I who in life stood upright. . . ." EP
"If You Got a Notion." TT
"Imperious Muse, your arrows. . . ." BE, ED
"In a Dry Season." HM, CT
"In a Prominent Bar in Secaucus One Day." ND, WI, BE, ML, CT
"In a Secret Field." BE, CT
"In Defense of New England." LM
"In Faith of Rising." ND
"In the Airport Bar." LM
"In the Holding Lounge at Frankfurt Airport." LM
"Inscriptions After Fact." ND, CT
"Intelligentsia." EP
"Interpreters at the UN." WT
"Intimate Disaster." EP
"Invasion and Retreat." DH
"Invitation to the Dance." WT
Japanese Beetles. BE, ED, CT (each volumes contains a slightly different selection of poems under this title)
"Jimmy Harlow." LM
"John." ML
"Joshua." HM, CT
"King Tut." ND, CT
"The Korean Emergency." GL, BE, CT
"Ladies Looking for Lice." ND, BE, CT
Landscapes with Set-Screws. ND, CT
"Last Child." BE, ED, CT
Last Lines. ED, CT (The epigrams under this title differ somewhat in each collection.)
"Last Lines for Athletes." CT
"Last Poem." FL
"Last Request." MP
"A Late Call for Armaments." CT
"Lazy Plumbing." GL
"Leaden, my thoughts. . . ." EP
"Leave of Absence." ND, WI
"Lecher." WT
"Lewis Carroll." ND, BE, CT
"Like a cheap candle. . . ." EP
"Like a loose dog who wets. . . ." EP
"Lilith." ND, BE, CT
"Lion." CT
"Literary Cocktail Party." CT
"Literati." EP

"Little Elegy." ND, WI, BE, ML, CT
"A Little Night Music." ED
"Lizabet's Song to the Senate and the House of Representatives." CT
"Long Distance." DH
"Loose Woman." GL, BE, CT
"Lost Ambition." MP
"Lyric." LM
"Main Road West." GL, BE
"The Man." ND
"The Man in the Manmade Moon." ND
"Maples in January." LM
"Mean Gnome Day." GL
"Meditation in the Bedroom of General Francisco Franco." LM
"The Medium Is the Message." GL, CT
"Mining Town." ED, CT
"The Minotaur's Advice." BE, ED
"Misanthrope." WT
"Miss Olive Leahy's Rooms and Cigar Divan." LM
"A Mobile." LM
"Monday." GL
"Mortal Landscape." FL
"Mother's Nerves." ML, CT
"The Moths Have Eaten My Butterfly Collection." TT
"A Movement." EP
"Mr. Longfellow's Iron Pen." LM
"Mustafa Ferrari." LM
"Naomi Trimmer." LM
"Narcissus Suitor." ND, BE, CT
"National Shrine." GL
"A New Formalist." EP
"The Nineteen-thirties." GL
"No Neutral Stone." CT
"None but the Spirit." ML, CT
"Not Marble." CT
"A Note on Contributors." CT
"Nothing in Heaven Functions as It Ought." GL, BE, CT
"Nude Descending a Staircase." ND, BE, ML, CT
"Obdurate Snow." LM
"Obscenity." LM
"October." GL (This poem is different from the other poem with the same title.)
"October." HM, CT

"Ode." GL, BE, ML, CT
"Of a Man Who Sent Off. . . ." EP
"The Old." GL
"Old Men Pitching Horseshoes." HM, CT
"Old Self-esteem can manage. . . ." EP
"On a Boxer." ED ("Stilled in his corner . . . " in CT)
"On a Child Who Lived One Minute." ND, BE, CT
"On a Dishwasher." EP
"On a Given Book." CT
"On a President." EP
"On Being Accused of Wit." WT, DH
"On his wife's stone. . . ." ED
"On Receiving a Book Manuscript from a Stranger. . . ." EP
"On Receiving a Mild Review." MP
"On Someone Who Had Part of His Corpse Flash-frozen." EP
"On Song." LM
"On the Liquidation of the Mustang Ranch by the Internal Revenue Service." DH
"On the Proposed Seizure of Twelve Graves in a Colonial Cemetery." ML, CT
"On the Square." DH
"Onan's Soliloquy." ED, CT
"One A.M. with Voices." ND, BE, CT
"One-Night Homecoming." CT
"Ool about to Proclaim a Parable." ML, HM, CT
"O'Riley's Late-Bloomed Little Son." GL, BE, CT
"Others." LM
"Overheard in the Louvre." ND, WI, CT
"Overnight Pass." DH
"Pacifier." WT, LM
"Palefaces." TT
"Parody: Herrick." BE, ED, ML, CT
"Peace and Plenty." GL, CT
"A Penitent Giuseppe Belli Enters Heaven." WT
"Perplexities." LM
"The Phantom of Woodland Homes." ND, CT
"*Physician,* who assisted suicide. . . ." EP
"Pie." LM
"Pierrot's Soliloquy." FL
"Pileup." WT, LM
"The Poets Learn of Their Posthumous Celebrity." WT
"Poets." GL, BE, CT
"Police Court Saturday Morning." LM

"Ponce de Leon." LM
"Pont Mirabeau." FL, DH
"Postmodernist Poetry." EP
"Pottery Class." GL, BE, CT
"Preacher." WT
"Proposal to the National Endowment for the Arts." MP
"Protest at a Conference of Educators." MP
"Protest." ED
"Pure Poetry." MP
"The Purpose of Time Is to Prevent Everything from Happening at Once." LM
"A Rail Traveler." EP
"Rat." DH
"Reading Trip." GL, BE, CT
"Reflection in Salt Lake City." EP
"Requiem in Hoboken." GL
"Reunion." CT
"Robert Frost Discovers Another Road Not Taken." CT
"Ron fades back and. . . ." CT
"Rondeau." ND (titled "Rondel" in CT)
"Rotten Reveille." DH
"Sailors with the Clap." LM
"Salute Sweet Deceptions." ED, LM
"Sappho to a Mummy Wrapped in Papyrus." CT
"Satori." WI
"A Scandal in the Suburbs." LM
"Schizophrenic Girl." ED, CT
"Scholar's Wife." GL
"Seance." ND
"Seine River Blues." ND
"The Self-Exposed." GL, BE, CT
"Sentimentalist's Song, or, Answers for Everything." TT
"Separated Banks." DH
"September Twelfth, 2001." LM
"Sex Manual." BE, ED, CT
"Sexual Combat." EP
"Sharing the Score." LM
"The Shorter View." GL, BE, CT
"Should All of This Come True." CT
"Shriveled Meditation." LM
"Similes." CT
"The Sirens." ND, BE, CT
"Sirens." FL

"Sisyphus: A Parable of the Writer's Lot." WT
"A Snapshot Rediscovered." LM
"Snapshots." GL
"Snowflake Soufflé." CT
"Snug." DH
"Solitary Confinement." ND, BE, CT
"Song to the Tune of 'Somebody Stole My Gal." CP, TT, CT
"Song: Enlightenment." DH
"Song: Great Chain of Being." BE, ML (see "Great Chain of Being")
"Sonnet for Hélène." FL
"Space." GL
"Speculating Woman." DH
"Sperm Bank." WT
"The Spoke." LM
"Staring into a River Till Moved by It." DH
"Stilled in his corner. . . ." CT ("On a Boxer" in ED)
"Street Moths." LM
"*Stud* has a way with women?. . . ." EP
"Summer Children." DH
"Sun." FL
"*Swap* got a wildly favorable review. . . ." EP
"Table Talk." MP
"Tableau Intime." DH
"Taking Aspirin." LM
"Talking Dust Bowl." TT, CT
"Terminals." LM
"Terse Elegy for J. V. Cunningham." WT, DH
"Teutonic Scholar." BE, ED ("For a Teutonic Scholar" in CT)
"The Theater of Dionysus." ND, CT
"Thebes: In the Robber Village." LM
"Then and Now." LM
"Theology." EP
"Time is that dentist. . . ." BE, CT
"To a Deceived Husband." EP
"To a Forgetful Wishing Well." CT
"To a Hard Core Porn-Film Leading Man." CT
"To a Now-Type Poet." BE, ED, CT
"To a Pilgrim Returned from a Tour of the Vatican." WT
"To a Young Poet." BE, ED, ML, CT
"To an Angry God." ED, CT
"To an Englisher." EP
"To an Unpopular Novelist." WT

"To Break a Marble Block." ND
"To Dorothy on Her Exclusion from the *Guinness Book of World Records.*" ML, HM, CT
"To His Lover, That She Be Not Overdressed." LM
"To Mary Baker Eddy. . . ." EP
"To Mercury." ML
"To Someone Who Insisted I Look Up Someone." BE, ED, CT
"To the One-Eyed Poets." CT
"To the Writers Forbidden to Write." DH
"Translator." BE, ED, CT
"Transparency." GL, CT
"Traveler's Warnings." CT
"Twelve Dead, Hundreds Homeless." WT, DH
"Two Apparitions." GL, BE, CT
"Two Doorbells." CT
"Two Lovers Proceed to Love Despite Their Sunburns." ML, CT
"Two Views of Rhyme and Meter." ED, CT
"Ultimate Motel." TT
"Uncle Ool's Song against the Ill-Paid Life of Poetry." TT ("Uncle Ool's Complaint Against the Ill-Paid Life of Verse" in CT)
"Veterinarian." DH
"Vietnamese." GL
"Vilma." MP
"Vision." EP
"A Visit to the Gingerbread House." ML, CT
"Visit." LM
"Voice from a Borne Pall." EP
"Vulture." CT
"War Newscast in St. Thomas." DH
"Watchmaker." WT
"A Water Glass of Whisky." CP
"The Waterbury Cross." DH
"A Well-Dressed Man Much Married." EP
"West Somerville, Mass." GL, CT
"What constitutes inviolable decorum. . . ." EP
"What She Told the Sheriff." GL, CT
"When Spinner writes he writes. . . ." EP
"Where Are the Snows of Yesteryear?" ND
"Where Will We Run To." CT
"Why does old *Rake* . . . ?" EP
"Winter Thunder." WT, DH
"Wish." GL
"The Withdrawn Gift." DH

"Woman in Rain." DH
"The Woodpile Skull." WT, DH
"A Word from Hart Crane's Ghost." HM
"A worn tradition. . . ." EP
"Writer." WT
"XXX-Film Star." WT
"Yet Another Anthology of New American Poets." EP
"You Touch Me." CT

Uncollected Poems

"Aftermath." *ELF: Eclectic Literary Forum* 4 no. 2 (summer 1994): 26.
"Alternatives." *Ante*, no. 2 (fall 1964): 43.
"An American Songbag." *Cat's Ear* 2, no. 2 (winter 1993): 25–26.
"Another Epitaph on an Army of Mercenaries." *Epitaphs, The Classical Outlook*, (fall, 1992) (cf. "Further Retort from an Army of Mercenaries," EP).
"Arizona Retirement Community." *Pivot* 45 (1997): 6.
"Ballad Shard." *Sewanee Review* 100, no. 2 (spring 1992): 271.
"Begetting Likened to a Crapshoot." *The New Press Literary Quarterly* (winter 1994–95): 5.
"A Crisis in the Cathedral." *Hampden-Sydney Poetry Review*, 25th anniversary number (winter 2000): 41.
"Death of a Window Washer." *Ontario Review* 35 (fall–winter 1991–92): 82.
"A Death's Head in the Park." *ELF: Eclectic Literary Forum* 4, no. 2 (summer 1994): 26.
"Destroying Old Love Letters." *South Coast Poetry Journal* 11 (winter 1991): 15.
"The Ghost of My Unfinished Ph.D." *Ontario Review* 35 (fal–winter 1991–92): 81.
"Gulls: Swan's Way" (translation of "Mouettes: Allée des Cygnes," by Scott Bates). *Delos: A Journal of World* Literature 4, no. 1 (spring–summer 1991): back cover.
"Harold Witt." *Blue Unicorn* 20, no. 1 (October 1996): 7.
"Harsh Days Kneel upon Wessex Agriculture." *Cincinnati Poetry Review* 16 (spring 1987): 60–61.
"In Reply to the Question 'How Are You?'" *Hampden-Sydney Poetry Review*, 25th anniversary number (winter 2000): 41.
"An Irish Prayer Versified." *Paintbrush* 25 (autumn 1998): 5.
"January Thaw." *Pivot* 40 (1992): 21.

"Japanese Beetles." *The North Stone Review* 11 (1993): 43–44.
"Kid Hoop Star." *From the Lily Pad: newsletter of the Nick Virgilio Haiku Association.* (winter 1993): 2.
"Lament for Capital Letters." *Blue Unicorn* 17, no. 1 (October 1993): 18.
"Last Log." *Sewanee Theological Review* 37, no. 4 (Michaelmas 1994): 407.
"Late Words from Hart Crane." *The New Press Literary Quarterly.* (winter 1994–95): 5.
"Leave of Absence." *Rhetoric Review* 8, no. 1 (fall 1989): 150.
"Like the Vineyard Watchman." (translation of "Wie Der Wachter in Den Weingelanden," by Rainer Maria Rilke). *Counter/Measures* 3 (1974): 161.
"Living Will." *The New Press Literary Quarterly* (winter 1994–95): 5.
"Love: A Neoplatonist View." *Paintbrush* 18, no. 36 (autumn 1991): 8.
"The Man of Blood's Ballad." *Gulf Coast* 5, no. 1 (summer 1992): 98.
"Meatloaf." *South Coast Poetry Journal* 4 (fall 1987): 16.
"A Minnesota Norseman Asks for a Viking Funeral." *New York Quarterly* 46 (fall 1991): 23.
"Normalcy." *Open Places* 38/39 (spring 1985): 183.
"Paul Stanwood's Bread." *Wrestling with God: Literature and Theology in the English Renaissance.* Edited by Mary Ellen Henley and W. Speed Hill. *EMLS Journal,* special issue 7 (May 2001): 9.
"Petrarchan Sonnet That Need Not Continue." *Journal of New Jersey Poets* 18, nos. 1–2 (summer 1996): 39.
"Poem of Banal, Cheap, and Worthless Feeling." *The Formalist* 2, no. 2 (1991): 32.
"Poet on the Make." *Paintbrush* 25 (autumn 1998): 6.
"The Poetry Mafia." *Paintbrush* 18, no. 36 (Autumn 1991): 8.
"Poets' Hearts." *North Stone Review* 11 (1993): 43.
"Possible Dyings." *Gulf Coast* 5, no. 1 (summer 1992): 102.
"Prom." *The Review* 1 (autumn 1995): 10.
"Raisins." *The North Stone Review* 11 (1993): 42.
"Reuben Farr." *The Southern California Anthology* 6 (1988): 77.
"Second-Hand Smoke." *Edge City Review* 15 (April 2001): 10.
"Sonnet with Immortality Written All Over It." *Sparrow* 59 (1992): 27.
"Stuart Davis: Premier, 1957." In *Heart to Heart: New Poems In-*

spired by Twentieth-Century American Art, edited by Jan Greenberg, 17. New York: Abrams, 2001.

"To His Proud Mistress." *The Formalist* 5, no. 1 (1994): 38.

"To Writers Forbidden to Write." *The North Stone Review* 11 (1993): 42.

"A Visit from St. Sigmund." *Light* 4 (winter 1992–93): 20.

"Walking through Walls." In *Divine Inspiration: The Life of Jesus in World Poetry,* edited by Robert Atwan, George Dardess, and Peggy Rosenthal, 155. New York: Oxford University Press, 1998.

"West Yorkshire Morning." *The New Press Literary Quarterly* (winter 1994–95): 5.

Uncollected Light Verse

All of the following poems were featured in *Light,* 3 (autumn 1992): 3–6.

"Apochrypha"
"Ancient Catastrophes Revisited"
"Cowhand Song"
"A Culinary Surprise"
"Drat These Brats!"
"Elizabethan Theater: A Suspicion"
"Ghastly Brats"
"History of Strong Drink"
"Medical Types of Personality"
"Naval Intelligence"
"Postscript to an Apocalypse"
"Reflection on Far Eastern Cuisine"
"Spooky Doings"
"Suffering Ungladly"
"Wild Death Purveyor"

The following poems appeared in *The Classical Outlook* (fall 1992): 19

"Epigrams: Various"
"Epitaphs"

Appendix D

Selected Prose by X. J. Kennedy

"About 'B Negative.'" In *Introspections: American Poets on One of Their Own Poems,* edited by Robert Pack and Jay Parini, 138–44. Hanover, N.H.: University Press of New England, 1997.

"Afternoon with a Geek." *The Texas Review* 18, nos. 1–2 (1997): 1–6.

"Andrew Marvell's 'To His Coy Mistress.'" In *Touchstones: American Poets on a Favorite Poem,* edited by Robert Pack and Jay Parini, 110–15. Hanover, N.H.: Middlebury College Press, University Press of New England, 1996.

"An Appreciative Essay by X. J. Kennedy." In *Hardening Rock: An Organic Anthology of the Adolescence of Rock 'n Roll,* edited by Bruce L. Chipman, 3–6. Boston and Toronto: Little, Brown, 1972.

Autobiographical essay. In *Contemporary Authors Autobiography Series* 9, edited by Mark Zadrozny, 73–88. Detroit: Gale Research, 1989.

Autobiographical essay. In *Something about the Author Autobiography Series* 22, edited by Gerard J. Senick, 105–24. Detroit: Gale Research, 1996.

"Comment." *Poetry* 151, nos. 1–2 (October–November 1987): 215–16.

"Consumer's Report." In *Fifty Contemporary Poets: The Creative Process,* edited by Alberta T. Turner, 164–67. New York: David McKay Company, 1977.

"CO-rrespondence." *The Hiram Poetry Review* 2 (spring–summer 1967): 4–5.

"The Devalued Estate." *Poetry* 114, no. 4 (July 1969): 266–74.

Discussion of "To Dorothy on Her Exclusion from the *Guinness Book of World Records.*" In *Poetspeak: In Their Work, about Their Work,* edited by Paul B. Janeczko, 167–69. Scarsdale, N.Y.: Bradbury Press, 1983.

"Disorder and Security in Nonsense Verse for Children." *The Lion and The Unicorn* 13 (1990): 28–33.

"Do Poets Need Subsidies?" *Harvard Review* 2 (fall 1993): 48–51.

"Does Poetry Have a History?" *Harvard Review* 2 (fall 1992): 31–33.

"Fenced-in Fields." *Counter/Measures* 1 (1972): 4–11. Reprinted in *Claims for Poetry*, edited by Donald Hall, 203–12. Ann Arbor, Mich.: University of Michigan Press, 1982.

"Foreword: Do Poets Need to Know Something?" In *Writing Poems*, 2d ed., by Robert Wallace, iii–vii. Boston: Little, Brown, 1987.

"Formal Verse and Fascist Deviousness." A rebuttal essay to "Pulse and Breath," by G. T. Wright. *The North Stone Review* 11 (1993): 65–71.

"'Go and Get Your Candle Lit!': An Approach to Poetry." *The Horn Book Magazine* 57, no. 3 (June 1981): 273–79.

"Guiding Myths for Teaching Writing Are Changing: Kennedy." *College English* 47 (February 1985): 158–59.

"How to Survive Gresham's Law." *Michigan Quarterly Review* 21, no. 1 (winter 1982): 43–47.

"Innocence in Armor." Review of *Hello, Darkness: Collected Poems* and *Innocent Bystander: The Scene from the '70's*, by L. E. Sissman. *Parnassus: Poetry in Review* 8, no.1 (fall–winter 1979): 48–63.

Introduction to *Contemporary New England Poetry: A Sampler*, edited by Paul Ruffin. Huntsville, Tex.: Texas Review Press, 1987.

Introduction to *Directory of American Poetry Books*, 3d ed., edited by Jane Preston. New York: Poets House, 1995.

Introduction to *Just What the Country Needs, Another Poetry Anthology*, edited by James McMichael and Dennis Saleh. Belmont, Calif.: Wadsworth Publishing Co., 1971.

Introduction to *Living in America*, by Anne Stevenson. Ann Arbor, Mich.: Generation, 1965.

"Is There a Vast, Untapped Audience?" *The New York Quarterly* 50 (1993): 93–99.

"John Ciardi's *Early Lives*." In *John Ciardi: Measure of the Man*, edited by Vince Clemente, 24–31. Fayetteville, Ark.: University of Arkansas Press, 1987.

"John Finlay's Personal Poetry." In *Light Apart: The Achievement of John Finlay*, edited by David Middleton, 129–33. Glenside, Pa.: Aldine, 1999.

"John O'Hara." *John O'Hara Journal* 3, no. 1 (fall–winter 1980): 150.

"Larkin's Voice." In *Philip Larkin: The Man and His Work*, edited by Dale Salwalk, 62–64. Iowa City, Iowa: University of Iowa Press, 1989.

"The Least Known Major American Poet." *Harvard Review* 3 (winter 1993): 103–6.

"The Light Tradition." Review of *The New Oxford Book of English Light Verse,* edited by Kingsley Amis. *Inquiry* 1, no. 19 (August 21, 1978): 27–29.

"Living with Whitman." In *Paumanok Rising,* edited by Vince Clemente and Graham Everett, 23–25. Port Jefferson, N.Y.: Street Press, 1981.

"A London View of Light." Review of *The Oxford Book of Comic Verse,* by John Gross. *Parnassus: Poetry in Review* 21, nos. 1/2 (1996): 131–35.

"The Loneliness of the Writer" (Padraic Colum lecture at Wesleyan University Writers' Conference). In *Facing the Lines: Writers on Life and Craft,* edited by Kurt Brown, 104–13. Boston: Beacon Press, 1996.

"Love 'Em and Leave 'Em." *This World* (Sunday magazine section of the *San Francisco Chronicle*), February 9, 1986, 13–14.

"Making a Name in Poetry." In *The Writer's Handbook,* edited by Sylvia K. Burback, 364–70. Boston: The Writer, 1988.

"Malcom Cowley, Poet." *The Visionary Company* (a double number) 2, no. 2; and 3, no. 1 (summer 1987): 55–61.

"The Man Who Hitched the Reindeer to Santa Claus's Sleigh." *New York Times Book Review,* December 5, 1993, 11.

"Marianne Moore." *The Minnesota Review* 2, no. 3 (1962): 369–76.

"Meter-Rattling." Review of *The Poems of General George S. Patton, Jr.: Lines of Fire,* edited by Carmine A. Prioli. *The Sewanee Review* 102, no. 1 (winter 1994): 148–52.

"New Harmony." Keynote speech at the Proceedings of the Tenth Annual Mid-America Conference on Composition, University of Southern Indiana, New Harmony, Ind., April 19, 1986.

"The New *King Kong,* or A Great Ape Double-Crossed." *The Writer's World: Readings for College Composition.* Edited by George Arms, William M. Gibson, and Louis G. Locke, 214–17. New York: St. Martin's Press, 1978.

"Orphan Asylum." Review of *Collected Poems, 1953–1993,* by John Updike. *The New Criterion* (April 1993): 62–65.

"Pelting Dark Windows." Review of *Collected Poems,* by David Wagoner. *Parnassus: Poetry in Review* 5, no. 2 (spring–summer 1977): 133–40.

"Piping down the Valleys Wild." *Parnassus: Poetry in Review* 12, no. 1 (1984): 183–89.

"Playing It Safe and the Outright Awful." *Arbor* 4 (1961): 1–5.

"Pleasure or Punishment: Hearing a Poet Read." *Poets and Writers Magazine* 25 (September–October 1997): 70–77.

"The Poet in the Playpen." Three reviews. *Poetry* 105, no. 3 (1964): 190–91.

"The Poetry: Form and Informality." In *Miller Williams and the Poetry of the Particular,* edited by Michael Burns, 43–53. Columbia, Mo.: University of Missouri Press, 1991.

"Prefatory Dialogue." In *Pegasus Descending: A Treasury of the Best Bad Poems in English from Matthew Arnold to Walt Whitman,* edited by James Camp, X. J. Kennedy, and Keith Waldrop, xii–xvi. New York: Macmillan Co., 1971.

"The Present State of American Poetry." *The New York Quarterly* 20 (1993): 93–99.

"Recurrences." Three reviews. *The Nation* 210, no. 12 (1970): 378–80.

Review of *Each in His Season,* by W. D. Snodgrass, and *Light While There Is Light,* by Keith Waldrop. *Harvard Review* 1 (spring 1995): 146–47.

Review of *The Oxford Book of American Light Verse,* edited by William Harmon. *The New Republic* 181, no. 12 (September 22, 1979): 49–51.

Review of *The Rag and Bone Shop of the Heart,* by Robert Bly. *Harvard Review* 3 (winter 1993): 188–9.

Reviews of nine poetry collections. *Poetry* 114 (1969): 266–74.

"Rhythmic Language." *Mississippi Review* 6, no. 1 (1977): 116.

"Rime." *New York Quarterly* 6 (spring 1971): 128–33.

"Roads in a Wood: The Choices Writers Make." *Gettysburg Review* 7, no. 2 (spring 1994): 289–303.

"Robert Frost Overheard." *Michigan Quarterly Review* 36, no. 1 (winter 1997): 129–38.

"Robert Wallace, Bringer of Light." *Light* 26 (autumn 1999): 49–52.

"Sameness and Individual Voice." *Harvard Review* 1 (spring 1992): 17–20.

"Say *Ah.*" *The Chariton Review* 21 (1995): 47–51.

"Seamus Heaney and the Tinsmith's Scoop." *Harvard Review* 1 (spring 1996): 164–65.

"Seeing New Englandly." Introduction to *Contemporary New England Poetry: A Sampler,* edited by Paul Ruffin. Huntsville, Tex.: Texas Review Press, 1987.

"A Selection of Notebook Entries by X. J. Kennedy." In *The Poet's Notebook,* edited by Stephen Kuusisto, Deborah Tall, and David Weiss, 121–33. New York: W. W. Norton, 1995.
"The Size of Snodgrass." In *The Poetry of W. D. Snodgrass: Everything Human,* edited by Stephen Haven, 301–4. University of Michigan Press, 1993.
"Statement on Poetry." *The Worcester Review* 9, no. 2 (1987): 43
"Strict and Loose Nonsense: Two Worlds of Children's Verse." *School Library Journal* 37, no. 3 (March 1991): 108–12.
"The Surprises of Rime." In *Books That Invite Talk, Wonder, and Play,* edited by Amy A. McClure and Janet V. Kristo, 259–61. Urbana, Ill.: National Council of Teachers of English, 1996.
"A Symposium of Poets." *South Dakota Review* 5 (1967): 12–13.
"A Symposium of Poets." *South Dakota Review* 5 (1987): 3–23.
"Taking Notes: From Poets' Notebooks." *Seneca Review* 21, no. 2 (1991): 103–9.
"A Tenth and Four Fifths." Review of five poetry collections. *Poetry* 141, no. 6 (March 1983): 349–58.
"That First Fine Careless Rapture." *First Intensity* 9 (summer 1997): 9–19.
"Tradition and Revolt: Recent Poetry for Children." In *The Lion and the Unicorn* 4, no. 2 (winter 1980–81): 75–82.
"Translations from the American." Review of the writings of James Merrill and A. R. Ammons. *The Atlantic* 231, no. 3 (March 1973): 101–4.
"Twelve from Small Presses." *Poetry* 99, no. 3 (February 1962): 313–19.
"Under Briggflatts." *English Language Notes* 28 (1998): 79–81.
"The Usefulness of Poetry." In *Poets' Perspectives: Reading, Writing, and Teaching Poetry,* edited by Charles R. Duke, 5–6. Nortsmouth, N.H.: Boynton/Cook, 1992.
"Who Killed King Kong?" In *The Writer's World: Readings for College Composition,* edited by George Arms, William M. Gibson, and Louis G. Locke, 211–14. New York: St. Martin's Press, 1978.
"The Writing Life: Three Fables" ("The Forbidden Library," "A Day at the Institute," and "Bait"). *New York Quarterly* 57 (1997): 37–38.
"Writing with a DECmate II: Building Sandcastles." In *The Bedford Reader,* 2d ed., edited by X. J. Kennedy and Dorothy M. Kennedy, 331–39. Boston: Bedford Books of St. Martin's, 1984.
"Why We Rejected Eight Hundred Thousand Poems." Symposium of Poetry Editors. *Writer's Digest* 42 (1962): 22–23, 77, 80.

"X. J. Kennedy Writes." *Poetry Book Society Bulletin* 71 (Christmas 1971).

"X. J. Kennedy." *The Place My Words Are Looking for: What Poets Say about and through Their Work.* Edited by Paul B. Janeczko, 35–37. New York: Bradbury Press, 1990.

Notes

Chapter 1: The Poetry of Design

1. Discussing light verse in "The Light Tradition," Kennedy interprets "form" to mean "rhyme and meter," as Kingsley Amis uses it. X. J. Kennedy, "The Light Tradition." Review of *The New Oxford Book of English Light Verse,* ed. Kingsley Amis, *Inquiry* 1, no. 19 (August 21, 1978) 29.

2. X. J. Kennedy, "Taking Notes: From Poets' Notebooks," *Seneca Review* 21, no. 2 (1991): 103.

3. Jim Svejda, "The Funniest Poet Alive: An Interview with X. J. Kennedy," *Syracuse Guide,* 9 (May 1976): 16.

4. "X. J. Kennedy on Form, Meter, and Rime," interview by John Ciardi, *Saturday Review* 4, no. 21 (May 20, 1972): 14, 19. A perceptive critic, John Gordon, sees that "Kennedy's adherence to traditional forms often seems a kind of quest, spurred by curiosity as much as anything, to discover the different permutations generated by the assimilation of modern experiences into the forms of the older, more permanent realities; the range is from melodious parody to the highest, wittiest sadness." Gordon sees Kennedy using traditional forms to express "the primal lub-dubs of ante-technocratic experience that Kennedy believes is abstracted into the old forms and ways. . . ." "Never Trust a Guy Whose First Name Is a Letter," *Boston Review of the Arts* 2, no. 4 (July 1972): 17, 77.

5. X. J. Kennedy, "The Poetry: Form and Informality," in *Miller Williams and the Poetry of the Particular,* ed. Michael Burns. (Columbia, Mo.: University of Missouri Press, 1991), 43–53.

6. Czeslaw Milosz, "The Writing Life," interview by Nathan Gardels, *Los Angeles Times,* July 25, 1999, 12.

7. Kennedy, *"Counter/Measures,"* 14, 19.

8. X. J. Kennedy, "Fenced-in Fields," *Counter/Measures* 1 (1972): 11.

9. Kennedy, *"Counter/Measures,"* 14, 19.

10. X. J. Kennedy, *The North Stone Review,* 44; in *The Epigrammatist* the first line is changed to read, "A worn tradition isn't hard to quit." Kennedy echoed this sentiment in an interview: "Many poets around the early Sixties got turned off by the old forms . . . They came to associate iambic pentameter with a dead aristocracy and to see open forms as more democratic, more fluid, more honest—more honest for them, that is. Just possibly their sense of honesty was affected by the fact that they had not mastered stricter forms to the point of feeling free within them . . . they have not let themselves experience containment and the power it can confer." Kennedy, *"Counter/Measures,"* 14, 19.

11. X. J. Kennedy, "Playing It Safe and the Outright Awful," *Arbor* 4 (1961): 1–5.

12. X. J. Kennedy, introduction to *Just What the Country Needs, Another*

Poetry Anthology, ed. James McMichael and Dennis Saleh (Belmont, Calif.: Wadsworth Publishing Co., 1971), ix–xii.

13. X. J. Kennedy, "A Symposium of Poets," *South Dakota Review* 5, no. 3 (autumn 1967): 12–3. He says that he is quoting from "the old jazz song."

14. X. J. Kennedy, "Sameness and Individual Voice," *Harvard Review* 1 (spring 1992): 17–20.

15. Svejda, "The Funniest Poet Alive," 17.

16. X. J. Kennedy, "Statement on Poetry," *The Worcester Review* 9, no. 2 (1987): 43.

17. The inscription to "Satori" reads: "Poem written to be read by 'Kenneth Kant' at the Wolgamot Society's beatnik poetry hoax, May 27, 1959." In the author's copy of this book, Kennedy penciled this comment beside the poem: "Never reprinted, of course!"

18. This poem appeared in *Ante* 2 (fall 1964): 43.

19. "X. J. Kennedy Writes," *Poetry Book Society Bulletin* 71 (Christmas 1971).

20. Critic Richard Moore thinks "The Withdrawn Gift" is especially effective in this regard, saying that Kennedy's persona disappears and that nothing stands between the beggar and the reader: "To *see* a beggar is to realize that you *are* a beggar" ("Lyrics of Wit." *Sewanee Review* 101, no. 1 (winter 1993): xlii–xliv).

21. Richard Moore explains why Kennedy's satire once made his poetry unfashionable, even threatening: "Satire's appeal is to a hypothetical general reader who is the opposite of the modern specialist. He is interested in society as a whole and in the human beings in it as sharing a common sense of life and destiny. Kennedy clearly writes for this reader (with apparent unconcern that such readers no longer exist), writes about the real sad/comic experience of ordinary people (in spite of the fact that ordinary people have given up on poetry). It all seems perfectly safe; but what if ordinary people ever did take an interest? What would happen to the marvelous edifice of contemporary poetry with its contests and awards, its committees and events, its attendant experts and critics? . . . [Kennedy's satire] is not merely distasteful to poetry's self-perpetuating officialdom, it poses a real threat, when Kennedy puts on his déclassé common man's voice" ("The Decline of Satire and the Specialist Society: Some Thoughts on the Poetry of X. J. Kennedy." *Light* 3 [autumn 1993]: 31–34). For further discussion of Kennedy's skillful use of epigrams, see David Middleton, "Stingers: X. J. Kennedy at Epigrams," *Paintbrush* 25 (autumn 1998): 92–99.

22. In a conversation with the author on July 20, 2001, Kennedy explained that this title refers to "little, shiny, nasty creatures that you can step on." He spoke with a mischievous twinkle in his eyes.

23. Some poems of his that Kennedy thought "work the best" are "In a Prominent Bar in Secaucus One Day," "Nude Descending a Staircase," "Little Elegy," "Ode," and a sonnet, "To Dorothy on Her Exclusion." X. J. Kennedy, "An Interview with X. J. Kennedy," by Jill Scherer, *Lodestar* 5 (1984): 49–50. Kennedy reprints "Ode" in four collections, starting with *Growing into Love.*

24. Forrest Read, "Notes, Reviews and Speculations," *Epoch* 11 (winter 1962): 257–58.

25. Ibid., 257.

26. Moore Moran, "*Cross Ties:* X. J. Kennedy," *Prairie Schooner* 60, no. 4 (winter 1986): 112–14.

27. Ibid., 2. Moran's reading sheds light on another instance of Kennedy's use of formal opposition to reinforce meaning and thereby increase the poem's

tension and irony. The effect not only gives a sense that Kennedy "is packing things a bit tight," as Moran observes, but creates meaning on many levels at once.

28. This poem was first published in *Poetry*. After the editor, Henry Rago, accepted the poem, Kennedy had second thoughts and hastened off a revision, which Rago rejected, printing the original version. Recalling the incident in 1987, Kennedy believed Rago's decision was "wise." See Kennedy's recollection of this incident in "Comment," *Poetry* 151, nos. 1–2 (October–November 1987): 215–16.

29. Ronald A. Sharp, "Kennedy's 'Nude Descending a Staircase,'" *Explicator* 37, no. 3 (spring 1979): 3.

30. Nancy Sullivan, "Perspective and the Poetic Process," *Wisconsin Studies in Contemporary Literature* 6, no. 1 (winter-spring 1965): 123. Not all critics could see the poem's complexities with an equally sensitive appreciation. In his reading of "Nude Descending a Staircase," Forrest Read believes that "while the nude dances in images of light, and Kennedy's mind agilely follows her motions for us, his self-consciousness interposes itself and prevents that further resonance of sound, rhythm, and tone which gives words the fullness of song, be it a chorale or a catch." ("Notes, Reviews and Speculations," 257). Fortunately, better readings have prevailed.

31. Kennedy alludes to Frost's idea in "John Ciardi's *Early Lives*," in *John Ciardi: Measure of the Man*, ed. Vince Clemente, (Fayetteville, Ark.: University of Arkansas Press, 1987): 24–31; and in "The Poetry: Form and Informality," in *Miller Williams*, 43–53.

32. In "Sameness and Individual Voice" Kennedy says that many poets represented in the current *American Poetry Review* "write in styles that seem interchangeable"; many are "insidiously easy to grind out. . . . And because you can just drone along in prose, chopping it up into lines, breaking a line whenever you come to a verb or a noun, few annoying technical demands are laid on you" (17–18). In the same essay, he cites Stanley Kunitz's remark that the doing away with rhyme and meter "has made poetry easier to write but harder to remember" and "has surely encouraged a vast murmur of indistinguishable free verse" (19). Elsewhere he sarcastically advises young poets seeking fame never to write in traditional forms, for they will slow production and reveal their lack of skill. X. J. Kennedy, "Making a Name in Poetry," in *The Writer's Handbook*, edited by Sylvia K. Burback. Boston: The Writer, 1988, 364–70.

33. Sam Hamill, introduction to *The Essential Basho: Matsuo Basho*, by Matsuo Basho, trans. Sam Hamill (Boston and London: Shambhala, 1999), 176–77.

34. X. J. Kennedy, *Poetspeak: In Their Work, about Their Work*, ed. Paul B. Janeczko (Scarsdale, N.Y.: Bradbury Press, 1983), 167–69.

35. The version of this poem printed in *Emily Dickinson in Southern California* contains the following three quatrains, numbered five, which are omitted in *Cross Ties*.

> I wrote all night—till break of Mind—
> Tongue thick—teeth clogged with Sludge—
> What decent words—were there to find?
> 'Oh flab!'—'Ah freeby fudge!'
>
> Some days you can't—do more than cant—
> My old White Owl died out—
> Then—Universe stood up in me
> To take a sharper—squint—

Impatient Lepers—queued for miles—
A split—hair more—thought—free—
And—I had healed 'em! Out winked—I—
And what was left but—me

36. This poem is printed in *Lords of Misrule: Poems 1992–2001*. The poem is also one of three that Kennedy reads on the CD-ROM that accompanies the "Interactive Edition" of Kennedy's textbook, *Literature*, eighth edition, with Dana Gioia.

37. See appendix A for a discussion of William Blake's influence on Kennedy's work.

38. In a note to the author, Kennedy says that "Ginsberg loved Blake's 'Songs,' even did an LP record on which he sang them."

39. Kennedy, "*Counter/Measures*," 14, 19.

40. In "Sameness and Individual Voice" Kennedy quotes from Thomas Hardy and Robert Frost to show that two poems written in identical form and syntax are very individual and very different (17–20).

41. "Reserves of Energy," *Times Literary Supplement*, 30 August 1974, 932. Earlier, another unsigned critic hints at a similar understanding of Kennedy's use of imagery, saying that "The denser or longer poems like 'Ant Trap,' 'The Ascent,' 'Golgotha,' 'Artificer,' 'Ode,' 'Last Child' have visible structures as elaborate as an espaliered tree, with the same life, growth, and tension" ("No Shortage of Satisfactions," *Times Literary Supplement*, December 24, 1971, 1602).

42. In a display of dull sense, Joseph Parisi says that "Mining Town" is an example of how Kennedy abandons "the gentle mockery for disquieting realism," and he adds blandly, "Clapboard houses occasionally plunge into the shafts of *Mining Town*," where "It takes a while to learn to sleep on edge" ("Coming to Terms," *Poetry*, 124 [September 1974]: 343–52).

43. Kennedy has displayed considerable interest in this poem, reprinting it in four collections, from *Breaking and Entering* (1971) to *Cross Ties* (1985). The word *Song* begins the poem's title in *Breaking and Entering* and *Missing Link* and is dropped in the other two printings.

44. Robert E. Bjork, "Kennedy's 'Nothing in Heaven Functions as It Ought,'" *The Explicator* 40, no. 2 (winter 1982): 6–7.

45. Ibid., 7.

46. Marden Clark, "Liberating Form," in *Liberating Form: Mormon Essays on Religion and Literature* (Salt Lake City, Utah: Aspen Books, 1992), 7.

47. David Shapiro, "Into the Gloom," *Poetry*, 128, no. 4 (July 1976): 226–27.

48. Ghita Orth says that "Separated Banks" "evokes the tension between connection and division in its form. In personifying the banks, however, and using diction redolent of the divorce court—'division of estate,' 'non-support'—Kennedy invests the ostensibly literal description with metaphoric implication; we seem to look at a marriage gone wrong" ("Rich in Discipline," *New England Review* 16 [spring 1994]: 172).

Chapter 2: The Book Collections

1. X. J. Kennedy, "Comment," *Poetry* 151, nos. 1–2 (October–November 1987), 215–16.

2. Lachlan Mackinnon noted this remarkable quality twenty-five years later,

saying that although *Cross Ties* "contains poems written from 1955 to 1984, it is impossible to tell early Kennedy from late[;] . . . like Frost, whose voice he deliberately takes on in a light poem, [Kennedy] demonstrates the virtues of consistency." ("High Fidelity," *Times Literary Supplement* 4303 [September 20, 1985]: 1039).

3. John Simon, "More Brass Than Enduring," *Hudson Review* 15 (autumn 1962), 464–65.

4. Forrest Read, "Notes, Reviews & Speculations," *Epoch* 11 (winter 1962): 257.

5. Theodore Holmes, "Wit, Nature, and the Human Concern," *Poetry* 100, no. 5 (August 1962): 321.

6. Thomas Goldstein, "X. J. Kennedy," *Dictionary of Literary Biography*, s.v. 5: 394. Goldstein contributed one of the longer reviews of Kennedy's career up to 1975, yet he clearly does not think much of Kennedy or his poetry. In addition to the attacks already quoted, he says that "Kennedy's poetry is often pugnacious," that "Another recurrent theme is a strident atheism"—he instances "First Confession" as one of the examples—and to a critic who referred to Kennedy's poetry as "'irreverent speculations' on a variety of themes," Goldstein replies: "when Kennedy turns to religion, his poems become more intolerant than irreverent. Rather than satirize the organization of religion, he often questions the authenticity of people's religious beliefs." Of *Breaking and Entering*, Goldstein says, "The title page contains a portentous quotation from T. S. Eliot. . . . Yet the seven new poems do not transcend, in either theme or scope, those of the previous books. It is difficult to imagine in what manner such a poem as 'In a Secret Field' may divert the mind." Goldstein is even less taken with *Emily Dickinson in Southern California*, in which Kennedy, "Rather than interpret the mayhem of Southern California as though through the ironic, cryptic, and refined sensibility of Emily Dickinson . . . is content to imitate her verse. The similarity gets no closer, however, than the frequent use of the dash, because Kennedy mocks the combination of depth of vision and teasing playfulness characteristic of Dickinson's verse. Ultimately, his poems only look like hers on the page." Goldstein thinks Kennedy's "most successful verse to date" may be found in *Celebrations after the Death of John Brennan* because "his subject . . . gives the poem direction and poignancy." (5: 396–97).

7. Ibid., 394.

8. Forrest Read, "Notes, Reviews & Speculations," 258.

9. Ibid., 259.

10. Holmes, "Wit, Nature, and the Human Concern," 321.

11. Kennedy identifies this work as a "brochure of poems by poets associated in Ann Arbor and Detroit, published by Burning Deck (at the time run by Donald C. Hope). The volume includes poems by James Camp, Donald Hall, D. C. Hope, John Heath-Stubbs, X. J. Kennedy, W. D. Snodgrass, and Bernard Keith Waldrop" (private correspondence with the author). W. D. Snodgrass adds that Kennedy and Keith Waldrop "—also a grad student—were joint heads of the John Barton Wolgamot Society. This organization, dedicated to the Principles of the Truly Awful and intended to offset the rigid propriety and stodginess of Michigan's English Department, was named for the worst poet they had yet discovered" ("Remembering Joe Kennedy," *Paintbrush* 25 [autumn 1998], 136).

12. David Harsent, "Poetae Sepulchrum," *Spectator* (February 12, 1972). Harsent is not alone on this point; sixteen years later, Moore Moran felt that in *Cross Ties* Kennedy's "cleverness sometimes borders on the cute. Or that such

a large swallow of traditional (and predictable) verse forms tires the palate a bit prematurely. But these are venial [sic] sins" ("X. J. Kennedy, *Cross Ties*," *Prairie Schooner* 60, no. 4 [winter 1986]: 113–14).

13. David Harsent is not favorably impressed by this widely praised epigram, saying that "it is always a pleasure to watch a craftsman at work—but it can become a questionable virtue when used for little more than a five-finger exercise, as in 'Ars Poetica'" ("Poetae Sepulchrum").

14. Kennedy would not reprint this poem in later collections, perhaps because his emotional ties to the poem's central event, the assassination of President John F. Kennedy, diminished over time.

15. Stephen Tudor, *"Growing into Love," Spirit* 37 (spring 1970): 38.

16. Ibid.

17. John Leggett, *Boston Globe*, 24 August 1969, 73.

18. Peter L. Simpson, "The Candor of Poetry," *St. Louis Post-Dispatch*, 7 December 1969, 16M.

19. Leggett, "Poems with a Temper of Mind," 73.

20. John Demos, "A Review of *Growing into Love*, by X. J. Kennedy," *Library Journal* 94, no. 15 (September 1, 1969): 2929.

21. Alan Brownjohn, "Dark Forces," *New Statesman* 28, no. 2009 (September 12, 1969): 347.

22. Knute Skinner, "Good Measures," *Northern Review*, XII, 95. Douglas Dunn also believed that this collection shows that Kennedy's "wit gets chronologically darker and sharper." *Encounter*, May 1972, 77.

23. Skinner, *Review* XII, 94. Thomas Goldstein says that the poem characterizes all those involved in such reading trips, including Kennedy himself, as "phony and culpable," adding that "his willingness to acknowledge his own part in the sanctimonious behavior of high literary circles does not exonerate him from the self-conscious cuteness that characterizes much of the poetry in this volume." *Dictionary of Literary Biography*, s.v. "Kennedy, X. J.," 396.

24. Thomas Tessier, "X. J. Kennedy's Poetry," *The New Haven Register*, 1969.

25. P. J. Ferlazzo is so struck by Kennedy's use of traditional forms, as evidenced in *Cross Ties*, that he says, "Not since the 18th century has one seen such a commitment to traditional forms," and although he admires Kennedy's "clear, sensible intelligence at work and at play on the page," Ferlazzo thinks that Kennedy has limited his audience: "He is writing essentially for the college crowd—readers, for example, who have studied the college textbooks he and his wife (Dorothy M. Kennedy), have edited and written over the years. Perhaps, one is tempted to say, he is writing for English majors. In sum, if Kennedy is an academic poet, he is one of the best" ("Kennedy, X. J. *Cross Ties*: Selected Poems," *Choice* 23 [October 1985:296). This comment is surprising in a review of *Cross Ties*, which appeared in 1985, by which time Kennedy was long past being considered an "academic" poet. For some readers, apparently, old—and outmoded—labels are difficult to put aside. Nevertheless, the belief persisted. Mark McCloskey ends his long review of *Cross Ties* on the same idea: "The range of poets to whom he alludes is wide . . . These and various allusions to such bookish things as Greek mythology and the Great Chain of Being tend to confine the focus of his work (notwithstanding the down-to-earth tone behind it) to an academic audience. All in all, though, Kennedy's work is first-rate within its confinement" ("*Cross Ties: Selected Poems*," in *Magill's Literary Annual*, ed. Frank N. Magill. [Englewood Cliffs, N.J.: Salem Press, 1986] 1: 203. R. S. Gwynn probably sensed that Kennedy's reputation as an academic poet would

be an issue when *Cross Ties* was published, for in his review of it, he sought to put the issue to rest: "Those who favor neat schisms in their –isms would call him an 'academic' poet, though Kennedy's ties to the university are now limited to guest lectures and readings and the continued success of *Literature*, one of the most popular of freshman textbooks ever" ("Swans in Ice," *Sewanee Review* 43, no. 4 [fall 1985]: lxxviii).

26. Ralph J. Mills, Jr., "Three Established Poets and a New One," *Chicago Sun-Times Book Week*, 19 October 1969, 10. Douglas Dunn, speaking of *Breaking and Entering*, also believes that Kennedy may seem "dry and academic" because he "writes carefully, usually in polished stanzas in which a dexterous technique complements a cultured wit and balanced sense of narrative episode, but the fineness of craft is never offensively obtrusive as the only reason for having written . . . and he prefers the mystery of feelings to showing off in metre." *Encounter*, May 1972, 77. Edward Lucie-Smith relegates Kennedy to the "academic wing of contemporary American poetry" and considers him to be, essentially, "an extremely witty lightweight, a poet with a cunning ear and a deft hand with rhyme and off-rhyme" (*Contemporary Poets*, 2nd edition, 1975).

27. Tessier, "X. J. Kennedy's Poetry."

28. James Carroll, "Blossoming Poet," a review of *Growing into Love*, by X. J. Kennedy, *Catholic World*, January, 1970, 183.

29. Henry Taylor, "'Singing to Spite This Hunger,'" *The Nation* 210 (2 February 1970): 122–24.

30. Louis L. Martz, "Recent Poetry: The End of an Era," *Yale Review* 59 (winter 1970): 265.

31. This poem is not collected before *Cross Ties*, but Kennedy places it among the poems written between 1978 and 1984.

32. Martz, "Recent Poetry," 264.

33. X. J. Kennedy, "X. J. Kennedy Writes," *Poetry Book Society Bulletin* 71 (Christmas 1971).

34. The table of contents designates the last seven poems as "New poems"; the poem preceding these seven did not appear in a previous collection and is listed thus: *Bulsh* (1970). In "X. J. Kennedy Writes," Kennedy adds that he has been writing song lyrics while would-be poems remain obstinate.

35. "No Shortage of Satisfactions," *The Times Literary Supplement* 3643, 24 December 1971, 1602.

36. Alan Brownjohn, "Light Fantastic," *New Statesman*, 52–53.

37. When Kennedy reprinted this poem in *Cross Ties*, he revised it so that each of the tag-lines is repeated. Another poem in *Breaking and Entering*, "To a Young Poet," would be reprinted in *Emily Dickinson in Southern California* three years later without its first four lines because, as Kennedy explained in a note to the author, the editor, Jan Schreiber, suggested that they be omitted, and Kennedy agreed.

38. X. J. Kennedy, "X. J. Kennedy Writes."

39. The three poems are "Last Child," *Japanese Beetles* (a sequence of epigrams), and *Last Lines*. In the earlier collection, *Last Lines* is part of *Japanese Beetles*. All three of these poems are reprinted in *Cross Ties* as well. In a note to the author, Kennedy says that this volume "Contains a couple of things not in *Cross Ties* — like 'A Little Night Music.' (Embarrassed to discover it in *Emily*: when I printed it lately in *New York Quarterly* as 'Sensual Music,' I thought I hadn't ever printed it before!) [.]"

40. Joseph Parisi, "Coming to Terms," *Poetry*, 124 (September 1974): 348.

41. "Reserves of Energy," *The Times Literary Supplement,* 30 August 1974, 932.

42. In an interview, Kennedy describes the history of his religious affiliation: "I sort of drifted out of the Church at the time I was thirteen. My old man was a Catholic, my mother was a Methodist and around adolescence the two sort of blanked each other out. Then I went to a Catholic college and took twenty credits of Scholastic philosophy and that really killed my faith altogether, so weak and namby-pamby a thing it was. Still, you can't pass through the Catholic Church, even nominally, without—Oh it sounds so crass and trite to say it!—without picking up a lot of useful symbols along the way. It does provide one with some important things to care about." Jim Svejda, "The Funniest Poet Alive: An Interview with X. J. Kennedy," *Syracuse Guide,* 26.

43. Joseph Parisi, *Poetry* 348.

44. The collection was printed by The Penmaen Press without a Table of Contents. The poem is divided into ten numbered sections, one section per page, and the collection is illustrated with three wood engravings by Michael McCurdy. In the notes at the end of the book, Kennedy says, in part: "These notes are offered for readers who did not know the subject of this poem and his circumstances. John Michael Brennan was born in 1950 in Denver and died in Denver in February 1973. He had been a student at Tufts University, located on a hill in Medford, Massachusetts, where I am a teacher. About a year before his death, John Brennan had dropped out of school to make a journey alone through England and Ireland. He returned home and in the summer of 1972 self-published his only book, *Air is,* a collection of poems, drawings, and photographs. In my poem, italics indicate quotations from that book."

45. David Shapiro, "Into the Gloom," *Poetry* 128, no. 4 (July 1976): 227.

46. Ibid., 226.

47. At the end of this poem is the note, "Translated by X. J. Kennedy and Keith Waldrop." The note does not indicate which parts Kennedy has written.

48. R. S. Gwynn asks rhetorically, "What other poet would even *think* of mourning the loss of a world-view, the collapse of the 'Great Chain of Being,' in the folk-measures of a chain-gang song?" *Sewanee Review,* lxxix.

49. Kennedy reprinted "Fall Song" in *Cross Ties* and "Pont Mirabeau" in *Dark Horses* along with another translation of Apollinaire's work, "Churchbells." Besides being an incorrigible reviser of his already published poems, Kennedy is very particular when it comes to choosing which of his poems to reprint. One measure of his opinion of a poem is to see whether he reprints it and how often. His poem "Cross Ties," for example, is printed in five of his collections, whereas "Down in Dallas" and other quite accomplished poems are printed in only one collection.

50. Above this poem in the author's copy, Kennedy wrote, "Worked on since 1955–56 in Paris and rewritten once more & I hope laid to rest in *Dark Horses.*"

51. In *French Leave,* these two lines are: "Evening come [space] be sounded hour," and the next line reads, "The days go running [space] I stand here." Several other relatively minor changes have been made. This discussion quotes from the version printed in *Dark Horses.*

52. In the author's copy of this poem, Kennedy drew a vertical line in the margin beside these three lines and wrote, "The best lines."

53. The dedication of this collection reads: "For Mary V. Toye, professeur de français extraordinaire." In the margin of the author's copy, Kennedy adds: "My high school French teacher, 86 years old in '92, & with whom I'm still in touch."

54. Kennedy explained that this "booklet of poems" was self-published "to give away at readings" since all books of his adult poetry were out of print. Private correspondence with the author.

55. Thomas Goldstein considered the theme of "First Confession" to be "strident atheism." *Dictionary of Literary Biography,* s.v. "Kennedy, X. J.," 396.

56. For a discussion of Crane's influence on Kennedy's work, see Appendix A.

57. Peter Wild, *Arizona Quarterly,* 279.

58. Ibid., 279–80.

59. A few years later, Kennedy said that he experienced great joy getting the *Los Angeles Times* Book Award for *Cross Ties.* Barbra Nightingale, "X. J. Kennedy: Poet for All Ages," *The South Florida Poetry Review,* 38.

60. "A Selection of Notebook Entries," *The Poet's Notebook,* ed. Stephen Kuusisto, Deborah Tall, and David Weiss (New York: W. W. Norton, 1995): 121–33.

61. Loxley Nichols says that "The mere structure of the book gives an inkling of the precision with which Kennedy writes. Not just an odd lot of poems left over or recycled, *Cross Ties* is a carefully constructed entity itself, a drama of sorts, wherein the poems, arranged chronologically over a span of thirty years, are divided into five sections, or acts, of major poems." "Facing the Gorgon," *National Review* 38, no. 13 (18 July 1986): 55.

62. X. J. Kennedy, "Interview with X. J. Kennedy: Keeping Merriment on the Boil," by Bruce Morgan, *Boston Literary News* 1, no. 6 (1986), 2. R. S. Gwynn, reviewing *Cross Ties,* sees vestiges of Kennedy's Catholicism: "Even the title *Cross Ties* cleverly puns on the persistence of a Catholic upbringing in the mind of an adult who is badly, to put it mildly, lapsed." "Swans on Ice," lxxviii.

63. In a note Kennedy says that this poem (or its title) "refers to Thomas Hardy's early lyric 'Neutral Tones.' Some think Hardy depicts the aftermath of his unsuccessful courtship of his cousin Tryphena Sparks."

64. Michael Collins concludes that Kennedy writes about the "ordered, diminished, undifferentiated urban world in which most Americans these days make their home and live out lives of quiet desperation." "The Poetry of X. J. Kennedy," *World Literature Today* 61 (winter 1987): 55–58.

65. R. S. Gwynn knows Kennedy's career well enough to be able to say that in his poems, Kennedy does not "look away from modern life; indeed [his poems] often describe such ubiquitous horrors as family violence . . . despair and suicide in nascent genius . . . and night-thoughts of a future where all is night . . . Through all this one never loses the sense that Kennedy has managed to strike a fair bargain between absolute pessimism and sheer escape." "Swans in Ice," lxxviii–lxxix.

66. In a note to the author at the front of the book, Kennedy writes: "Items checked (√) were faces on the cutting-room floor when John Irwin pared down the manuscript for *Dark Horses.* The Belli sonnet & "Pacifier" are dear to me, and I hope to work them into a future book." The following poems have been checked: "A Penitent Giuseppe Belli Enters Heaven," "Pacifier," "Pileup," "Sisyphus: A Parable of the Writer's Lot," "Invitation to the Dance," and "Epigrams." Among these, only "Pacifier" and "Pileup" made it into *Lords of Misrule.*

67. Kennedy says that this poem is "supposed to celebrate work and striving: the speaker chooses to endure, like a tree that keeps putting out leaves" (Note to the author).

68. Reviewer Bruce Bennett said of the collection, "Ultimately, despite its

pervasive wit and verve, *Dark Horses* is a somber and unsettling book." *Harvard Review*, no. 3 (winter 1993), 192.

69. Robert B. Shaw, "*Dark Horses.* (book reviews)," *Poetry* 158, no. 1 (October 1993): 42.

70. As noted in a previous reference, the decision to omit the poem from *Dark Horses* was not Kennedy's.

71. David Middleton discusses epigrams in general and some of Kennedy's epigrams in particular in "Stingers: X. J. Kennedy at Epigrams," *Paintbrush* 25 (autumn 1998): 92–99. Richard Moore adds his keen insights as well in "The Decline of Satire and the Specialist Society: Some Thoughts on the Poetry of X. J. Kennedy." *Light* 3 (autumn 1993): 31–34, and in "Lyrics of Wit." *Sewanee Review* 101, no. 1 (winter 1993): lxiii–xliv.

72. In a note to the author, Kennedy explains: "It may strike you that, unlike *Dark Horses,* this book has a number of comic poems in it—'Then and Now,' 'The Blessing of the Bikes,' 'A Curse on a Thief,' 'Horny Man's Song.' That's one reason I like this book better than *Dark Horses.*" The reason for the comic poems, he adds, is that "This time, John Irwin [editor at Johns Hopkins University Press] and I saw practically eye to eye, and he let me keep everything that I thought really mattered."

73. Kennedy explains that "The Lords of Misrule were those officials who presided over Christmas revels in England in the late Middle Ages, their job being to keep revelers from getting too obnoxious. In the 'Invocation,' a new poem to stand at the front of the book, I take the lords as a metaphor for strict form in poetry, which does a similar job—a force presiding over riotous emotions. (The riotous emotions had better be there, though, or the result isn't poetry.) By happy accident, in an earlier item, 'For Allen Ginbsberg,' I call Ginsberg 'misrule's lord' (private correspondence with the author). Kennedy may be having further fun by going to England, to medieval England no less, for his spirits, going as far from the spirits of contemporary free verse as decency would allow. If Robert Bly, echoing Walt Whitman, believes that traditional forms are alien to the American poetic spirit, here is Kennedy's answer, in part. For more of Bly's argument, see Robert Bly, "Reflections on the Origins of Poetic Form," *Field* 10 (spring 1974): 32.

Chapter 3: Themes and Subjects

1. John Gordon writes: "With the necessary caveat about taking 'autobiographical' poems too literally . . . , still there is a poem called 'Poets' . . . which seems to know what it's talking about very well, which perhaps we can take as at least some kind of reflection of the young XJK." "Never Trust a Guy Whose First Name Is a Letter," *Boston Review of the Arts* 2, no. 4 (July 1972): 16.

2. In a reply to the author's query about the meaning of this quotation, Kennedy wrote: "The line 'Le vierge, le vivace, et le bel aujour'hui' is the opening line of Stéphane Mallarmé's sonnet about the swan with its feet frozen in ice, its wings battering the sky. (The title of Mallarmé's poem is the same as its first line). The swan in this sonnet has been interpreted as a symbol of the poet's condition: locked in earth, aspiring heavenward. Kate Flores, in an old Anchor Books anthology, renders the line: 'The pristine, the perennial, and the beauteous today' altho I think 'The virginal, vivacious, and beautiful present day'

would be more literal, or, in better words, maybe, 'The virginal, lively, and lovely here-and-now.'"

3. According to *The Compact Edition of the Oxford English Dictionary*, *quenched* means extinguished, stifled, suppressed, squashed, even destroyed.

4. John Gordon quotes Kennedy saying "'I've never been able to talk about my own life for any length of time and tell the truth without being tempted to lie a little or jazz it up a little bit'" ("Never Trust a Guy," 16). Presumably, what Kennedy says here applies to writing autobiography into his poetry as well.

5. M. L. Rosenthal's discussion of this poem focuses on its relation to what he calls "the Romantic challenge." Rosenthal begins by saying that "Kennedy, in any first reading, seems clearly of the order of Classical ironist: worldly, satirical, wry, astringent," but, according to Rosenthal, "Poets" belies that impression. Some of Kennedy's work, such as "Poets," "is so passionate in its sense of life and art that, despite his surface amusement at romantic mystification and its magical symbols, [Kennedy] exposes himself as vulnerable and sympathetic to their magnetism after all." Rosenthal concludes his discussion of "Poets" thus: "What emerges is a view of swan and poet in Romantic perspective after all. A great deal rides on such words and phrases as 'smoldering,' 'beautiful,' 'dreams,' and 'sun-silvered,' on the sheer weight of the form despite the apparent tone, and on the evocation of Lawrence's feelings against the repression ('quenching') of psychic energies and of Mallarmé's marvelous poignancy and pride." *Shenandoah*, XXIV, 90–1.

6. Critic David Harsent admired "Artificer" for its "economical, near-vernacular line: by turns acerbic, lilting, or racy," but he saw the poem representing "urban life" rather than the artist's self-created world, and that urban life becomes "a nightmare of manufactured objects." *Spectator*, 12 February 1972.

7. Kennedy explains that "as in the poem 'Ambition,' this parable sees a writer as *needing* his own endless toil. The attitude toward Sisyphus is respectful, not unlike that of Albert Camus, to whom Sisyphus is a hero" (private correspondence with the author).

8. Kennedy's own explanation of this poem differs somewhat from the author's: "At the end of the poem the speaker makes a discovery: that the love of a woman is better than the pride of authorship. Like the poor in spirit whom the Beatitudes call blessed, he now feels himself one with his fellow poor, and has come down from his vanity" (a private note to the author).

9. Kennedy probably means Georges de La Tour, 1593–1652, who often employed in his paintings geometric planes that suggest horizontals and verticals.

10. "Singing to Spite This Hunger," *The Nation* 210 (2 February 1970): 123.

11. Ibid.

12. Stephen Tudor, "*Growing into Love*," *Spirit* 37 (spring 1970): 37. On the other hand, critic Louis Martz thinks that "Reading Trip" is one of Kennedy's weaker poems and shows Kennedy's tendency to write "mere society verse—superficial, imperceptive pieces." He advised Kennedy not to pursue this vein (*The Yale Review*, 266). John Heath-Stubbs defended Kennedy on this point, saying that although one might dismiss Kennedy's poetry as *vers de societé*, "again and again it is saved by a kind of seriousness which cuts very near the bone," ("*Breaking and Entering*, by X. J. Kennedy," *Aquarius* 5 [1972]: 91).

13. The question of literary influences on Kennedy's poetry is the focus of appendix A, which includes a long statement by Kennedy himself on the subject. In this part of the book, my chief purpose is to trace the evidence of Kennedy's interest in other writers and to examine how that interest is revealed.

14. Like Walt Whitman, though with less bravura, Kennedy sees himself as a representative man, the heir of past traditions and the progenitor of future ones. Like Whitman, he is also both voyager and observer. In 1981, Kennedy described the impact Whitman's poetry had on him as early as 1943—Kennedy was fourteen years old. He said that later, Lionel Trilling awakened him to Whitman's "subtle sound-effects and mastery of metrical rhythms . . . " ("Living with Whitman." In *Paumanok rising*, eds. Vince Clemente and Graham Everett. Port Jefferson, NY: Street Press, 1981: 23). Whitman's influence, too, may be found in one of the lines in "Theater of Dionysus," "A blackbird faintly warbles" (l. 10).

15. In "Living with Whitman," Kennedy explains that when he was a child, his house contained three books of poetry: *Song of Myself*, Harriet Monroe's anthology, *Poems for Every Mood*, and *The Rubaiyat*, which he describes as "another dangerous work!" (23). See appendix A for other influences on Kennedy's poetry.

16. On his way back to the United States from Mexico by ship, Crane jumped overboard and drowned.

17. The inveterate reviser changes these lines in *Cross Ties* to read thus: "Asia's rumor of despair / Beyond a wall of Salt —". Of his penchant for rewriting, Kennedy has said, "I never get done rewriting it seems, and some poems I thought were my best and were finished I have lately found fault with[;] I will probably always keep rewriting until I cash in my chips." Jill Scherer, *Lodestar* 5 [1984]: 49–50). Loxley Nichols sees Kennedy's revisions as evidence of Kennedy's artistic growth and responsibility: "That some of the selections from previous volumes appear here in slightly altered form reveals the poet's attention to detail. But more than that, it bespeaks a belief in the inherently organic nature of poetry and the creative process. Such considerations might also illuminate Kennedy's readiness to undertake translations. . . . In other words, Kennedy proves that what has been made can be remade, not only from the reader's point of view, but from the poet's as well." *National Review* 38, no. 13 [18 July 1986]: 55).

18. Joseph Parisi, "Coming to Terms," *Poetry*, 124, 347. Kennedy's collection is reviewed along with five other books in this article.

19. Ibid., 348.

20. R. A. Benthall's essay, "The Kneeling Ox: Catholicism in the Poems of X. J. Kennedy," argues this point quite persuasively, bringing in Kennedy's children's verse in support of his position, citing comments by Kennedy himself, and studying a couple of poems in depth, including "Cross Ties."

21. In "Poetry" (*The New Orleans Review* 2, no. 1 [1970]: 88–90), Ralph Adamo thinks this poem exposes one of Kennedy's faults: "occasionally, though he is obviously feeling his subject deeply, he does not make the reader feel it as deeply. It is this detachment that makes it difficult sometimes for the reader to be as completely inside the experience as Kennedy himself seems to be." Adamo instances the following stanza from 'Down in Dallas':

> The big bright Cadillacs stomped on their brakes,
> The street fell unearthly still
> While smoke on its chin, that slithered gun
> Coiled back from its window sill.

22. Tudor, "*Growing into Love*," 37.

23. Martz, "Recent Poetry," 264.

24. Kennedy printed only two lines of this poem's fourteen lines in *Cross Ties*, placing them with his epigrams in *Japanese Beetles*: "Great Yahweh fingered through His Bible, / Thought on it. And filed suit for libel." By paring down "Apocrypha" and not reprinting "Down in Dallas" and "Carol," Kennedy may have wanted to distance himself even fruther from his early Catholicism, thereby becoming even more of an "ex-Catholic."

25. The poem refers to the biblical story of Joshua's victory while the sun and moon stood still.

26. R. S. Gwynn detects further evidence of doubt in the philosophical stance Kennedy assumed after putting aside his Catholic faith: "Yet Kennedy, for all his outward rejection of the supernatural, cannot quite escape the thought that, just possibly, there are some things a purely existentialist philosophy cannot account for . . . Merely to doubt is one thing; to doubt one's own doubt is far more serious" ("Swans in Ice," *Sewanee Review* 42, no. 4 [fall 1985]: lxxviii).

27. Michael Collins sees many references in this poem to the Vietnam war: "'Golgotha' . . . sets the ordered, suburban world of the speaker . . . against the chaos of war in Vietnam." One of the papers that the professor reads "evokes images of war. Suddenly, the torn-up hill on campus and the defoliation of the jungle are joined as destruction in the apparent service of good. While the dormitory nears completion, the students who would live in it are drafted for service in Vietnam" (*World Literature Today*, 58).

28. Loxley Nichols says these lines exemplify Kennedy's going "too far in his intellectual wordplay," entangling his poems "in conceits that border on the absurd." This entire poem "is ruined by the last lines," and after quoting them, Nichols asks: "(Or have I missed the joke?)" "Facing the Gorgon," *National Review*, 55. Mr. Nichols has not missed the joke: he has missed the point.

29. Roger Mitchell seems to disagree. Reviewing *Cross Ties*, he makes much of Kennedy's adherence to traditional forms, believing that Kennedy is "a social historian of his corner of existence," which lies in the past, although Mitchell says that "Emily Dickinson in Southern California" measures "the vapidities of California culture." Kennedy's work, according to Mitchell, "is much better at rendering the vapidities than the spiritual life." Mitchell continues in this contradictory manner: Kennedy is a poet "for whom the modern world is dreary and shallow . . . The culture does not like what he cares for, so he is reduced to being a kind of monk in the Dark Ages keeping the great poets and their forms alive by copying them into large unread books. Or, into books read only by students who are told to by their teachers." Again we hear the echo of Kennedy's being an "academic"—that he is *only* an academic poet. Mitchell thinks that Kennedy has stuck to the ideals of the seventeenth century. "A Romantic revival has occurred since then, and he, almost alone, has not gone along with it." Putting the matter more pictorially, Mitchell continues: "If he is driving a horse and buggy in the age of the automobile, it is an elegant, well-made buggy, and the animal is gorgeous and well-groomed . . . The good-hearted Irish Catholic backwater out of which Kennedy writes, to say nothing of the literary tradition he is implicit spokesman for, does not have a comfortable relationship with our world. If we want to know what we are today, let me say 'now'—an obligation poetry cannot ignore—we must read elsewhere." ("Nine Poets," *Poetry* 147, no. 4 [January 1986]: 233–34). A much more astute assessment was made by Michael J. Collins at the end of his review of *Cross Ties*: "Kennedy is a remarkably accomplished poet, whose best work, distinguished by its skilled and witty use of language, reflects, with rare insight and sympathy, the desperate, undifferen-

tiated, suburban world in which most Americans these days make their home" ("X. J. Kennedy. *Cross Ties*," *World Literature Today* 60 [summer 1986]: 473).

30. Kennedy reprinted only three quatrains of this poem in *Cross Ties*, giving them the title, "Lizabet's Song to the Senate and the House of Representatives." The reprinted portion contains Lizabet's song, which recounts a dream in which she sees an image of her lover, "a featureless face full of outer space / On a neck like a jet exhaust" (ll. 11–12). The final surreal image blends the space program with the woman's private grief over the loss of her lover. Her "song" injects a human element in the political and scientific atmosphere of the space program, and the final image suggests that the space program kills and distorts the human element, turning lovers and astronauts into doll-like effigies no longer recognizable. Although the poem is clearly meant to poke fun at both romantic love and the space program, it did not seem to amuse reviewer John Gordon very much: he saw the poem as a "bizarre fantasy . . . written in the double-thud dragoon-beat meter of 'The Ballad of Sam McGee. . . '" ("Never Trust a Guy," 17).

31. Kennedy and G. T. Wright debate this point in *The North Stone Review* 11 (1993): 63–71.

32. An epigraph within parentheses explains the inspiration of these lines: "(on the photography of the planet's terrain by Mariner flights)." Mariner 10 passed Mercury three times, twice in 1964 and once in 1965, photographing the surface of the planet and transmitting data back to Earth. This poem was collected only in *Missing Link*.

33. In an autobiographical piece, Kennedy wrote: "Now and again [while in the navy] I got a taste of genuine salt: I was packed off on destroyers to take pictures of sailors for their hometown newspapers. This led to cruises . . . and best of all, a five-month cruise of the Mediterranean aboard the destroyer Compton, going from Gibraltar to Ixmir, Turkey, with intervening stops at Nice . . . Athens. . . . Later I wrote a poem ("Theater of Dionysus") about sitting in a sailor suit in the open-air theater beside the Acropolis, entertaining urchins by drawing cartoons, contrasting my puny show with those of Sophocles and Aristophanes" (*Contemporary Authors Autobiography Series*, vol. 9, ed. Mark Zadrozny [Detroit: Gale Research, 1989]: 73–78). The whole series of five poems begins with pre-historical events, through Greek myths of Odysseus in "The Sirens" and Leda and the swan in "Narcissus Suitor," to current history in "Theater of Dionysus," in which Kennedy recalls visiting the theater while in the navy. When he reprinted Inscriptions in *Cross Ties*, he excluded "Declare War Against Heaven" and replaced the title, "Inscriptions After Fact," which had been dropped when he reprinted "Lilith," "The Sirens," and "Narcissus Suitor" in *Breaking and Entering*.

34. Several of Kennedy's early poems show traces of Villon's influence, in particular those that indicate a preoccupation with death and those that employ irony and ribald humor. A more direct influence may be found in "Ballad of the Hanged," which Kennedy placed in *The Lords of Misrule* with the epigraph, "after François Villon." See appendix A.

35. Emily Grosholz notes this aspect of Kennedy's poetics, saying of *Dark Horses* that the poems are "as usual quite formal, and in this context it is as if strict rules were required to rein in chaos. The poetry is mordant, funny, and even sometimes rather frightening" ("Poetry Chronicle," *The Hudson Review*, 45 [autumn 1993], 575).

36. Forrest Read, "Notes, Reviews & Speculations," *Epoch* 11, (winter 1962): 257.

37. Kennedy's affection for this poem is unmistakable. He has reprinted it in five collections and takes pleasure in actually singing this song in social gatherings.

38. Critic Mark McCloskey sees the portrait in this poem as that of a type of woman who has lost her youth. "*Cross Ties: Selected Poems*," in *Magill's Literary Annual*, ed. Frank N. Magill (Englewood Cliffs, N.J.: Salem Press, 1986), 1: 199–203.

39. Theodore Holmes, "Wit, Nature, and the Human Concern," *Poetry* 100, no. 5 (August 1962): 320–21.

40. Loxley Nichols secularizes the poem further, saying that the phrase "cross ties" "signifies both the despair and the hope of the modern-day Odysseus who is tethered not by propriety or ropes, but simply by the vestiges of custom" ("Facing the Gorgon," 56).

41. This poem is a thorough revision of "A Glass of Whisky," which Kennedy did not reprint after its publication in *A Controversy of Poets*. The earlier poem, "A Glass of Whisky," consists of four quatrains; "Main Road West" consists of two six-line stanzas. The Rite Nite Motel becomes the Oak Motel; the "near-beer bar's sign" in the earlier poem is changed to "used cars"; and "An old famous head in the screen / Facelifted" is transformed into "A screen star ancient as this Oak Motel / Undergoes facelifts." Despite these drastic revisions, Kennedy has retained the earlier poem's vivid description of the town as well as the poem's central point. Both poems depict a part of the American landscape that has become isolated and lost.

42. *Times Literary Supplement* 3643, 24 December 1971, 1602.

43. It is among the series in *Growing into Love*, where it stands between "Best Seller" and "What She Told the Sheriff." In *Cross Ties*, it is among poems from 1962–1968.

44. Kennedy first collected this poem in *Emily Dickinson in Southern California* and made the following changes in it before placing it here:

> ". . . Clasp dirt for dear life" = ". . . Hug dirt for dear life." (l. 2)
> "Who ever thinks that Kitchen Kounter World" = "Who recollects that Kitchen Kounter World . . . " (l. 9)
> "Thick coaloil-colored clouds = "Dull coaloil-colored clouds" (l. 10)
> "It takes a while to learn to sleep on edge = Born in this town, you learn to sleep on edge" (l. 12)
> "these townsmen like their trees" = "to grow up like a tree" (l. 13)
> "the wind's steep angle" = "the wind's sharp angle" (l. 14)

These changes illustrate some of the ways Kennedy revises his reprinted poems.

45. This line echoes Theodore Roethke's admiring image of another woman: "(She moved in circles and those circles moved)" from the poem, "I Knew a Woman."

46. Michael Collins illustrates how Kennedy combines the playful and serious elements in creating this portrait of John Dowd: "The bounding regularity of the tetrameter lines and the insistent rhymes (particularly "tongue out" and "flung out") of the first three stanzas help create an essentially comic tone. In the last stanza, however, the stressed syllables side by side in the first two lines slow the poem down and give "stared straight at his killer" an unexpectedly serious connotation. The perverse integrity of John Dowd, affirmed by the emphatic rhythms of the second line, becomes the norm against which we see the compromises of the others horseradish makers. The heavier stress on the words

of the sequence "white turnip filler" in the last lines closes the poem with a tone of quiet contempt that, through the rhythm, evokes assent." ("The Poetry of X. J. Kennedy," 56).

47. Collins says that "If the talents of Professor Backwards are finally small and even absurd, he nonetheless brought them to a kind of perfection all too rare in this fallen world" ("The Poetry of X. J. Kennedy," 56).

48. Kennedy's wife's name is Dorothy, so presumably the poem is addressed to her.

49. R. S. Gwynn, "Swans in Ice," lxxix.

50. This phrasing has been changed from "clutching fast, gathering gold," in *Winter Thunder.*

51. Mark McCloskey thinks the portrayal of these old men is negative; they "hold on to the illusion of the skill and power they no longer have." McCloskey places this poem among other poems that make the old man a "major type," which includes the "alcoholic bum" in "B Negative," the drinker in "The Aged Wino's Counsel," the drunk in "Ool about to Proclaim a Parable," the "subject of 'Flagellant's Song,' who needs violence and pain to be sexually aroused," and the old performer in "The Death of Professor Backwards" (*Magill's Literary Annual,* 200).

52. David Ray is particularly bothered by Kennedy's darker subjects, saying that Kennedy "seems to adopt the duty to scorn. Juvenalian and Swiftian, he uses wit and metrical precision . . . with a pugnacious bitterness rare to modern verse. . . . I have known Mr. Kennedy's work for years, and as is often the case with literary pessimism—even when dished up with delicious wit—there is a puzzling quality to it. One wonders why, particularly if 'Cross Ties' contains 'every poem that the poet cares to save,' as the publisher claims, he cannot more frequently break out of the bondage of metrics and cleverness. What is behind all this scorn, one wonders, and why is there not more often delight and merriment and versatility? We can share his hates now and then—but all the time?" ("Heroic, Mock-Heroic," *New York Times Book Review* 90 [24 November 1985]: 28). If we read David Ray correctly, he would assign each poet a quota of pessimism and at least an equal amount of "delight and merriment." Moore Moran, on the other hand, defends Kennedy: "But wait a minute. Who ever said a poet has to be merry? Or even optimistic? Emily Dickinson wasn't all that jolly, and she doesn't seem to be chasing readers away" ("*Cross Ties*: X. J. Kennedy," *Prairie Schooner* 60, no. 4 [winter 1986]: 112–14).

53. In Appendix A Kennedy's discusses the influences on this poem. He thinks so much of it that he reprinted it in five of his collections, beginning with *Nude Descending a Staircase* and ending with *Cross Ties.* Nevertheless, the poem did not win universal praise. David Harsent sees in it "woefully inadequate language" that induces "a stultifying cuteness," as in the lines, "Here lies resting, out of breath, / Out of turns, Elizabeth / Whose quicksilver toes not quite / Cleared the whirring edge of night" ("Poetae Sepulchrum").

54. Michael Collins expertly connects some of the poem's structural features to the poem's meaning, saying, in part: "the falling rhythms of the entire poem (with three and a half trochaic feet in each line) gently reinforce the tone of sadness. The use of *quite* to rhyme with *night* and the stress the rhythm puts on the word both intensify the irony, the absurdity of the child's death. In the second stanza, with a traditional elegiac turn, the poem widens its vision to those who live within earth's whirling circles of night and day. While 'lightest limbs' suggests (in part through alliteration) the loveliness of the living child, it also recalls our own fragile hold on life. The poem here playfully imagines each

of us skipping, like Elizabeth, over the diurnal circles of the earth. The last two lines, a prayer for Elizabeth and for all the living, in part through the final rhythmic shift to three consecutive stressed syllables, end the poem with a sad, almost bitter repudiation of death in a lovely, fragile world" ("The Poetry of X. J. Kennedy," 55).

Chapter 4: X. J. Kennedy as Critic

1. *Literature: An Introduction to Fiction, Poetry, and Drama*, 7th ed. Ed. X. J. Kennedy and Dana Gioia (New York: Longman, 1999); *The Bedford Guide for College Writers*, 5th ed. Ed. X. J. Kennedy, Dorothy M. Kennedy, and Sylvia A. Holladay (Boston: Bedford Books of St. Martin's, 1999); and *The Bedford Reader*, 7th ed. Ed. X. J. Kennedy, Dorothy M. Kennedy, and Jane E. Aaron (Boston: Bedford Books of St. Martin's, 2000).

2. In a review of *Collected Poems, 1953–1993*, by John Updike, Kennedy says that Updike expresses a similar view, saying that rhyme is "intrinsically comic" and "antithetical to realism" ("Orphan Asylum," *The New Criterion* [April, 1993], 62–65).

3. X. J. Kennedy, a review of *The Oxford Book of American Light Verse*, ed. William Harmon, *The New Republic* 181, no. 12 (22 September 1979), 50.

4. X. J. Kennedy, "After the Bombs Subside," a review of *American Free Verse: The Modern Revolution in Poetry*, by Walter Sutton, *Counter/Measures*, no. 3 (1974), 187.

5. X. J. Kennedy, a review of *The Oxford Book of American Light Verse*, in *The New Republic* (22 September 1979): 51.

6. "Taking Notes: From Poets' Notebooks," *Seneca Review* XXI, no. 2 (1991): 105. When asked in a recent interview whether he feels "out of step with the times, out of fashion," Kennedy replied, "Absolutely. But who cares? I'd go nuts if I worried about being in fashion." Foster Mancini, *Paintbrush* XXV (autumn 1998), 21.

7. X. J. Kennedy, "*Counter/Measures*: X. J. Kennedy on Form, Meter, and Rime," by John Ciardi, *Saturday Review* 55, no. 21 20 May 1972), 14, 19.

8. X. J. Kennedy, "Fenced-in Fields," *Counter/Measures*, no. 1 (1972), 6.

9. X. J. Kennedy, "Formal Verse and Fascist Deviousness," *The North Stone Review* (1990), 65–71.

10. "Fenced-in Fields," 6–7. Kennedy repeated this reference to Robert Lowell a few years later in an interview "The Funniest Poet Alive: An Interview with X. J. Kennedy," by Jim Svejda, *Syracuse Guide* 9 (May 1976): 16.

11. Kennedy, "Fenced-in Fields," 7.

12. Kennedy, "Taking Notes," 105.

13. Kennedy, "Fenced-in Fields," 9.

14. "Living with Whitman," in *Paumanok Rising*, ed. Vince Clemente and Graham Everett, (Port Jefferson, NY: Street Press, 1981), 23–25.

15. X. J. Kennedy, "A Self-demanding Englisher," a review of *Sappho to Valery: Poems in Translation*, by John Frederick Nims, *Counter/Measures* 2 (1973): 194.

16. Kennedy, "Fenced-in Fields," 7.

17. Ibid., 8.

18. Ibid., 5.

19. Ibid., 5–6.

20. X. J. Kennedy, "Recurrences," three reviews in *The Nation* 210, no. 12 (1970), 378.
21. As quoted in X. J. Kennedy, "Formal Verse and Fascist Deviousness," 65.
22. Ibid., 67.
23. Ibid.
24. Ibid., 68.
25. Ibid., 69.
26. G. T. Wright, "Pulse and Breath," *The North Stone Review* 11 (1993): 63–64.
27. Kennedy, "Recurrences," 373, 379–80.
28. X. J. Kennedy, "Marianne Moore." *The Minnesota Review* 2, no. 3 (1962): 369–76.
29. In a note to the author, Kennedy comments: "A form in itself ain't weak—only bum poems written in it." Unlike Kennedy, who welcomes "every kind of excellence," including poetry in open form, Robert Bly seems unwilling to allow that formal poetry written today has any value. In an exchange with Kennedy, published in *The North Stone Review* in 1993, G. T. Wright seems to agree with Bly, at least in part. Wright asserts that "Something in American speech goes relatively flat in English iambic meters . . . The well-made metrical poem now has all the cultural impact of a well-turned pot." One of the problems in this controversy, Kennedy has argued for years, at least implicitly, is that critics such as Bly and Wright have created a bogus either-or, us-and-them argument that pits writers of free verse against traditionalists. The issue is whether a poem, tightly structured or loosely formed, has those rhythms that free-verse writers often lose when they reject structured poetry entirely. Kennedy repeatedly argued that open forms are quite able to capture those essential rhythms that he believes all good poetry has. As he said more than a decade ago: "I have nothing but dumb admiration for poets who triumph in open forms. I wish I could do so, but I always fall flat on my snoot without the support and the challenge of old-fangled technical difficulties. The poems I like (whether or not they're mine) are impassioned, surprising, concise, full of music and low seriousness." ("Statement on Poetry," *The Worcester Review* 9, no. 2 [1987], 43). The significant element in this list is of course "full of music." Kennedy had already confessed in a 1976 interview that he had "a dumb, dog-like admiration for poets who are able to [write in both open and closed forms], or poets who are able to achieve triumphs in open forms" (Kennedy, "The Funniest Poet Alive," by Svejda, 16).
30. X. J. Kennedy, "Twelve from Small Presses." *Poetry* 99, no. 3 (February 1962): 313–19.
31. Ibid.
32. X. J. Kennedy, "The Devalued Estate." *Poetry* 114, no. 4 (July 1969): 266–74.
33. See appendix A for Thomas Hardy's influence on Kennedy's work.
34. Kennedy, "A Self-Demanding Englisher," 192.
35. Ibid., 195.
36. Ibid., 189.
37. Kennedy, "After the Bombs Subside," 193.
38. Kennedy, "The Funniest Poet Alive," by Svejda, 16.
39. X. J. Kennedy, "The Poetry: Form and Informality" in *Miller Williams and*

the Poetry of the Particular, ed. Michael Burns (Columbia, Mo.: University of Missouri Press, 1991): 43–53.

40. Kennedy, "A Self-Demanding Englisher," 194.

41. X. J. Kennedy, "Rime," *New York Quarterly* 6 (spring 1971): 128–33.

42. X. J. Kennedy, "The Least Known Major American Poet," *Harvard Review* (winter 1993): 103–6.

43. Robert Bly, "Reflections on the Origins of Poetic Form," *Field* 10 (spring 1974): 32.

44. X. J. Kennedy, "Rhythmic Language," *Mississippi Review* 6, no. 1 (1977): 116.

45. Published in *The Lords of Misrule.*

46. X. J. Kennedy, "Rhythmic Language," 116.

47. X. J. Kennedy, "Fenced-in Fields," 9–10.

48. Appendix A discusses the influences of these and other contemporary poets on Kennedy's writing and includes some of his own words on the subject.

49. X. J. Kennedy, "Ritual Repetitions," *Counter/Measures* 3 (1974): 189. This article contains a review of *Four Poems in Measure* by John Heath-Stubbs.

50. Kennedy, "*Counter/Measures,*" by Ciardi, 14, 19.

51. Ibid.

52. As quoted in X. J. Kennedy, "Sameness and Individual Voice," *Harvard Review*1 (spring 1992): 19.

53. Kennedy, "The Poetry: Form and Informality," in *Miller Williams,* 45.

54. Rainer Maria Rilke, "Wie der Wachter in den Weingelanden," trans. Robert Bly and X. J. Kennedy, *Counter/Measures* 3 (1974): 160–61.

55. Hofmannsthal, Hugo von, "Die Beiden," trans. Robert Bly and X. J. Kennedy, *Counter/Measures* 3 (1974): 174–75. Kennedy reprinted his translation in *Hangover Mass,* where he titled it "Goblet" and added an epigraph, "from *Hugo von Hofmannsthal.*"

56. X. J. Kennedy, "How to Survive Gresham's Law," *Michigan Quarterly Review* 21, no. 1 (winter 1982): 43–47. Kennedy adds in a note: "This piece was a talk given at the 50th anniversary Hopwood Festival, Univ. of Mich., April 9–11, 1981."

57. X. J. Kennedy, "Foreword: Do Poets Need to Know Something?" in *Writing Poems,* 2d ed., by Robert Wallace (Boston: Little, Brown, 1987): iii–vii.

58. Kennedy, "How to Survive Gresham's Law," 43–47.

59. Kennedy "Foreword: Do Poets Need to Know Something?" iii–vii.

60. X. J. Kennedy, "Making a Name in Poetry," in *The Writer's Handbook,* ed. Sylvia K. Burback (Boston: The Writer, 1988): 364–70.

61. X. J. Kennedy, "Is There a Vast, Untapped Audience?" *The New York Quarterly* 50 (1993): 93–99.

62. Ibid., 97.

63. Ibid.

64. Ibid., 99.

65. Kennedy, "Rime," 128–33.

66. Kennedy, "*Counter/Measures,*" by Ciardi, 14, 19.

67. Kennedy, "Fenced-in Fields," 4–11.

68. Kennedy, "Taking Notes," 109.

69. X. J. Kennedy. "*Counter/Measures*: X. J. Kennedy on Form, Meter, and Rime." By John Ciardi. *Saturday Review* 4 (20 May 1972): 19.

70. Barbra Nightingale, "X. J. Kennedy: Poet for All Ages," *The South Florida Poetry Review* 7, no. 3 (1990): 39.

Chapter 5: X. J. Kennedy and Light Verse

1. X. J. Kennedy, "Interview: X. J. Kennedy: Keeping Merriment on the Boil," *Boston Literary News* 1, no. 6 (1986): 2.

2. X. J. Kennedy, "The Funniest Poet Alive: An Interview with X. J. Kennedy," by Jim Svejda, *Syracuse Guide* 9 (May 1976): 17.

3. X. J. Kennedy, "The Light Tradition," review of *The New Oxford Book of English Light Verse*, ed. Kingsley Amis, *Inquiry* 1, no. 19 (August 21, 1978): 27–29.

4. *The New Republic*. (22 September 1979): 49.

5. Henry Taylor, "Singing to Spite This Hunger," *The Nation* (2 February 1970): 123. In a longer review of *Growing into Love*, Taylor continues to praise Kennedy's poetic skills, concluding with a summary statement that aptly connects the light and serious in Kennedy's poetry: "Kennedy is at his best when he is thinking seriously within playful frameworks" ("Growing into Love," in *Magill's Literary Annual*, ed. Frank N. Magill [Englewood Cliffs, N.J.], 1: 157).

6. Kennedy quotes from Hardy and Frost to show that two poems written in identical form and syntax are very individual and different ("Sameness and Individual Voice," *Harvard Review*, 1 [spring 1992]: 17–20).

7. Kennedy explains that this poem is "about a hypocrite who aspires to become Pope, while being a letcher [sic], a swine, a liar, a back-biter and so on. "Bulsh" was the name of the central character, which was supposed to be short for a well-known epithet and I was inspired by one of my favorite works of literature, Alfred Jarry's *Ubu Roi*, which is about a monstrous human swine, who in the original production resembled a large piece of excrement" (Kennedy, "The Funniest Poet Alive," by Svejda, 26).

8. W. D. Snodgrass describes one of Kennedy's performances in which he sang this song. "Remembering Joe Kennedy," *Paintbrush* 25, 138. The "Interactive Edition" of Kennedy's textbook, *Literature*, eighth edition, with Dana Gioia, comes with a CD-ROM showing Kennedy and Gioia reading their poetry and Kennedy singing "In a Prominent Bar in Secaucus."

Chapter 6: X. J. Kennedy's Literature for Children

1. X. J. Kennedy, "Interview with X. J. Kennedy: Keeping Merriment on the Boil," by Bruce Morgan, *Boston Literary News* 1, no. 6 (1986): 2. In a note to the author, Kennedy writes: "I started writing for kids because poets I admired were doing it—Ciardi, Roethke, W. J. Smith. The children's poems in *Nude Descending* antedate my marriage [and having children of my own]." Kennedy discusses some of his experiences in and ideas about writing children's literature in an interview with Foster Mancini, "X. J. Kennedy: An Interview," *Paintbrush* 25 (autumn 1998): 18–20. For a review of some critical statements about Kennedy's verse for children, see *Children's Literature Review*, vol. 27, ed. Gerard J. Senick. Detroit, Mich.: Gale Research, 1992.

2. X. J. Kennedy, "Disorder and Security in Nonsense Verse for Children," *The Lion and the Unicorn* 13, no. 2 (December 1989): 28–33.

3. X. J. Kennedy, "Talking with X. J. Kennedy," an interview by Jack Prelutsky. *Instructor* 102, no. 2 (September 1992): 26.

4. X. J. Kennedy, "Staying Human," a review of *When You Are Alone/It Keeps You Capone, an Approach to Creative Writing with Children,* by Myra Cohn Livingston, *Counter/Measures* 3 (1974): 190.

5. "*Dark Horses,* by X. J. Kennedy," *Publishers Weekly* 239, no. 49 (November 9, 1992): 79.

6. X. J. Kennedy, 'Go and Get Your Candle Lit!' An Approach to Poetry," *The Horn Book Magazine* 57, no. 3 (June 1981): 273–74.

7. X. J. Kennedy, "The Poet in the Playpen," three reviews, *Poetry* 105, no. 3 (1964): 190.

8. In another review, Kennedy chides James Broughton for failing at the task: "Much of the time, Broughton underestimates the difficulty of emulating Mother Goose, and his whimsy results in doggerel" ("Old Wine, New Wrinkles," *Counter/Measures* 3 [1974]: 200).

9. In "X. J. Kennedy's Poetry for Children: A User's Guide," *Paintbrush* 25 (autumn 1998): 111–8, Bruce Bennett explains how effective Kennedy's children's verse is when read aloud to children.

10. X. J. Kennedy, "Strict and Loose Nonsense: Two Worlds of Children's Verse," *School Library Journal* 37, no. 3 (March 1991): 112.

11. In a letter to the author dated May 20, 1999, Kennedy describes this volume as "a book to read aloud to wee tots who can't read for themselves yet, not a book for young adults (a phrase that in kidlit means teenagers). Probably its choice of poems is not fraught with much deep significance, and anyhow, the choice was half Dorothy's."

Chronology

1. Kennedy adopted the pseudonym "X.J." Kennedy" when he began publishing his work. As he explained in an interview, "the X really doesn't stand for anything. My real name is Joe Kennedy, but if you live in Massachusetts with that name, you're perpetually kidded. I added the X years ago just to be different from all those other Kennedys." X. J. Kennedy, "Talking with X. J." Kennedy," by Jack Prelutsky, *Instructor* 102, no. 2 (September 1992): 26. In a humorous vein, Kennedy used "Xerox" as his first name in *Pegasus Descending*." An editor at *Times Literary Supplement* (7 April 1972), apparently missing the humor, listed him among the editors of *Pegasus* as "Xerox Kennedy."

2. See appendix A, "Influences," for John Heath-Stubbs's influence on Kennedy's work.

3. Kennedy explains how he came to write children's books and textbooks and describes some of his experiences in that field in "X. J. Kennedy: An Interview," by Foster Mancini, *Paintbrush* 25 (autumn 1998): 12–22.

Appendix A: Influences

1. This narrative is previously unpublished.

2. Stephen Tudor sees the influence of Robert Lowell in the way Kennedy

"gives a Latin polish to his diction." "*Growing into Love*," *Spirit* 37 (spring 1970): 39.

3. Many critics have seen the influence of Robert Frost on Kennedy's poetry, particularly "Frost's knack for sketching people, some of his brand of wisdom and a kindred metrical skill" (Stephen Tudor, *Spirit*, 39).

4. Gordon, John. "Never Trust a Guy Whose First Name Is a Letter." *Boston Review of the Arts* 2, no. 4 (July 1972): 16.

5. Ibid., 17.

6. Raymond Oliver, "X. J. Kennedy's Poems Revel in Humor, Humanity," *Christian Science Monitor* 77, 7 August 1985, 21–22.

7. Ibid.

8. Lachlan Mackinnon, "High Fidelity," *Times Literary Supplement* 4303, 20 September 1985, 1039.

9. Loxley Nichols, "Facing the Gorgon," *National Review* 38, no. 13 (18 July 1986): 55.

10. Ibid., 56.

11. Moore Moran, "*Cross Ties*: X. J. Kennedy," *Prairie Schooner* 60 (winter 1986): 112–14.

12. Michael True, *Contemporary Poets*, 6th ed. (Detroit: St. James Press, 1996), 575. True's comments do draw attention to the difference between Kennedy's being influenced by a writer—William Butler Yeats, for example—and his imitating an author's style or form, as he does in "Emily Dickinson in Southern California." True points out that Kennedy occasionally "parodies an earlier versifier—Robert Herrick, Lewis Carroll, or Robert Frost—or appropriates a Greek myth to his own purposes, as in 'Narcissus Suitor.'" The difference between influence and deliberate imitation is sometimes indistinguishable, but influence tends to be more subtle and pervasive than parody or imitation. Influence, too, issues from a desire to appropriate as one's own a perspective, style, or attitude, and usually implies admiration and affection, whereas imitation or parody may imply the opposite.

13. Bernard Keith Waldrop, "Squibs," *Burning Deck* 2 (spring 1963): 92.

Works Cited

Adamo, Ralph. "Poetry." *The New Orleans Review* 2, no. 1 (1970): 88–90.

Basho, Matsuo. *The Essential Basho: Matsuo Basho.* Translated by Sam Hamill. Boston and London: Shambhala, 1999.

Bennett, Bruce. "*Dark Horses* by X. J. Kennedy." *Harvard Review* 3 (winter 1993): 191–92.

———. "X. J. Kennedy's Poetry for Children: A User's Guide." *Paintbrush* 25 (autumn 1998): 111–18.

Benthall, R. A. "The Kneeling Ox: Catholicism in the Poems of X. J. Kennedy."

Bjork, Robert E. "Kennedy's 'Nothing in Heaven Functions as It Ought.'" *The Explicator* 40, no. 2 (winter 1982): 6–7.

Bly, Robert. "Reflections on the Origins of Poetic Form." *Field* 10 (spring 1974): 31–35.

Brownjohn, Alan. "Dark Forces." *New Statesman* 78, no. 2009 (September 12, 1969): 346–47.

———. "Light Fantastic." *New Statesman* 83, no. 2130 (January 14, 1972): 52–53.

Carroll, James. "Blossoming Poet." Review of *Growing into Love,* by X. J. Kennedy. *Catholic World,* January 1970, 183.

Clark, Marden J. "Liberating Form." In *Liberating Form: Mormon Essays on Religion and Literature,* 1–15. Salt Lake City, Utah: Aspen Books, 1992.

Collins, Michael J. "The Poetry of X. J. Kennedy." *World Literature Today* 61 (winter 1987): 55–58.

———. "X. J. Kennedy. *Cross Ties.*" *World Literature Today* 60 (summer 1986): 473.

"X. J. Kennedy." *Contemporary Authors Autobiography Series,* vol. 9. Edited by Mark Zadrozny. Detroit: Gale Research, 1989: 73–88.

Copeland, Jeffrey S., ed., *Speaking of Poets: Interviews with Poets Who Write for Children and Young Adults.* Urbana, Ill.: National Council of Teachers of English, 1993.

"*Dark Horses,* by X. J. Kennedy." *Publishers Weekly* 239, no. 49 (November 9, 1992): 79.

Demos, John. Review of *Growing into Love,* by X. J. Kennedy. *Library Journal* 94, no. 15 (September 1, 1969): 2929.

Dunn, Douglas. "A Bridge in Minneapolis." *Encounter* 38, no. 5 (May 1972): 77.

Ferlazzo, P. J. *Choice* 23 (October 1985): 296.

Goldstein, Thomas. S. V. "X. J. Kennedy." *Dictionary of Literary Biography.* Vol. 5: American Poets since World War II. Detroit: Gale Research, 1980.

Gordon, John. "Never Trust a Guy Whose First Name Is a Letter." *Boston Review of the Arts* 2, no. 4 (July 1972): 11–17, 77.

Grosholz, Emily. "Poetry Chronicle." *The Hudson Review* 46 (autumn 1993): 570–78.

Gwynn, R. S. "Swans in Ice." *Sewanee Review* 93, no. 4 (fall 1985): lxxviii–lxxix.

Harsent, David. "Poetae Sepulchrum." *Spectator* (February 12, 1972).

Heath-Stubbs, John. *Aquarius* 5 (1972): 91.

Hofmannsthal, Hugo von. "Die Beiden." Trans. Robert Bly and X. J. Kennedy. *Counter/Measures* 3 (1974): 174–75.

Holmes, Theodore. "Wit, Nature, and the Human Concern." *Poetry* 100, no. 5 (August 1962): 319–24.

"Kennedy, Joseph Charles." *Contemporary Authors: New Revision Series*, vol. 30. Edited by James G. Lesniak. Detroit: Gale Research, 1990: 212–14.

Kennedy, X. J. "After the Bombs Subside." Review of *American Free Verse: The Modern Revolution in Poetry*, by Walter Sutton. *Counter/Measures* 3 (1974): 186–87.

———. "Comment." *Poetry* 151, nos. 1–2 (October-November 1987): 215–16.

———. "*Counter / Measures*: X. J. Kennedy on Form, Meter, and Rime." By John Ciardi. *Saturday Review* 4 (May 20, 1972): 14, 19.

———. "The Funniest Poet Alive: An Interview with X. J. Kennedy." By Jim Svejda. *Syracuse Guide* 9 (May 1976): 14–17, 26.

———. "An Interview with X. J. Kennedy." By William Baer. *The Formalist* 11 (2000): 19–34.

———. "An Interview with X. J. Kennedy." By Jill Scherer. *Lodestar* 5 (1984): 49–50.

———. "Interview with X. J. Kennedy: Keeping Merriment on the Boil." By Bruce Morgan. *Boston Literary News* 1, no. 6 (1986): 2–3.

———. "Old Wine, New Wrinkles." *Counter/Measures* 3 (1974): 200.

———. "The Poet in the Playpen." Three reviews. *Poetry* 105, no. 3 (1964): 190–91.

———. "The Poetry: Form and Informality." In *Miller Williams and the Poetry of the Particular*. Edited by Michael Burns. Columbia, Mo.: University of Missouri Press, 1991: 43–53.

———. "A Self-Demanding Englisher." Review of *Sappho to Valery: Poems in Translation*, by John Frederick Nims. *Counter/Measures* 2 (1973): 193–94.

———. "Staying Human." A review of *When You Are Alone / It Keeps You Capone, an Approach to Creative Writing with Children*, by Myra Cohn Livingston. *Counter/Measures* 3 (1974): 190.

———. "Talking with X. J. Kennedy." By Jack Prelutsky. *Instructor* 102, no. 2 (September 1992): 26.

———. "X. J. Kennedy: An Interview." By Foster Mancini. *Paintbrush* 25 (autumn 1998): 12–22.

Leggett, John. "Poems with a Temper of Mind." *Boston Globe*, August 24, 1969, 73.

Lucie-Smith, Edward. *Contemporary Poets*. 2d ed. New York: St. Martin's Press, 1975.

Mackinnon, Lachlan. "High Fidelity." *Times Literary Supplement* 4303, September 20, 1985, 1039.

Martz, Louis L. "Recent Poetry: The End of an Era." *Yale Review* 59 (winter 1970): 252–67.

McCloskey, Mark. "*Cross Ties: Selected Poems.*" In *Magill's Literary Annual,* edited by Frank N. Magill. Englewood Cliffs, N.J.: Salem Press, 1986. 1: 199–203.

McGann, Jerome. "Poetry and Truth." *Poetry* 117, no. 3 (December 1970): 195–203.

Middleton, David. "Stingers: X. J. Kennedy at Epigrams." *Paintbrush* 25 (autumn 1998): 92–99.

Middleton, Francine K. "Introduction of X. J. Kennedy as the 1996 Fletcher Lecturer at Nicholls State University, Thibodaux, Louisiana, 11 April 1996." *Paintbrush* 25 (autumn 1998): 103–4.

Mills, Jr., Ralph J. "Three Established Poets and a New One." *Chicago Sun-Times Book Week,* 19 October 1969, 10.

Milosz, Czelsaw. "The Writing Life." By Nathan Gardels. *Los Angeles Times,* 25 July 1999.

Mitchell, Roger. "Nine Poets." *Poetry* 147, no. 4 (January 1986): 232–34.

Moore, Richard. "The Decline of Satire and the Specialist Society: Some Thoughts on the Poetry of X. J. Kennedy." *Light* 3 (autumn 1993): 31–34.

———. "Lyrics of Wit." *Sewanee Review* 101, no. 1 (winter 1993): xliii–xliv.

Moran, Moore. "*Cross Ties*: X. J. Kennedy." *Prairie Schooner* 60, no. 4 (winter 1986): 112–14.

Nichols, Loxley. "Facing the Gorgon." *National Review* 38, no. 13 (18 July 1986): 55–56.

Nightingale, Barbra. "X. J. Kennedy: Poet for All Ages." *The South Florida Poetry Review* 7, no. 3 (1990): 33–39.

"No Shortage of Satisfactions." *The Times Literary Supplement* 3643, 24 December 1971, 1602.

Oliver, Raymond. "X. J. Kennedy's Poems Revel in Humor, Humanity." *Christian Science Monitor* 77, August 7, 1985, 21–22.

Orth, Ghita. "Rich in Discipline." *New England Review* 16 (spring 1994): 168–73.

Parisi, Joseph. "Coming to Terms." *Poetry* 124 (September 1974): 343–52.

Ray, David. "Heroic, Mock-Heroic." *New York Times Book Review* 90, 24 November 1985, 28.

Read, Forrest. "Notes, Reviews and Speculations." *Epoch* 11 (winter 1962): 257–60.

"Reserves of Energy." *Times Literary Supplement,* 30 August 1974, 932.

Review of *Dark Horses,* by X. J. Kennedy. *Publishers Weekly* 239, no. 49 (November 9, 1992): 79.

Rice, William. "A Conversation with X. J. Kennedy." *Sparrow* 62 (1995): 48–57.

Rilke, Rainer Marie. "Wie der Wachter in den Weingelanden." Trans. Robert Bly and X. J. Kennedy. *Counter/Measures* 3 (1974): 160–61.

Rosenthal, M. L. "Poetic Power—Free the Swan!" *Shenandoah* 24, no. 1 (fall 1972): 88–91.

A Selection of Notebook Entries. In *The Poet's Notebook,* edited by Stephen Kusisto, Deborah Tall, and David Weiss, 121–33. New York: W. W. Norton, 1995.

Senick, Gerard J., ed. *Children's Literature Review,* vol. 27. Detroit, Mich.: Gale Research, 1992.

Shapiro, David. "Into the Gloom." *Poetry* 128, no. 4 (July 1976): 226–27.

Sharp, Ronald A. "Kennedy's 'Nude Descending a Staircase.'" *Explicator* 37, no. 3 (spring 1979): 2–3.

Shaw, Robert B. "*Dark Horses* (book reviews)." *Poetry* 163, no. 1 (October 1993): 42–44.

Simon, John. "More Brass Than Enduring." *Hudson Review* 15 (autumn 1962): 455–68.

Simpson, Peter L. "The Candor of Poetry." *St. Louis Post-Dispatch,* December 7, 1969, 1–16M.

Skinner, Knute. *Northern Review* 12, no. 2 (spring 1972): 94–96.

Snodgrass, W. D. "Remembering Joe Kennedy." *Paintbrush* 25 (autumn 1998): 136–38.

Sullivan, Nancy. "Perspective and the Poetic Process." *Wisconsin Studies in Contemporary Literature* 6, no. 1 (winter-spring 1965): 114–31.

Taylor, Henry. "*Growing into Love.*" In *Magill's Literary Annual,* edited by Frank N. Magill. Englewood Cliffs, N.J.: Salem Press, 1970. 1: 154–57.

———. "'Singing to Spite This Hunger.'" *The Nation* 210 (February 2, 1970): 122–24.

Tessier, Thomas. "X. J. Kennedy's Poetry." *New Haven Register,* 1969.

True, Michael. *Contemporary Poets,* 6th ed. Detroit: St. James Press, 1996.

Tudor, Stephen. "*Growing into Love.*" *Spirit* 37 (spring 1970): 36–39.

Vinson, James, ed., *Contemporary Poets.* 2d ed. London: St. Martin's Press, 1975.

Wakeman, John, ed. *World Authors, 1950–1970.* New York: H. W. Wilson, 1975.

Waldrop, Bernard Keith. "Squibs." *Burning Deck* 2 (spring 1963): 92.

Who's Who in America. 54th ed. S. V. "Kennedy, X. J." New Providence, N.J.: Marquis, 2000. 1: 2576–77.

Wild, Peter. *Arizona Quarterly* 41 (autumn 1985): 279–80.

Wright, G. T. "Pulse and Breath." *The North Stone Review* 11 (1993): 63–64.

"X. J. Kennedy." *American Poets Since World War II.* Detroit: Gale Research Company, 1980.

"X. J. Kennedy." *Contemporary Authors Autobiography Series,* vol. 9. Edited by Mark Zadrozny. Detroit: Gale Research, 1989: 73–88.

Index